PULLMAN

THE URBAN LIFE IN AMERICA SERIES

RICHARD C. WADE, GENERAL EDITOR

STANLEY BUDER
PULLMAN: An Experiment in Industrial Order
and Community Planning, 1880–1930

ALLEN F. DAVIS
SPEARHEADS FOR REFORM: The Social Settlements
and the Progressive Movement, 1890–1914

LYLE W. DORSETT
THE PENDERGAST MACHINE

KENNETH T. JACKSON
THE KU KLUX KLAN IN THE CITY, 1915–1930

MELVIN G. HOLLI
REFORM IN DETROIT: Hazen S. Pingree and
Urban Politics

ZANE L. MILLER
BOSS COX'S CINCINNATI: Urban Politics in the Progressive Era

PETER J. SCHMITT
BACK TO NATURE: The Arcadian Myth in Urban America,
1900–1930

PULLMAN

An Experiment in Industrial Order
and Community Planning
1880–1930

STANLEY BUDER

OXFORD UNIVERSITY PRESS
NEW YORK   LONDON   TORONTO

To My Parents

Foreword

To the present generation the word "Pullman" usually connotes only labor strife, a bitter strike in 1894, and the feudal paternalism of the town's founder and owner, George Pullman. But to Americans of the 1880's the word was synonymous with innovation, enlightenment, and success. Pullman was best known, of course, for his development of the sleeping car, which made railroad travel comfortable and even elegant. Earlier, in the 1850's, he had earned a more than local reputation by his part in physically raising Chicago buildings out of the mud. By the eighties, however, Pullman's name was bound up with the "model town" he created due south of Chicago for the production of railroad cars and the housing of his workers.

Pullman himself often described his model town, with disarming plainness, as a profit-making enterprise. "A man who can bring his mind down to understand the simplest business proposition can fathom the Pullman scheme very easily," he once told a reporter. "It is simplicity itself—we are landlord and employers. That is all there is of it." Yet the experiment always carried with it greater implications. The planned town, with its model housing and clean and pleasant surroundings, would also provide an answer to the persistent industrial warfare that characterized nineteenth-century society. "With such surroundings and such human regard for the needs of the body as well as the soul," he said, "the disturbing conditions of strikes and other troubles that periodically convulse the world of labor would not be found here." Or as a company official put it, "the building of Pullman is very likely to be the beginning of a new era for labor."

The town of Pullman was thus an attempt to establish a new system of labor relations as well as an experiment in town planning. Stanley Buder has examined both of these dimensions of the Pullman story. For the first time the strike is set convincingly in the context of the development of the community; hence it becomes something more than an ugly episode in management-labor relations. He finds the tangled roots of the conflict not only in the depression of 1893 but also in a decade of growing difficulties in the town. As a result he presents a fresh view of the events of 1894 and a more satisfying account than we have had before.

Mr. Buder's volume is also important for the student of urbanization, since it contains a detailed analysis of a "model town" from its conception to its transformation into an ordinary urban neighborhood. Pullman was designed to be everything Chicago was not. It was to be planned rather than haphazard, orderly rather than chaotic, green and antiseptic rather than concrete and sooty. Moreover, the new environment would elevate the character of its residents by reducing drunkenness, strengthening family life, and encouraging thrift and ambition. In the broadest sense, the town was to be an agent of fundamental social reform.

The gradual decline of the paternal utopia is one of the large themes of this book. Mr. Buder explains not only what Pullman expected, but what the residents experienced. He asks the right questions: who lived in Pullman, why did they come, and, just as important, why did many leave so quickly? In addition, he analyzes the "model town" in relation to its less-than-model neighbors, Kensington and Roseland. And, throughout, the author sees Pullman as part of the natural growth of metropolitan Chicago. Though located well outside the built-up area in 1880, it was engulfed by the expanding city within two decades.

Finally this volume has a peculiar relevance to our own times. For never before have urban problems and planning had the attention they now command. Public officials, architects, planners, academic specialists, and experts of all kinds are busily attempting to control and order the future of the modern metropolis. Inevitably, one of the responses of those frustrated by the intractability of the present city is to start all over again and build "new towns" in the vicinity of existing cities. In a sense, this is what Pullman tried to do. Paternalism is only a partial explanation of his defeat; other elements of the failure are deeply embedded in the nature of American urban development itself. Mr. Buder, in examining this historic experiment, also illumines the broader urban currents that flow so forcefully today.

RICHARD C. WADE

GENERAL EDITOR

URBAN LIFE IN AMERICA SERIES

Chicago, Ill.
June 1967

Preface

French observers at the Philadelphia Centennial Exposition of 1876, wanting to convey their awe at the exhibited American products, described them as "Pullman car style." By perfecting and promoting the sleeping car, George M. Pullman (1831-1897) revolutionized rail travel and built a prosperous company. His name entered several languages as a near synonym for luxury and comfort, and both here and abroad it became a byword for American business genius. Asked the secret of his success, he usually referred to the "Pullman system."

Like other nineteenth-century entrepreneurs, Pullman was obsessed with the need for system. Through attention to account book and workshop, he strove to develop uniformity in production, design, and service. In addition, he sought ways to keep his product before the public. Part inventor and businessman, part promoter and financier, Pullman's versatility gave birth to a system which was not only a way of getting things done, but also a technique to attract favorable attention. His work was successfully identified with science and social progress. The beauty and elegance of the sleeping car became a visible symbol of the material promise of American industry and ingenuity.

Though a naturally reticent man, Pullman was always eager to talk about his system. On first consideration, however, it appears little more than disappointing generalities: a confident assertion that businessmen must search for order and control through innovation and expansion. But this is only because his ideas are now common knowledge and matter of fact. In its application the Pullman system was new and impressive if not always successful.

This system was given dramatic setting in a model town built in 1880 to prove its validity for community as well as factory. Pullman wished to demonstrate that American industry could plan and construct a town which would solve the social problems of the time by providing adequate housing for workers and thus encourage their development of proper middle-class standards. At a distance from Chicago, the model town was to be both the company "showplace" and the solution to its labor problems.

Long dismissed as mere paternalism, Pullman's town was actually his effort at employing a business system for public as well as personal ends. He hoped to show that industrialization need not lead to social disintegration and that the chaotic concentration of men and machinery in unmanageable urban neighborhoods could be reversed by the planned order of an industrial community. The model town was an experiment in reform, but one placed in a business context and intended to illustrate that social reform and good business practices were complementary. This, then, is a study of George Pullman and the application of his system to factory and town.

S. B.

Chicago, Ill.
June 1967

Acknowledgments

The author wishes to express his gratitude to the following people. Mrs. Amy Nyholm, manuscript librarian of the Newberry Library, was always kind and helpful. Professors Mark Abrahamson and Fred Jaher and Mrs. Marlene Wortman aided me at various times in the writing, and Mr. Abrahamson also guided my use of statistical measurements. Dr. and Mrs. C. Phillip Miller allowed me access to important material and the hospitality of their home while making no effort to influence my treatment of George M. Pullman, who was Mrs. Miller's grandfather. A Faculty Fellowship, which reduced my teaching responsibilities for a term, was generously granted by the Illinois Institute of Technology. Professor Walter Johnson read an early draft, and offered numerous useful suggestions. My teacher, friend, and editor, Richard C. Wade was steadfast in his invaluable support and constructive advice. Mr. Glen Roth, a student assistant, very largely prepared the index. My wife, Rachel Buder, through her interest, comments, and companionship made the exacting tasks of research and writing an enjoyable and unforgettable experience.

Contents

Plates

Figures

Tables

I

THE PULLMAN SYSTEM

1

Development and Promotion
of the Sleeping Car

In every respect the nature of American society . . . favored
the enterprise of businessmen. No intrenched clergy or nobility
overshadowed them in national life or branded their labors . . .
with the stamp of contempt.

Charles and Mary Beard, *The Rise of American Civilization*

Andrew Carnegie's *Triumphant Democracy* was an encomium for
his adopted country with the highest accolade, "typical American,"
given to the sleeping-car king, George Pullman. Pullman's background had the simple lines of the self-made man common to the
heroes of the Horatio Alger novels. His early years are the tale of
rapid rise from humble origin to fame and riches through industry
and ability. It was a story that the nineteenth-century American
wanted to consider typical of the nation's successful businessmen.

George Mortimer Pullman was the third born of the eight children of James Lewis and Emily Minton Pullman. The father had
been raised in central New York State, but dissatisfied with farming, went to Auburn, New York, where he learned the carpenter's
trade and married in 1825. A conscientious, hard-working man, his
skill as a house builder enabled him to provide adequately for a
large family.

Shortly after George's birth on March 3, 1831, the family moved
from Brocton, Chatauqua County, to the nearby town of Portland,
where the boy grew up. On the day the father joined the Universalist Church, James Pullman assembled his family, read from the
Bible, and implored God's aid in their Christian rearing. He suc-

3

ceeded in impressing his earnest convictions on his children, who were raised in a strict and religious manner. Disobedience, idleness, and extravagance were quickly punished. They were counseled, "you can succeed nowhere except as an honest man; have the power of your convictions." [1] All did well, and two of the sons became prominent Universalist ministers. The most famous of the six boys, George, always believed that "character"—meaning by this honesty, devotion to work, and acceptance of family and religious duties—was the key to success.

George Pullman's formal education at a small country school ended in his fourteenth year, and in 1845 he went to clerk in a small general store at Westfield, New York, for forty dollars a year plus board. The family moved to Albion along the Erie Canal and George joined them there in 1848. For a while he worked as a cabinetmaker in his older brother Albert's shop. When in the early 1850's the New York State Legislature decided to widen the Erie Canal, his father won several contracts from the state to move homes that were too near the canal's banks at Albion. But falling ill he died in November 1853. George, the oldest unmarried son, was left the financial care of his mother and the younger children, and after his father's illness took over the contracts.

With the house-moving work nearly finished in 1855, Pullman decided to go to Chicago, then America's fastest growing city.

Started as a trading post on a muddy plain, Chicago had been incorporated as a town in 1833 with a population of three hundred and fifty. At mid-century it had close to thirty thousand people, and this would increase ten-fold by 1870. The lake city vied with the older river city St. Louis for the profit of trading between east and west. Not content to be only a purveyor of goods, Chicago was rapidly developing its own industry and financial institutions. Fortunate in its geographic location, it early attracted the attention of the railroad, and would be one of the few American cities to meet the high expectations of its "boosters."

In the early 1850's Chicago had a serious problem in that much of its land was only a few feet above the level of Lake Michigan, making it difficult to keep cellars dry or streets drained. The new importance of the city as well as requirements of health demanded paved streets, and yet it was feared they would be washed away. The only solution was to elevate the streets along the lake and the Chicago River four to seven feet, which meant buildings would also have to be raised. Property owners disturbed by the costs fought the city government's plan in the courts. By 1855, however, the way had been cleared, and work began.

Pullman, arriving in late 1855 to raise buildings, opened an office and shop on Madison Street west of LaSalle, not far from the river and the Chicago and Alton railroad tracks. When in April 1858 the Tremont Hotel, the city's finest, was lifted, Pullman was first in his field and consequently was awarded the contract. Under his supervision, heavy timbers were propped along the cellar's walls and ceiling, and a thousand men and five thousand jackscrews were placed in position to lift the four-story brick hotel. Pullman stood at a distance giving directions to foremen who relayed them to the workers in and around the building. On his command the men turned the jackscrews a set number of notches. At intervals the process was repeated, and quickly the structure rose. Within an hour it was at the desired height. People and furniture had remained in the hotel undisturbed. The cost of moving the building was reported as high as $45,000.[2] On another occasion, Pullman raised simultaneously the entire block of brick stores on Lake Street, between Clark and LaSalle. Not a pane of glass was broken. After such feats he soon had more business than he could handle. By the end of the year, the twenty-seven-year-old businessman was worth $20,000 and known by Chicago's more important citizens.

Fernando Jones, a realtor, who met Pullman at this time, described him as "a lordly man." "He was always quick, ready, and wanted his men to work fast."[3] George M. Pullman was of average height and build, five foot seven and 160 pounds. He had a round face, which made him look young for his age, a high forehead, brown hair, and exceptionally bright brown eyes. In later years he grew a chinbeard to give himself a more mature appearance. His dress was immaculate and in conservative taste, and a reporter noted, "you can see that he refers his speech to his mind before he utters it." A practical and ambitious man with little interest in idle conversation, he tended to be brusque with those wasting his time. Though always polite, he was also reserved and deliberately gave the impression of a man in full command of himself.

When the cold weather froze the ground and brought work to a stop, Pullman returned east. The trip from Chicago to New York by railroad was long and difficult. He would later say that it was on one of these uncomfortable journeys that he resolved to build an improved sleeping car. This story became legend, but his decision to manufacture sleeping cars actually occurred under more prosaic circumstances.

The idea of a railroad car with sleeping facilities was first presented by R. F. Morgan in 1829, a year before the introduction of railroad passenger service to America.[4] Described as a "land barge," Morgan's proposed sleeping car was bizarre and unrealistic. There were two decks, the top one covered with awnings and intended as a promenade while the bottom one contained five berths. The early railroad coach had been kept as close as possible in design and terminology to the stagecoach. Morgan, for all his far-fetched plans, recognized that the relatively large size of the railroad coach might allow for the introduction on land of the amenities known formerly only in sea travel. His "land barge" came to nought, but from the beginning beds aboard a train were known as berths. By a twist of metaphor, however, the early sleeping car was often called a "bunk car."

In 1836, the Cumberland Valley Railroad experimented with putting beds in their regular coaches. Two years later the first patent for a sleeping car was taken out by a Charles McGrew. By 1855 various lines in different parts of the country were running cars advertised in the newspapers as "sleepers," and several companies soon came into existence to manufacture cars specifically constructed for this purpose. The most promising of these were the Wagner Sleeping Car Company and the Woodruff Sleeping Car Company. Webster Wagner, a New York station master, designed a car in 1856 and gained Commodore Vanderbilt's support to build it for the latter's railroads. At about this time, T. T. Woodruff, a master car builder of the Terre Haute and Alton line, also incorporated a car building company with the then impressive capitalization of $100,000.

Interest in the sleeping car paralleled the remarkable expansion of the railroad. Between 1850 and 1860 rail mileage tripled to thirty thousand. Most of the new construction occurred in the Midwest and connected the cities of the east with those on the Great Lakes and along the Mississippi-Ohio rivers. Everyone expected that a transcontinental line would shortly link the coasts, and common sense suggested that as railroad trips became longer in distance and in time, people would grow more concerned with traveling conditions. Rapid growth had left many rough spots in need of honing, passenger comfort being particularly backward. Railroads offered greater speed and cheaper cost than other means of transportation, but little else. Pullman described the three-and-a-half-day trip between New York and Chicago as a "nightmare." Since there was no through service, passengers had to travel by several different railroads, the roundabout route making the distance between the two cities over thirteen hundred miles. When the terminal point of a line was reached, the traveler collected his baggage and moved on to another station where he purchased a ticket and waited for a train to carry him on the next leg of his journey. Often he spent a night or two in hotels along the way while awaiting connections.

Conditions in the coaches were primitive. Narrow seats with wooden backs and hard springs did little to cushion the jolts caused by the lowness of the car's floors over the rails. Rattling windows, noises from the engine, and the clicking sound of moving wheels made conversation or resting difficult. In summer the passenger could choose between opening the windows and choking on dust, or keeping them closed and sweltering. Two small wood-burning stoves at either end of the car offered little heat in winter but did frequently cause accidents. A trip of a few hours under these circumstances was barely tolerable, while one of several days was enough to make a strong man blanch. If possible a sensible traveler planned his schedule so as to spend his nights in local hotels. It was

obvious to many that passengers would gladly pay for railroad accommodations which allowed them to travel at night in comfortable circumstances.

By the 1840's the railroad car already had assumed the shape of a
long narrow box. The first sleepers were ordinary coaches with a
few crude extras added. Three wooden shelves were permanently
fixed to the sides in a tier arrangement so that the sleeper could not
be used for day travel. Lacking privacy and adequate bedding, the
passenger would climb fully dressed onto a shelf. In time a hard
mattress of curled hair with a greasy headrest and a rough blanket
were supplied, but still women, children, and many men concerned
with comfort and appearance would not travel on a sleeper.

There was no dearth of ideas on what was needed to improve
railroad travel; most passengers considered themselves experts on
the subject. As early as 1842 the *American Railway Journal* predicted that "erelong [trains] will furnish board and lodging as well
as mere passage." [5] Everyone knew that the problem was to build a
sleeping car that could be used comfortably day and night. What
was lacking, however, was the know-how. The first practical step
toward the design of such a convertible sleeping car came in 1854
when H. B. Meyer patented a folding coach chair which a mechanic could adjust into a bed. In the next few years, others worked
on more practical versions of the hinged chair.

While Pullman was moving buildings at Albion in the early
1850's, he met a politician and businessman named Benjamin Field,
who was at that time a member of the New York Senate. After leaving the legislature in 1856, Field acquired the right to run sleepers
on the Chicago and Alton and the Galena and Chicago Union railroads. In the winter of 1857-58, Pullman went home to Albion. He
must have been concerned about his future since the construction
work in Chicago would be completed shortly. A partnership was
struck between Field, his brother Norman, and Pullman to construct and operate sleeping cars for the two Illinois lines.

Pullman, on his return to Chicago, went to the Bloomington, Illinois, works of the Chicago and Alton Railroad. There he selected
two passenger cars to make over as sleepers and hired Leonard

Siebert, an experienced railroad mechanic. The two, with an occasional helper, worked on the cars through the summer of 1858 and by September they were finished. The men had not used a blueprint, but "worked out the details and measurements as [they] came to them." [6] The cars were each forty-four feet long with room for ten upper and ten lower berths. Simply designed, hinged chairs were installed. About these iron rods ran from floor to ceiling from which were suspended ropes and pulleys attached to the upper berths. At night the upper berths were lowered halfway to the floor, while in the day they hugged the ceiling. Each car contained toilets at either end and a linen closet. To make the cars more attractive and durable, the interiors were finished in cherry wood. The total cost of remodeling was $2,000. When the sleepers were added to the regular trains of the two companies, a passenger wanting to use them would pay his regular fare and an additional charge of fifty cents. For a while Pullman employed a special conductor for his cars, but business did not warrant keeping him.

The early Pullman sleepers were not much different from others constructed at this time; if anything, they were less attractive and functional than the Woodruff and Wagner cars which were built specifically as sleepers. By 1860 Pullman had renovated several more sleepers and persuaded a third road, the short-lived Dixon Air Line, to use them. His cars were running between Chicago and Freeport, Bloomington and Dubuque, Iowa, when the Civil War started. At first business continued as usual. Early in 1862, a sleeping car was built from scratch at a cost of $7,000 for the Chicago and Alton. It had sixteen wheels, instead of the usual eight, which made for a smoother ride. Shortly after, however, the Union Army requisitioned the Pullman cars for use as troop transports.

With business temporarily halted, Pullman decided to go to the gold fields of Colorado. From the spring of 1862 to the spring of 1863, he operated a trading post in Central City, serving an area known as Gregory Gulch thirty miles southwest of Denver. Supplies brought from Denver were sold at a high profit to miners who had plenty of gold but little to spend it on. During this year, Pullman maintained his interest in the sleeping car and used his spare time to work out an idea for a hinged upper berth which would swing into the car's side. Convinced that there were many Americans of "wealth and refinement" who would gladly pay for the best, Pullman resolved to build the "biggest and best car ever." [7]

On his return to Chicago, he secured use of a repair shed of the Chicago and Alton located on the present site of the Union Station. Twenty thousand dollars were used to "fit-up" a plant, acquire the necessary materials, and hire assistants. Through the winter and spring of 1864 Pullman's small crew of carefully selected carpenters and mechanics built, under his watchful eye, a car that became a classic of American railroad history. To emphasize the revolutionary design, it was called the "Pioneer." Longer, wider, higher, and heavier than any other car, it had two cast-iron trucks, or bogeys, each with eight wheels. These were topped with coiled springs reinforced by blocks of solid rubber. Above was a raised deck on which rested the car's body.

The interior of the "Pioneer" was considered a "wonder of the age." Brocaded fabrics covered the seats, and doorframes and window sashes were of hand worked and polished woods. There was a plush red carpet, and several gilt-edged mirrors reflected the light of silver-trimmed coal-oil lamps. During the day the hinged upper berths, cleverly concealed behind ornamented wood paneling, were used to store bedding, which, consistent with the car's luxury, was of the finest quality. The "Pioneer" cost $20,000—five times the price of the ordinary car.[8]

The impressive size of the sleeping coach—a foot wider and two and one-half feet higher than any car in service—presented problems. A confident Pullman had gone ahead and built the "Pioneer" without obtaining a contract for its use by a railroad, assuming that its beauty and superiority would quickly gain the car a place. To run the "Pioneer," however, railroads would have to adjust trestles and platforms to its size, and none were eager to do this.

An extraordinary event gave Pullman an opportunity to introduce his car. After the tragic death of Lincoln, the martyred President's body was brought by a slow, roundabout route from Washington to Springfield, Illinois. Everywhere a nation in deep mourning attended the pomp and ceremony of the cortege.

The arrangements in Chicago and the trip from there to Springfield was largely handled by a committee headed by Colonel James H. Bowen, Republican State Central Committee Chairman.[9] A man of indefatigable energy and drive, Bowen was the proprietor of a large Chicago general merchandising concern. During the Civil War, he became a leader of the Union Defense Committee, which organized and equipped volunteer companies. In 1865, Bowen was also president of the Third National Bank of Chicago.[10] It is not known what Pullman's connection with the bank was at this time, but a few years later he was its principal depositor. When the Third National Bank folded in the Panic of 1873, it was known as "Pullman's bank." [11]

Bowen's committee selected the "Pioneer" to be part of the train carrying the casket from Chicago to Springfield along the route of the Chicago and Alton. Bridges were raised and platforms narrowed to accommodate the car, and on May 2, 1865, the funeral train with the "Pioneer" attached pulled out of Chicago. The engine bell tolling, the train stopped at the more important towns, taking several days to arrive in Springfield. Thus the maiden voyage of the "Pioneer" attracted national attention, and started Pullman's fame as a car builder.

The "Pioneer" proved that a well-designed car could serve with equal ease and comfort as a sleeper and day coach. As one astute observer reported, Pullman had placed the car's machinery behind the scene, "leaving only the beautiful at the fore." His job now was to convince the railroads to use the car on his terms, for Pullman intended to own and operate the sleepers: he would take the entire extra charge for the sleeper while the railroad received the passenger's regular fare. Under these conditions a line would carry his cars only if they attracted new business.

Without doubt, the "Pioneer" would have received considerable attention on its own. Pullman, however, preferred not to leave this to chance and the car was conspicuously displayed. The Chicago and Alton, impressed by the publicity at the time of Lincoln's funeral, put the new sleeping car into service on May 25, 1865. At this time the line was extended into St. Louis and its name was accordingly changed to the Chicago, Alton and St. Louis. The "Pioneer," when not in use, was placed on exhibit in the two cities, where long lines of people admired the car, while newspapers hailed its obvious superiority.[12]

Pullman quickly proved his ability as a promoter. There were excursion trips aboard the "Pioneer" for prominent citizens and reporters with free passes liberally given. The car was placed at the disposal of important civic groups, and early in June a delegation from the St. Louis Board of Trade went to Boston on the "Pioneer" as Pullman's guests. On their return, they issued a statement extolling the car's many comforts and recommending its use to all.

By August 1865 Pullman was negotiating with an important trunk line, the Michigan Central, which ran from Detroit to Chicago. This railroad already had its own sleepers and was in no hurry to replace them with Pullman's. There was also concern that travelers would view Pullman's two-dollar surcharge as too high. Discussion was at an impasse when Ulysses S. Grant reached Detroit on his way to Chicago and a hero's return to his home in Galena. By now Pullman had built additional cars even more expensive and "plush" than the first, and one was offered for Grant's use. On his acceptance it was quickly rushed to Detroit to be exhibited. A story on this car even appeared in the far-off *New York Herald* (August 22, 1865), which dramatically claimed that Pullman had found the "nostrum" for the discomforts of travel. The overwhelming approval given the car by press and public persuaded the railroad to sign a contract. The Michigan Central's own cheaper sleeping cars were soon deserted by passengers, substantiating Pullman's contention that the traveling public would gladly pay for luxury.

The success of Pullman's sleeping cars on two lines brought other railroads into his fold. By the end of 1866, the Chicago, Burlington and Quincy; the Great Western, a Canadian trunk line; and a portion of the New York Central were running his cars. Pullman now could offer through service to his passengers, who remained in their sleeper while it was switched from one track to another. This feature proved highly attractive and Pullman for obvious reasons was a leading proponent of the movement for standardization of track gauges and correlated schedules. In turn the desire of railroads to use his sleepers helped promote these advances.[13]

Accolades from the public poured into Pullman's offices. The Reverend Albert Ellis, a missionary, wrote: "I have no hesitation to state that of all the cars I have ridden . . . [yours are] by far the smoothest, and the most comfortable. They truly make traveling a pleasure, and a recreation." [14] General Philip Sherman told a company conductor, "this is the smoothest car I ever rode on." [15] Newspapers described Pullman as the "prince of railroads" and "a public benefactor," while a writer for the *Chicago Republican* (April 17, 1867), called him "a missionary of civilization," who introduced his patrons to beauty and good taste.

By May 1866 there were twenty-one cars in operation, and five awaiting use were introduced to the public in a way calculated to draw attention. On May 19, the five cars along with several older ones carried five hundred people, representing the cream of Chicago society, on a picnic. Twelve miles west of the city the train stopped at Haare's Park. Tables, chairs, and provisions were unloaded and arranged. An elaborate hot meal prepared by Chicago's finest restaurant, the Opera House, was served by white-jacketed waiters as the guests selected their dishes from silk menus. Champagne was served with the dinner, and cigars and cognac were freely offered after. Then Judge Thomas Drummond of the U. S. Circuit Court of Appeals proposed a resolution unanimously accepted by the party:

> Resolved: That the completion of the magnificent sleeping coaches marks a notable epoch in the history of railway travel and that the thanks of the entire traveling public are due to Mr. George M. Pullman, the originator of the sleeping car enterprise, whose energy, liberality and abundant means have enabled our railways to supply their patrons with every possible convenience, whereby a journey by rail becomes both a comfort and luxury.

The picnic ended with a brief speech by Pullman, thanking the guests for their compliments.

The reserved and shy Pullman did not feel comfortable in the role of a celebrity. Though pleased with his new fame and keenly aware of the need to publicize his sleepers, he carefully guarded his private life from scrutiny. His reputation among newspapermen was that of a busy man who was difficult to see,[16] interviews if granted being short and to the point. He was usually truthful but also very careful to say only what he wanted known. Pullman was very concerned with his dignity, and his formality and success virtually demanded and usually received the respect of others, though there were some who found him proud and rigid. In 1866, Pullman's brother, Albert, three years older and extremely close to him, joined the business. A relaxed and friendly man, he would act as a buffer between George Pullman and the public.

By the end of 1866, Pullman with forty-eight cars in operation dominated the sleeping-car industry in the Midwest and was now interested in pushing into the national market. In 1866, he and two wealthy young men organized the Pullman, Kimball and Ramsey Sleeping Car Company at Atlanta, Georgia,[17] to serve the southern trade. Southern railroads eager to rebuild and expand after the war's devastation quickly adopted Pullman's sleepers, and by 1868 ten major lines had contracts with the new company.

But Pullman's advances toward eastern roads were deftly blocked by two rival sleeping-car companies backed by powerful railroad men. These were the Wagner Car Company, controlled by Commodore Vanderbilt, and the Central Transportation Company which was primarily owned by Tom Scott and Andrew Carnegie of the Pennsylvania Railroad. Pullman, though, was more interested in the west coast than the east. There the Central Pacific and the Union Pacific were jointly building a transcontinental railroad which was to be completed in 1869. The western roads with their great distances were made to order for the sleepng car. Coast to coast trips requiring a week of uninterrupted travel with few accomodations available along much of the way clearly required the services that Pullman had perfected. He was nearly ready to act.

2

Pullman's Palace Car Company, 1867-80

Pullman monopolized everything. It was well that it should be
so. The men had arisen who could manage, and the tools belonged to him.

Andrew Carnegie, *Triumphant Democracy*

Well aware of the railroad's future role in settling the plains and
mountains of the West, Pullman was eager for capital to expand.
He had previously bought out his partners, Benjamin and Norman
Field, and in the fall of 1866 he decided to incorporate. This would
facilitate raising funds and, selectively offered, the stock would
gain the new company influential friends. On February 22, 1867,
the Illinois State Legislature issued a charter to "Pullman's Palace
Car Company." The company's initial offering of one million dollars in capital stock was quietly sold to railroad leaders and Chicago businessmen. On August 1, an organizational meeting was
held in Chicago, which elected five men to the board of directors,
including George M. Pullman, who was appointed President and
General Manager.[1]

When a few weeks later Thomas C. Durant, President of the
Union Pacific, visited Chicago, Pullman approached him on behalf
of the new company but found that the Union Pacific intended to
accept an offer of sleepers from the Central Transportation Company. Durant was persuaded to postpone his decision until the
Union Pacific's board meeting in September. Pullman's rival was to

be represented by Andrew Carnegie. The two men knew each other only slightly, but already Carnegie considered Pullman, "one of those rare characters who can see the drift of things, and was always to be found . . . swimming in the main current where movement was the fastest." The future steel magnate preferred a deal to fighting.

The two formed a company known as the Pullman Pacific Car Company with Carnegie's interests receiving stock in return for canceling their offer to the Union Pacific. The Union Pacific now signed a 15-year contract with this new company in October 1867.[2] A short time later, Carnegie and Pullman arranged for the Pullman Palace Car Company to acquire control of the Central Transportation Company, including its contract with a major eastern trunk line, the Pennsylvania Railroad. Pullman was now established nationwide.

The Pullman Palace Car Company's charter permitted the purchasing, manufacturing, operating, and leasing of railway cars. Pullman did not, however, build sleeping cars until 1870. After the "Pioneer" he contracted out his construction with a number of Midwest yards that built the cars according to his plans. In the fall of 1867, the Pullman Palace Car Company rented two floors of a building on Randolph Street and Michigan Avenue in Chicago, across the way from the Michigan Central Depot. The front part of one floor consisted of offices for Pullman, six company officials, two clerks, and a telegraph operator, who communicated with lines carrying Pullman's cars. Behind these was a large upholstery storeroom. The upper floor contained facilities for the manufacture and repair of "Palace" car furnishings. A bare car was brought from the manufacturer to the Michigan Central Depot. There it was inspected by the sleeping-car company, furnished, and sent out.

Pullman intended the company eventually to have its own yards. In 1868 and 1869 he purchased several large lots in Chicago, including one on Michigan Avenue and Adams Street. H. R. Hobart, editor of the *Chicago Evening Post*, told a New York reporter that the company planned a car manufactory on this site. Instead, when a

Detroit company offered its yard for a low price in 1870, Pullman bought it.

The shop, consisting of three old buildings, was located on a large block, Crogham Street and Sequindre, intersected by the Detroit and Milwaukee Railroad tracks. The buildings were considerably improved and enlarged. By 1875 the work force had grown from two hundred to six hundred men, and in 1880 the capacity of the yard was one thousand men who could produce 114 cars a year. The company also purchased a yard in Elmira, New York, where a few hundred men built and repaired cars for eastern lines, principally the Erie. To save hauling cars great distances, a network of repair shops was established. Most were railroad yards that contracted for work, but a few were owned by the company.

The manufacturing of sleeping cars was straightforward and simple as compared to their operation. Lacking a precedent, Pullman slowly developed a system by which passengers with their baggage could be carried comfortably and safely throughout the country in stylish cars equipped for continuous travel and attended by trained personnel. The Pullman Palace Car Company became a national company in both scope and service, whose passengers always knew what to expect. Judge A. O. Lochrane, the company's counsel, stated: "The essential element of the Pullman system was its entire and absolute uniformity." [3]

In 1867, a Negro porter was added to the conductor aboard each Pullman car. Conductors sold and collected tickets and enforced company rules, such as the one forbidding passengers to wear boots in bed. Porters prepared the berths for use, cleaned the cars, and rendered innumerable small services to patrons. Both were trained in the way the company expected them to perform. Their chores were prescribed in minute detail in a rule book, and they wore uniforms purchased from the company.

The company, to maintain high standards, hired "spotters" who traveled on the cars incognito to check the honesty and efficiency of the personnel. Conductors and porters were fined for such things as drinking on duty or allowing soiled washbasins. The *St. Louis*

Daily Democrat (February 28, 1873) called this a ". . . most dis-
agreeable system of espionage, that is utterly repulsive and despi-
cable to every high-minded and honorable man." "Spotters," however, also protected the valuables of sleeping travelers.

Great care was taken in servicing each car after its run for fear
that diseases and epidemics might otherwise be spread. All movea-
ble objects were removed, beaten, and exposed to the sun. Char-
women scrubbed the interior with soap and disinfectant. Each car
was equipped with one hundred sheets and pillowcases, thirty hand
towels, ten roller towels, and forty blankets. Berths were made
fresh each night with clean supplies being picked up along the way.
Laundering was a substantial part of the companys' operating expenses. The *Louisville Medical Journal* claimed that "nine out of
ten when they step into a Pullman car step into far better hygienic
conditions than when they step into their own homes." [4]

For administrative purposes the company was divided into six
regional districts, each in the charge of a superintendent.[5] The Detroit and Elmira shops were kept apart under their own superintendents, and as much as possible, the manufacturing of cars was
separated from their operation. The company, desiring the best
people as officers, paid well; even so, there was a high turnover.
Pullman, a perfectionist who kept tight control over the company's
many activities, was not an easy boss.

The P.P.C.C.'s headquarters always remained in Chicago, and
to the city's "boosters," a Pullman car upon the nation's roads
preached "the enterprise and greatness of Chicago." When the
building on Michigan and Randolph was destroyed by the "Great
Fire" of 1871, a three-story brick structure was built on Michigan
Avenue and Fourteenth Street to house the company's headquarters.

To other businessmen Pullman had done the impossible. They
believed it common sense for railroads to run their own sleepers.
Yet this car company, dependent upon others for motor power and
rails, survived and flourished. Carnegie observed, "I do not know
anyone but [Pullman] who could have . . . retained some rights
the railways were bound to respect." [6] According to the contracts

signed with the railroads, the Pullman Palace Car Company supplied all the sleeping cars that demand warranted; maintained upholstery, bedding, and carpets; and guaranteed against negligence of Pullman employees or imperfect construction of the cars. The railroads in turn kept the outside of the cars in good order and appearance. The company received all the proceeds from the sale of tickets to its cars above the regular fare for the train. If sales averaged over $7,500 per annum for each Pullman car on a line, the railroad was relieved of responsibility for the cars' exteriors. An option was offered a road to buy half interest in cars it regularly used. The contracts varied only in length of time, some being for ten years but most for fifteen.

In 1874 when the Senate Transportation Committee asked Pullman what public service his company performed, he replied in a letter:

> The aim of the Pullman Company is . . . to do work in connection with the railroad companies which they separately could not so well perform. An organization was needed to amicably right all the different interests for the better service of the public, and to combine, in one class of car and one system, as only a single company could, all needful improvements . . . so as to enable the public to use the different railway lines as though they all were under the same management.[7]

Of necessity, Pullman worked hard to sell his sleeper to the public. His strength in dealing with the railroads rested only upon the general demand for his product.

In the fall of 1875, the Michigan Central, under pressure from Commodore Vanderbilt, replaced Pullman's cars with Woodruff's. Deprived of access to New York, Pullman helped organize a new trunk line which soon carried more Chicago-New York passengers than the Michigan Central. The newspapers attributed its success to the public's desire to travel Pullman,[8] and it was generally accepted that "the Pullman cars, in point of combination, elegance, solidity and every other advantage are unrivaled." Through courting the public, the company had become so powerful that a railroad could cross it only at great risk.

At a time when other businessmen throttled rivals through ruthless price cutting, George M. Pullman rarely altered his fares. He competed only in services and remained firm in his conviction that Americans would gladly pay for quality. His cars were always equipped with the newest improvements and their interiors reflected the latest style in decor. Costs were cut by eliminating inefficiencies in the cars' manufacture and operation but never through reducing service. And any savings, to Pullman's way of thinking, rightfully belonged to the company.

Long before the age of "Madison Avenue," Pullman brilliantly created a "corporate image." "The reputation for first-class work which this company enjoys is unique. It is no exaggeration to say that anything that bears the name Pullman instantly secures favor and is immediately accepted as the fashion." [9] The outside of the cars was painted a dark olive with the company's name featured in bold lettering along both sides. The interiors were made as different as possible and people enjoyed talking about the distinctive merits of their favorite cars. Not having the national media now open to advertisers, Pullman promoted his cars at fairs, through excursion trips, and above all, by numerous innovations which were conscientiously sought for and dramatically introduced. Using this system Pullman successfully built his company, revolutionized railroad transportation, and completely altered the public's view of travel. According to the St. Louis Daily Times of March 8, 1871, "What was once really tedious [has] become a pleasure."

One such innovation, the car "Western World," loaded with notables, left the Detroit factory for New York City on April 8, 1867. Newspapers made much of the unusual feature of this otherwise conventional sleeping car: a small, six-by-three-foot kitchen. The journey of this "first hotel car had all the features of a grand ovation." A passenger wanting dinner pulled a string ringing a silver bell which summoned a waiter. A portable table was placed before him and formally set. The traveler selected his meal from a menu that included beefsteak, mutton, and ham; oysters—raw, fried, or roasted; and eggs—boiled, fried, scrambled, or cooked with rum; each item cost forty cents. There was also a choice of imported wines. "The tableware was of the nicest description and made especially for car use. . . . Vessels in which tea, coffee, and wines were served was [sic] so constructed that they did not slop their contents, and the cars moved so steadily that nothing was displaced." New York's *Rochester Daily Union* (April 10, 1867) described the "Western World" as "totally eclipsing anything in the way of passenger comfort."

Writing of the hotel car, one Chicago newspaper called Pullman, "a satiated Alexander, with no more worlds to conquer." That they underestimated the man became apparent a short time later when in April 1868 he unveiled the dining car "Delmonico." This had a six-foot-square kitchen in its center and was manned by a crew of two cooks and four waiters. The rest of the car contained tables and chairs and small cupboards inset between the windows. Every inch of space was cleverly used, and original paintings and white tablecloths made an attractive scene. The car could serve 250 meals a day. Before the introduction of the dining car, trains made frequent "twenty-minute stops." At station restaurants passengers would "bolt" a meal of "tough meats, cold vegetables, soggy bread, boiled tea, and swill coffee." Now fewer and briefer stops could be scheduled, considerably shortening travel time. A train with sleeping quarters and eating facilities was virtually self-sufficient and paused only for passengers and supplies.

These innovations occurred none too soon. For on May 10, 1869, at Promontory Point, Utah, six miles east of Ogden, the tracks of the Union Pacific and Central Pacific were joined together to establish the first transcontinental railroad. Long distance travel in the United States had entered a new phase with speed and comfort more important than ever. At 6:30 A.M., July 17, 1869, the Pullman sleeping car "Wahsatch" left Sacramento, California, with thirty passengers who each paid $136.00 in gold for a ticket to New York. The "Wahsatch" arrived only one week later at 8:00 A.M., though it had had to wait at several places for connections and crossed the Mississippi River on a ferry. *The New York Times* (July 25, 1869) began its story of the car's arrival: "A new era in railroad travel begins. Twenty years ago, 118 days were necessary to compass the trip by doubling the Horn. Now, from ocean to ocean, a little over six days are consumed." One of the first to journey over this new route wrote of Pullman's contribution in perhaps exaggerated terms: "The Continental Railroad would be almost worthless but for the labors of George Pullman. . . . My prayer to heaven is 'God bless George Pullman.'" [10]

The sleeper and the diner made the long ride to California "a genuine pleasure excursion . . . affording many of the comforts of home to the traveler." For the first time, at least within the United States, people traveled great distances not out of necessity but for pleasure. Men, families, and even unescorted women went west for a visit; eastern papers were filled with reports of returned travelers extolling the ease of the journey and the wonders of the scenery. Pullman had made travel comfortable, inexpensive, and safe enough for the middle class.

For those able to afford extra luxury, the Pullman Company introduced an "excursion" car in April 1870. This was a smaller version of the "hotel" car with a crew of four—steward, cook, and two waiters—which was rented for a period by an individual or group. The steward acting as purchasing agent made all necessary arrangements with railroads. Ticket agents now spoke of the educational value of a route, as well as its speed.

To demonstrate the wonders of modern travel, Pullman staged his most ambitious promotional excursion trip in the spring of 1870. A train called the "Pullman Hotel Express" went from Boston to San Francisco: "Faneuil Hall to the Golden Gate." This was the first through train to cross the continent. Aboard were 129 members of the Boston Board of Trade and George and Albert Pullman. Fifty thousand people inspected the train during a two-day layover in Boston before its departure, and large crowds viewed the cars in the towns and cities en route. Among the passengers was a journalist, W. R. Steele, hired to publish a daily journal, *The Transcontinental,* on a new Gordon press aboard the train.[11]

Steele described the carriages as "the most elegant . . . ever drawn over an American Railway." First was a baggage car supplied with five large ice closets and a refrigerator. The second in line contained Steele's office, a wine room, a smoking room, and a barber shop. Next came four hotel and sleeping cars, and finally the dining cars, "St. Cloud" and "St. Charles." According to *The Transcontinental*, the cars were "equipped with every desirable accessory that may tend in the least to promote the ease of the passengers," including two libraries and two Burdett organs.

The "Pullman Hotel Express" left Boston on May 23. Ten days later it pulled into San Francisco, where a bottle of Boston Bay water was ceremonially emptied into the harbor. The New Englanders toured the northern part of California before returning home on June 25. They saw buffaloes, sequoias, teepees, and army posts; and spoke to Indians, miners, Mormon elders, and businessmen seeking capital to develop the new section. Judged by newspaper coverage, the excursion succeeded in focusing attention on the ease and interest of western travel. Subsequently, the train, with all equipment except the press, was put in use on the Omaha to Ogden, Utah, run of the Union Pacific.

The Pullman Palace Car Company entered the lucrative day-coach business in 1875. Passengers paid an extra fare to sit in a "parlor" car's easy chairs with pillows for their heads and hassocks for their feet. Mounted on a swivel, the chair turned to face a window or a fellow passenger while a lever adjusted the back to the desired incline. Parlor cars found particular favor with women and the elderly, who thought them more genteel than day coaches. A number of other different types of cars were later introduced, but these were by and large variations of the sleeper, hotel, and parlor cars, or a combination of the three.

The years 1868 to 1873 were a time of rapid expansion and improvement for the railroad industry. Thirty-three thousand miles of rails were laid, and many lines were double-tracked with steel rails beginning to replace iron. George Westinghouse's air brake, invented in 1868, was widely adopted, making the use of more powerful locomotives possible. Pullman's designers reduced the weight of their cars and improved ventilation, heating, and lighting. The advent of the dining car made moving from one car to another necessary, and the company engineers worked on ways to make this safe. Trains carried several types of Pullman cars, each offering a different service. The Pullman sleeper was often called a "French flat," a term for a tenement. Now as passengers slept in one car, dined in another, had their hair cut in a third, and used the library or organ in a fourth, the whole train became a temporary community. One amazed French editor called it a "rolling village."

Although overbuilding of railroads contributed to the Panic of 1873, which depressed business conditions until 1878, the Pullman company weathered the bad times in good shape. Revenue from the operation of cars remained steady, but over-all profit declined slightly[12] because of Pullman's decision in 1875 to manufacture baggage and passenger cars for sale to railroads. A drop in these orders caused him in June 1878 to reduce wages in his Detroit plant.

With the return of business confidence in 1879, many businessmen, including George Pullman, considered the stage set for another phenomenal period of railroad growth. By summer the Detroit shops, working at capacity, could not meet the demand for cars, and wage rates were restored. It was now decided to expand into freight-car manufacturing. Throughout October reports circulated that the Detroit shops would be greatly enlarged. The next month, however, it was announced that a new plant was to be built elsewhere. The company wanted to increase efficiency and economy in servicing cars by spreading facilities. St. Louis was an ideal location, and in mid-November Pullman visited there to look for a site.

He wanted several hundred acres adjacent to railroad and water transportation. A large tract near the Pacific Railroad tracks interested him, but the price of $2,500 an acre was too high. After Pullman left St. Louis, negotiations continued on two other sites while the St. Louis Republican (November 25, 1879), stressing the factory's importance to the city, asked the real estate owners to be reasonable. This plea was ignored and as speculation forced prices higher the company lost interest. Disappointed in St. Louis Pullman turned his attention to Chicago. Several company officials considered the city too near Detroit for advantageous spacing of facilities, but he believed its industry and transportation offered compensation. The solution was found when, in December, Pullman, with his family and several friends, traveled to Long Branch, New Jersey, for Christmas, and included among the guests was Pullman's old acquaintance Colonel Jim Bowen.

Bowen was in Long Branch to discuss a site for the new plant. In 1868, he had formed a company to sell land for industrial use in the Calumet region, an area south of Chicago along Lake Michigan and the Indiana border. Soon after, Congress had allocated funds to build a harbor where the Calumet River flowed into Lake Michigan, and federal money was sought to dredge the river from its mouth to Lake Calumet, but the depression postponed any real development of the area. By 1879, Bowen's Calumet and Chicago Canal and Dock Company had been pushed into bankruptcy and its land tied up in legal suits.

Pullman had good reasons for selecting the Calumet region for his new plant. Land prices in Chicago were prohibitive, and even long established firms were going to the suburbs. Calumet offered cheap land, low taxes, and excellent transportation. The nearby mills made iron and steel readily available, and wood, the principal material used in car construction, could be easily brought by barge from the forests of northern Michigan.

The shortest entry into Chicago for railroads coming from the east and south passed through the Calumet region, and by 1880 six crisscrossed the area. As economic recovery brought industry to this area, these roads vied for the carrying trade. Plans were put forward for a belt line circling Chicago with its southern terminus at South Chicago, a town which had sprung up along Calumet Harbor. In 1879, the North Chicago Rolling Mills moved to Calumet, and it was quickly followed by other steel works, which needed large tracts of flat land near water. Iron ore was shipped down Lake Michigan from Michigan and Minnesota mines, while coal was brought by rail from Indiana and southern Illinois. Within ten years the Calumet region was to be America's second largest steel center.

Pullman, acting on Bowen's suggestion, had already purchased land along Lake Calumet's west bank in 1869,[13] but now he wanted

additional acreage for the factory site. To avoid a repetition of the
St. Louis speculation, Bowen was instructed to buy the land for a
secret owner.[14] When Pullman and Bowen returned to Chicago in
January 1880, plans commenced for the rapid acquisition of several
thousand acres on the north, south, and west banks of Lake Calumet. The major problem was that the land was in small parcels
owned by many people. Though Bowen moved quickly, the trans-
action still took several months, during which time the company
carefully tried to cloak its interest.

Reporters who questioned company officials concerning Pullman's intentions were told that he could not decide between Indi-
anapolis, Kansas City, St. Louis, and Chicago. But by February the
shrewdest surmised that Chicago had the "plum." The giveaway
was the announcement on January 26 by the Allen Paper Wheel
Company of New York that a factory was to be built in the Chicago
area. The Pullman Palace Car Company was the largest buyer of
their product—a car wheel filled with compressed paper—and had
recently obtained control of this company. It was obvious that the
plant would be in proximity to the new Pullman works. Many observers guessed that the shops would be in Calumet. They knew the
area had what the company needed and there were reports of large
sales in the vicinity of Calumet Lake where Pullman owned land.
The company stepped up its deception. Albert Pullman denied that
the factory would be in Calumet, and a special car filled with company personnel roamed the countryside looking at various sites.

In early April, Pullman revealed the general plans of the factory,
but still insisted no city or site had been selected. Despite this denial, excitement ran high among Chicago realtors, and speculators
began buying in Calumet. Then on April 24, George M. Pullman
called a press conference and announced the location. The *Chicago
Tribune* for April 25 reported, "this is the most important enterprise, as far as real estate goes, that Chicago has yet seen, and its
effects will be great and lasting."

In four months the company had purchased over four thousand
acres at a price of $800,000.[15] Altogether there had been seventy-
five individual transactions; the last completed only days before the

announcement. Much of the land was swamp, a habitat for ducks and hunters, still the cheapness of the price provoked surprise and was viewed as evidence of Bowen's shrewdness. Within three years land bought for $75 to $200 an acre was valued at $1,000 to $3,000 an acre. Chicagoans, however, would soon learn that the importance of the purchase far exceeded its effects on local real estate, for George Pullman was preparing to build a model town adjacent to his new factory.

3

George M. Pullman and the Social Problems of His Time

Though placing business obligation above all else, Pullman found time for a private life. Early in 1867 he met Harriet Sanger, the small, darkhaired, and attractive daughter of a prosperous Chicago railroad contractor. Her lively, outgoing personality captivated the reserved businessman ten years her senior, and after a brief courtship they were married quietly on June 13, 1867. The marriage proved enduring and happy, and in time two daughters and twin sons were born, the eldest daughter, Florence, being the father's favorite. Pullman was a dutiful husband and father, whose relations with his fun-loving but often ailing wife were always close even though she knew little about his business activities. The only serious contention between husband and wife was in Pullman's high expectations for his sons, who keenly disappointed him.

Mrs. Pullman's charm, enhanced by wealth and her husband's prestige, made the family a leader in Chicago society. They entertained often and lavishly, making their home a "magnet for the wealthiest, wittiest and most favored." The family's style of life surpassed that of families with considerably greater fortunes. Believing that attractive surroundings and elegance were important, Pullman readily indulged his wife's expensive tastes, and the children received the finest of private school educations here and abroad.

In 1873, the Pullmans commissioned John M. Dunphy, a Chicago architect, to build a mansion at 1729 Prairie Avenue. This southside street across the Illinois Central tracks from Lake Michigan was little more than a cow path running through sand dunes when Marshall Field, "Chicago's Merchant Prince," built his home there in 1873. Others soon followed and "a double line of brick or stone dwellings [arose], some built in blocks, others—the grander ones— standing proudly aloof behind iron picket fences in their own grounds with stables." [1] Prairie Avenue became "the very Mecca of Mammon, the Olympus of the great gods of Chicago."

Additions in 1879 enhanced Pullman's home, and it was acknowledged "grandest of all," newspapers estimating its value between $350,000 and $500,000. A three-story greystone with mansard roof, it was set in a private garden adorned by lighted fountains and a large conservatory. Its interior was ornamented with teak paneling, marble, and expensive furnishings, and the house contained a music room with pipe organ, a library, and a small theater in the attic. Fond of music, Pullman frequently hired organists to play for the family and friends. Several hundred people could easily be entertained; and when the daughters made their debut in 1893, a thousand guests attended an afternoon and evening reception.

The P.P.C.C.'s success in becoming a national, and later international, company required Pullman to travel extensively. He estimated that about half his time was spent away from Chicago, and in 1876 a private car costing $38,000 was built for him. This "mansion on wheels" became a valued status symbol of the day, and was used on occasion by every American president from Grant to McKinley as well as by such visiting dignitaries as the Brazilian Emperor Dom Pedro and Princess Eulalie of Spain. Often the family came east in early June and remained until late September. Their grand style of travel was described by a *Chicago Tribune* reporter who noted that they occupied the private car, while twelve servants and baggage were in two following cars, with yet a fourth car holding five riding horses.

Pullman owned an islet with an imposing stone house, "Castle

Rest," in the St. Lawrence River, and a home in Albion, New York. But summers were usually spent in "Fairlawn" an estate in Long Branch, New Jersey—near the Atlantic Ocean, and only thirty miles south of New York City. At this time, Long Branch was a well-known watering place, famous for its scenery and excellent carriage roads. When Pullman came in 1869, it was being transformed as businessmen, made rich by the new importance of industry and transportation, built summer homes there.

The sleeping-car king commuted frequently between "Fairlawn" and the city. A suite was permanently retained in his friend Charles Waite's Windsor Hotel on Forty-sixth Street, and he used the company's office in the Mills Building, Broad Street and Exchange, in the center of the financial district. Pullman had several interests in New York, perhaps the most important being a company that built and operated an elevated railroad along Third Avenue.

The Chicagoan also visited Washington often, and knew prominent politicians of both parties. With some he exchanged advice on the stock market for information on legislation pertinent to his company.[2] He was particularly interested in high tariffs, hard money, enforcement of patent rights, and avoidance of regulation of sleeping-car rates, all of which he viewed as essential to the economy in general and his company in particular. Pullman, an ardent Republican, believed this party's success important for business prosperity, and contributed heavily to its presidential campaigns. Not far from "Fairlawn" was Ulysses S. Grant's "Summer White House," and General Horace Porter, who resigned as Grant's presidential secretary in 1872 to join the car company, carefully nurtured the friendship between his old and new employers.[3]

Twice in the 1870's George Pullman visited Great Britain and the Continent, remaining several months on each occasion. The first time was in December 1872 when the Midland Railroad, which ran from London to Liverpool, contracted for his sleepers. Encouraged by this success, Pullman hoped to extend his activities elsewhere in Europe, but his efforts were blocked by a newly formed Belgian company that featured cars designed by an American, Colonel William D'Alton Mann. A shop to build Pullman cars for use on Italian lines was established in Turin, Italy, but elsewhere on the Continent Colonel Mann's "boudoir car"—each compartment having an entrance of its own—was preferred.[4]

When at home in Chicago, Pullman arrived at his office between eight and nine in the morning. He worked at a meticulously ordered desk until one o'clock and then joined Marshall Field, John Crerar, A. O. Sprague, and Phillip Armour at the "millionaire's table" in the main dining room of the Chicago Club on Michigan Avenue. Pullman was highly regarded by his peers, who considered him a forceful, strong-willed man of considerable business foresight,[5] and many of them held stock in his company and sat on its Board of Directors.

Returning to his office at three, Pullman remained until six. Often he came to work on Sundays after church services. He was known to be eager for new ideas and spent a great deal of his time with visitors. A reporter who came for an interview found the reception room crowded with men holding clumsily wrapped inventions on their knees. A visiting French economist noted with astonishment that it was customary "to doff one's hat when waiting for Mr. Pullman" which "may seem a simple matter to a French reader, but an American . . . stands stupefied when he sees all the heads uncovered. Indeed, I have seen plenty of people take it more at ease when with President Harrison." [6]

Pullman's office employees viewed him with a mixture of fear, fondness, and respect. One recounted: "I never knew a man so reserved. He was always mighty good to me, and I think he'd have liked to treat others that way and make them his friends. But he couldn't. He just didn't know how." [7] His men knew it was difficult to put anything over on him. The smallest mistakes came to his attention, and the malefactor would receive a cutting tongue lashing. A wrongdoer who had this experience described Pullman as being "about as hot as an ice crusher in the winter out on the lake." On occasion, however, he could loose a monumental rage which often left him apologetic in its wake.

While Pullman showed little interest in the private lives of his men, he paid high salaries, and certain of his actions indicated con-

cern of a kind with their welfare. In May 1873, he had his brother
Albert charter the Pullman Mutual Benefit Association. Employees
who joined paid an initiation fee of two dollars and were taxed a
dollar upon the death of a member with the funds providing for the
family of the deceased. Two months earlier, Pullman had announced plans for the construction of a company building which
included unusual facilities for employees. A restaurant would furnish a "cheap and convenient place for the working force . . . to
get their dinners and to cultivate a society . . . of harmony and
good feeling." In addition, there were to be bathing facilities, a
library, and family rooms. All of this would be available to the men
on their days off, as well as after work. Pullman explained his intentions by stating that "whatever tends to make the [company's]
headquarters attractive to the employee has the effect to make
them more useful." [8] Actually the building was not constructed
until ten years later and by this time Pullman had achieved a more
grandiose setting for his ideas.

Despite his frequent absences, Pullman participated fully in Chicago's social and civic life. He helped organize the Calumet and
Commercial clubs and served them as an officer; he was also a
member of the Chicago and Union clubs. The Commercial Club,
started in December 1877, with membership limited to sixty, met
once a month for a dinner and speeches. According to the charter
the club's purpose was "to advance by social intercourse and by a
friendly interchange of views the prosperity and growth of this
city." The members concerned themselves with honest urban government, increasing educational facilities, and improving the city's
housing, sewerage, and transportation. The other three clubs were
primarily social, each maintaining a club house. The Calumet Club
house on Twentieth Street and Michigan was only two blocks from
Pullman's home, and he often came there in the evening.

⌊Pullman gave time and money, often anonymously, to many civic
causes, particularly to efforts concerned with improving young
workingmen.⌋The Young Men's Christian Association was created
at a public meeting on October 17, 1871. On its Board of Directors
from the inception, Pullman was elected president in 1872 and

served until 1874. During his presidency, the name was changed to Chicago Athenaeum and the purpose was narrowed from general philanthropy to education. A building was acquired and equipped with classrooms, a library, bathrooms, and a gymnasium. Courses intended for practical use, ranging from bookkeeping to modern languages, were offered members for a nominal fee.

Pullman also served as a vice-president of the Citizens' Law and Order League. The League enforced laws prohibiting the sale of liquor to minors by instituting court cases against saloons which were in violation. It was organized in 1877 in reaction to the sight of intoxicated youths joining in the labor disturbance of that year, and it soon became the model for groups in other cities. Interested in the training as well as morals of young men, Pullman and his close friend Marshall Field were influential forces in the Commercial Club's sponsorship of the Chicago Manual Training School in 1883 and were on the school's Board of Trustees. Here students from working-class families paid low tuition for a three-year program that trained them to be skilled mechanics. Along with traditional courses in mathematics and English, there were others in mechanical drawing and the use of tools. Pullman's sustained interest in the education of workingmen may have been influenced by his own early deprivations. Clearly it reflected his concern as an employer with what he considered the poor quality of American labor. It also rested, however, on the deep conviction that no "question was more important to American society than [that of the] taste, health, cheapness of living and comfort among the artisan class." [9]

Josiah Strong described the American city of this time: "Here . . . is the congestion of wealth severest. Dives and Lazarus are brought face to face; here in sharp contrast are the ennui of surfeit and the desperation of starvation." The industrialization that occurred at a rapid, unplanned pace after the Civil War had many effects on the country. The 1870's witnessed the erection of New York's Fifth Avenue, San Francisco's Nob Hill, and Chicago's Prairie Avenue. These streets were a physical representation of the rise of the American millionaire from a handful in the 1860's to over four thousand by 1892.[10] On the other hand, this period also saw a dramatic intensification in the numbers of the urban poor, as people with little capital and few useful skills came to the American cities from farms and foreign countries in search of employment. A thin line of homes for the wealthy and the comfortable sprang up along Chicago's lake front, but to the west stretched the hovels of the poor. Slum and mansion had become part of the American-cityscape, the two offering vivid illustration of the promise and the price of industrial society.

The cities grew at a phenomenal rate. In 1870, Chicago's population was 298,977, but within ten years this swelled to 503,185. By 1882, Dr. Oscar De Wolf, Chicago's Health Commissioner, reported with apprehension a "dangerous overcrowding in all the poorer districts." [11] Land and construction costs had risen rapidly and most of the people coming to the city, in particular immigrants from southern and eastern Europe, could not afford to build or buy a home. In consequence, according to De Wolf, "the building of tenements on speculation" was now "a regular and profitable means of investing capital." Speculators in a hurry for profit erected flimsy structures on unimproved land distant from services. In addition, antiquated buildings originally intended for single residences were being converted into tenements, housing as many as a dozen families. De Wolf found "several [immigrant] families living huddled together in one room, with mere boards and curtains for partitions between their scanty goods."

Congestion, dirt, poor sanitation were held responsible for diseases such as cholera and tuberculosis. Not only did this mean high death rates and ill health for the poor and their children—in itself an economically and morally reprehensible situation—but it offered the specter of contagion running throughout the city. Mary Reilly, the Irish servant girl, could visit her family on Sunday and on Monday return to Prairie Avenue bringing the dreaded cholera with her.

The slums offered other potential for trouble. Crime, prostitution, and violence were laid at the doorsteps of poor housing, while alcoholism was singled out as a particularly pernicious product of the slum. De Wolf reported that the many saloons were well patronized in these areas. The passerby in the early evening would find small clusters of men sitting on stairs and curbs, who later, singly and in pairs, would make their way to the tavern. According to De Wolf they could not go to homes that offered no space for relaxation or even "standing room . . . until the smaller children are packed away in the corners after the evening meal." A letter writer to the *Chicago Tribune* (October 11, 1872) thought alcoholism among the poor primarily due to "the pressing want of decent and good homes."

During the decade from 1870 to 1880 Chicago did not experience a year free of labor disturbances. The danger present in this situation became obvious in July 1877, when disorders touched off by a strike on the Baltimore-Ohio Railroad occurred in a score of cities. In Chicago conflicts between mobs and police persisted for four days and left thirteen men dead and hundreds injured. The local newspapers reported the trouble under such flaming headlines as "Civil War," "Horrid Social Convulsion," and "Red War." To men of wealth and position, the events of July 1877 were a frightening harbinger. According to historian James Ford Rhodes, they "had hugged the delusion that such social uprisings belonged to Europe and had no reason of being in a free republic where there was plenty of room and an equal chance for all." It was now painfully clear that strikes and disorders were a consequence of a growing chasm between workingmen and employers. By 1880 fear of social upheavals that could rend the very fabric of society was widespread.

One reaction was to strengthen the police power of the state. Congress and state legislatures were petitioned to increase the militia and build new armories. Marshall Field, for instance, asked that a large standing army permanently guard against a recurrence of the riots. But there was also increased concern with the causes of labor unrest and a fresh impetus to do something about them. Many attributed the poverty and terrible living conditions of the working class to the lack of such virtues as frugality, industriousness, and temperateness. It was assumed that a man who had these standards could better himself and his children, and that only the lazy and improvident need remain poor. Therefore, the general solution to the problems of the workingman was to elevate his character. Yet there was growing recognition that the workingman's environment made the acquisition of desirable values difficult. Overcrowded homes lacking privacy "broke down the barriers of self-respect and prepar[ed] the way for direct profligacy," [12] while personal cleanliness and respectable dress were understood to be almost impossible without proper sanitation. The need now began to be stated in terms of aiding the workingman to achieve "comfortable homes and decent surroundings" so that he and his children might develop middle-class values. More and more the reformer and social critic concerned himself with housing and education for the worker.

Pullman had a serious interest in the labor problem as early as 1872. In that year, while aboard a ship for England, he read and then reread a popular novel of the day, Charles Reade's *Put Yourself in His Place*. This Victorian romance opens with a description of the English town of Hillsborough, which was an accurate depiction of conditions in many other industrial communities in America as well as Europe:

> Industries so vast . . . on a limited space had been fatal to beauty . . . The city is pock-marked with public houses and bristles with high chimneys. They are not confined to a locality, but stuck all over the place like cloves in an orange. They . . . belch forth messy volumes of black smoke that hang like acres of crepe over the place, and veil the sun and the blue sky.

Here was the grim stage upon which an unremitting and violent conflict was fought between capital and labor. The employer in Reade's novel callously viewed his labor force as but a cog in the wheel of production. His employees organized into secret trade unions and asserted their will through bombing factories and terrorizing workers who would not join them. Each side viewed the other as an enemy and was indifferent to the general welfare. A learned and kindly doctor urges each to consider the other's position—"put yourself in his place." He influences a young inventor, who through hard effort had risen from workingman to owner. The inventor applies scientific principles to production, bringing higher profit to the owners, safer and pleasanter working conditions for the men, and an improved product for the public. While Reade blamed both sides for the social problems described in his novel, there can be no question that he considered the terrorist practices of unions as being the main immediate concern. On returning home, Pullman frequently told friends that Reade's novel had convinced him that capital and labor must learn to co-operate for their mutual benefit.

In their quest for business success, the entrepreneurs of the Gilded Age inadvertently touched off a whirligig of social change. Pullman was hardly alone in believing something had to be done. By the end of the 1870's many were urging either reform or rejection of a system which in its emphasis on individual freedom appeared indifferent to social wrongs. Disturbed by the evident disparity between the conditions of the rich and those of the poor a Senate committee in 1883 even suggested limiting the money spent for mansions. Though fully enjoying the perquisites of wealth, George Pullman was deeply disturbed that the circumstances of common life had become dangerous and deplorable. Seeing nothing wrong in a society oriented toward the profit motive, his intention was only to apply principles of business efficiency to meet the needs of his own workers. These ideas were promoted with the same verve as earlier had been lavished on the sleeping car. Pullman wanted to perfect, not alter, free enterprise.

4

Industrial Expansion and a Planned Community

It was the need for a new factory that offered George Pullman the opportunity to do something about his ideas on capital and labor. When he announced its site in late April 1880, he also unveiled plans to include houses for the workingmen. However, little attention was awarded this news as brush-fire speculation had started in the Calumet region, and the plant's impact on land values preempted public interest. The *Chicago Tribune* (April 25, 1880) duly noted that there would be 320 dwellings, occupying sixteen blocks, and commented that "the good taste and sense of beauty Mr. George M. Pullman has brought the public to expect . . . will be a characteristic feature of his new establishment." Few apparently knew the car manufacturer's intention of building a model company town.

The rising cost of urban property had pushed Chicago companies toward the suburbs early in the 1870's. With the economic revival of 1879, this tendency increased. Suburbs offered cheap land, lower taxes, and elbow room, but usually could not provide the needed labor. Companies that relied primarily on unskilled workers assumed that men would follow the job supply and led the move to the suburbs. Most simply left their employee's housing needs to contractor and speculator, but a few, such as the McCormick

Reaper Works, built inexpensive cottages in order to offer workers shelter at a minimal rent or sale price.

Industries, such as car works, which required skilled mechanics, were chary of leaving the city. In May 1882 William Henry Osborn, the former president of the Illinois Central Railroad, wrote to his successor: "The desideratum in establishing large workshops is to have them at a settlement large enough for good schools, churches, and other appliances, which the better class of workmen and superior officers demand for themselves and families." [1] Osborn explained that he had selected Chicago as the location for the railroad's principal shop because it contained "all the necessary comforts of modern life." He wondered, however, if the "moral status and character" of the workers might have been improved had the company placed the yard on the "bare prairies" away from the "seductive city." He urged his successor, William Ackerman, to weigh carefully the advantages and disadvantages of the city for workingmen in choosing any future shop sites. Other businessmen also viewed the city as a cause of labor unrest. They were troubled by the proximity of bar and brothel, criminals and labor agitators.[2]

The strikes of 1877 had forced business leaders to consider their employees and to show a greater interest in their feelings. In the 1880's a few American companies began to use "social secretaries" or "welfare managers" whose function was to improve employee morale.[3] William Ackerman wrote in 1882 that he believed the last few years had seen "a gradual improvement in the morale of railway employees throughout the country . . . owing largely to the efforts made by officers of the leading lines in the country to afford their men the advantages of reading rooms and other conveniences." [4] The concept of employee morale as a factor in production had struck root in the American business mind.

Businessmen prided themselves on managerial skill in enterprises of size and complexity, and desired to impose central control. A reporter for the *New York World* (December 25, 1892) found "Mr. Pullman's bump of order . . . developed to an astounding degree. He simply cannot endure litter and confusion. . . . The love of order is the keynote to a great system, wide in scope and based

upon broad and often very bold ideas." The sleeping-car king ab-
horred inefficiency resulting from workingmen's drinking to excess,
dissipating their time and health, and moving pointlessly from job
to job. Like many, he believed these practices too costly to be tolerated. In his opinion, it "was to the employer's interest to see that his
men are clean, contented, sober, educated and happy," but he wondered how this could be done when urban circumstances "com-
pelled [workers] to live in crowded and unhealthy tenements, in
miserable streets, and subject to all the temptation and snares of a
great city." [5] Concerned with the general conditions of labor, particularly as they affected his own people, Pullman, in the early
1870's, became an interested observer of the model tenement movement.

The leading spokesman for this movement was Alfred T. White,
a wealthy resident of Brooklyn, New York. White intended to in-
volve the "intelligent and wealthy" in the problem of housing for
workingmen through dramatizing the seriousness of the situation
and the simplicity of its solution. It was White's conviction that the
poor were paying high rents for hovels which made their owners
rich. Accordingly, a public-spirited man could erect well-designed
and decently constructed buildings which offered clean, light, and
ventilated rooms while still receiving a reasonable 7 per cent return
on his investment.[6] White thought the solution was to aid the worker
to help himself: "The reception of a home as a specie of charity
is quite as harmful as to the poor, quite as destructive of self-
respect, quite as discouraging to the industrious, as is the direct
receiving of alms without adequate return in labor. Fair return for
fair rents, simple justice and not which is falsely called charity, is
what the industrious laboring classes ask [for], and what they are
entitled to."[7] Every effort was to be made to protect the landlord's
investment. Rents were to be paid promptly and in advance, while
an elaborate rule book restricted a tenant's activity so as to safe-
guard property and avoid inconvenience to others. In return the
landlord would show self-restraint and charge only enough to show
a proper profit. White hoped that the success of the model tenement would force less enlightened property owners to raise stand-

ards or face vacancies. As a recent study has pointed out, "the model tenement movement represented no challenge whatever to economic orthodoxy. It was a painless and ostensibly effective solution to the housing problem." [8] The worker acquired a decent home while the landlord rendered a public service and received a profit for his trouble. Everyone was to gain and no one to lose.

By 1879, White had erected two housing compounds for workingmen—one of tenements, the other of single-family cottages— and published a pamphlet, *Improved Dwellings for the Laboring Classes: The Need, and the Way to Meet It on Strict Commercial Principles*. . . . This work attracted attention and generated substantial enthusiasm. Many of New York's ministers delivered sermons concerning the housing problem on Sunday, February 23, 1879. Public meetings about this subject were commonly held in large cities. A trade magazine, *Plumber and Sanitary Engineer*, in 1878, sponsored a well-publicized contest for the best design of a model tenement, which is remembered by the historian for having produced the notorious dumbbell tenement.

The actual accomplishments of the model tenement movement proved negligible. Though many among the "intelligent and wealthy" praised it, only a handful invested money, and the few projects erected could not set standards for the general housing market. But, in 1879 and for many years after, its promises seemed bright. It had helped intensify the growing public concern with slums and their adverse effect on health and morals. The strikes and riots of the 1870's suggested a dramatic connection between labor unrest and poor urban conditions. Any effort to mitigate these would naturally attract attention.

The houses to be erected by Pullman were such an attempt. Pullman agreed with those who thought workingmen could afford decent homes.[9] He also respected the opinion that adequate housing was essential for social well-being, and in time he came to the conviction that good homes for his employees would solve his labor problems. While the model tenement movement intended to use commercial means to reach a philanthropic end, Pullman took many of its premises and placed them in a strictly business setting:

The object in building Pullman was the establishment of a great manufacturing business on the most substantial basis possible, recognizing . . . that the working people are the most important element which enters into the successful operation of any manufacturing enterprise. We decided to build, in close proximity to the shops, homes for workingmen of such character and surrounding as would prove so attractive as to cause the best class of mechanics to seek that place for employment in preference to others. We also desired to establish the place on such a basis as would exclude all baneful influences, believing that such a policy would result in the greatest measure of success . . . from a commercial point of view. . . . Accordingly the present location of Pullman was selected. That region of the country was then sparsely populated.[10]

In building on a prairie, Pullman needed to provide stores, churches, and schools, for his tenants could not depend upon the neighborhood for services as did model tenements in the cities. Of necessity he constructed a community which provided a place for shopkeeper and professional, as well as laborer and clerk. In range of skills and types of occupations, the new town's inhabitants differed little from the people in many other American communities. The town stood apart in that the major employer owned all the buildings and land. Pullman told a reporter: "A man who can bring his mind down to understand the simplest business proposition can fathom the Pullman scheme very easily. It is simplicity itself—we are landlord and employers. That is all there is of it." [11]

Pullman wanted his town distinguished for its beauty and order. According to Lewis Mumford, the common practice was that "the location of factories, the building of quarters for the workers, even the supply of water and the collection of garbage, should be done exclusively by private enterprise seeking for private profit. . . . None of these needs was regarded as worthy of rational appraisal and deliberate achievement." [12] The proposed town was not to be the result of casual growth, but a planned creation, reflecting forethought and taste. Pullman intended to hire an architect, a landscape designer, and sanitary engineers to anticipate and prepare for all human needs. Utility and attractiveness were to be their criteria in constructing the town.

The model tenement movement, concerned with keeping rents low, substituted "sanitary" for "foul" dwellings. Aesthetics, though not completely ignored, was underplayed as adding to cost. Pullman intended to go further and build attractive homes. The French economist, Paul de Roussiers, who had interviewed him, commented on the businessman's deep conviction in the "Anglo-Saxon idea, that exterior respectability aids true self-respect." [13] To Pullman aesthetics had a virtue and function of its own which he called the "commercial value of beauty." He said this principle had been derived from his business experience, and he frequently recalled how people had scoffed at the expensive appointments in sleeping cars, predicting abuse by the "rougher element." Instead, passengers had responded to the cars' beauty by being exceptionally well behaved and considerate of property. The company's experience demonstrated, according to Pullman, that beauty improved the individual, and that a businessman who understood this could profit from his insight. American society had tended to ignore beauty only because its financial value was not obvious. The success of his company and now of the town would demonstrate the importance of aesthetics as a civilizing force which had commercial as well as social implications.[14]

Those who spoke about the physical environment's influence on "character" usually limited themselves to showing the harmful effects of poor surroundings. A few went beyond this to emphasize the corollary that good conditions were beneficial. Pullman firmly believed an aesthetic town setting would have a dramatic and lasting impression on a community, "ennobling and refining" it. For this reason, all buildings—commercial, industrial, and residential—were designed to be ornamental as well as practical; to Pullman they were obverse sides of the same coin. The town's appearance was to be carefully cultivated and conscientiously maintained.

The press was told: "I have faith in the educational and refining influences of beauty, and beautiful and harmonious surroundings, and hesitate at no necessary expenditure to secure them." Actually, there was never any intention of the company paying for the entire cost of the town, but only for the works. The expense of building and beautifying the residential area would be met by charging rents set to return a 6 per cent profit on capital invested. According to Pullman, people did not appreciate what was handed them. He shared the prevalent view that giving something for nothing was injurious to the integrity of all concerned. The people of the town would benefit immeasurably from the concern and foresight of their employer. But they were not to expect gifts. As with passengers in a sleeping car, they paid a surcharge for beauty.

Pullman deliberately spoke of his town as a "strictly business proposition." He risked his company's money only because he believed it was a safe investment and would bring a profit, as well as less tangible gains. The town was expected to attract and retain a superior type of workingman, who would in turn be "elevated and refined" by the physical setting. This would mean contented employees and a consequent reduction in absenteeism, drinking, and shirking on the job. Furthermore, such workers were expected to be less susceptible to the exhortation of "agitators" than the demoralized laborers of the city slums. His town would protect his company from labor unrest and strikes. Pullman went out of his way to make these practical considerations clear to all.

The community was expected to attract visitors, and the public would be made aware that the "Pullman system," which had succeeded in railroad travel, was now being applied to the problems of labor and housing. Its success would present dramatic testimony of the wisdom of one man and his company. Both could not help but benefit from their sponsorship of a town widely known for beauty and functionalism. The desire to join the two qualities inseparably in the public mind with the town and the company probably led its founder to name the community "Pullman." Without question the town was intended as a showplace.

Repeatedly denying any philanthropic motivations, Pullman justified his actions as a practical response to pressing business needs. The company was furthering its interests by helping the employees.

It was a unilateral and costless gesture by capital to help labor aid itself for their mutual benefit, and this to Pullman was the scheme's genius. From knowledge of his associates, he commented: "capital will not invest in sentiment, nor for sentimental considerations for the laboring classes. But let it once be proved that enterprises of this kind are safe and profitable and we shall see great manufacturing corporations developing similar enterprises, and thus a new era will be introduced in the history of labor." [15] The town of Pullman would point the way for less perceptive businessmen to follow.

As the town became well known, many began to compare it with certain model company towns in Europe: Saltaire, England; Guise, France; and the Krupp's work in Essen, Germany. Some went so far as to claim that Pullman derived his original ideas from one or another of these, but Pullman denied this. For him the town had been a simple and logical extension of his business experience. A pamphlet prepared by the company for distribution at the Columbian Exposition of 1893 stated: "The story of Pullman naturally divides itself into three parts—the building of the car, the building of the operating system, and the building of the town. Each of these stages is the natural logical sequence of the other. Through them all runs the same underlying thought, the same thread of idea."

II

THE MODEL TOWN, 1880-93

5

Physical Planning of Town and Factory

> In the spring of 1880 . . . the west shore of Lake Calumet, nine miles south of Chicago, was a wilderness of grass turning from the browns of winter to grays, greens and yellows. Its solitary inhabitant was the transient duck alighting for a moment in its flight from the marshes of the Kankakee. No sign of human life was to be seen except the smoke rolling from the steel mills of South Chicago, several miles to the east, some straggling houses to the south, at an insignificant station on the Illinois Central, and far to the north the busy chimneys of Chicago.
>
> Henry Demarest Lloyd, "Pullman" [1]

Four years later this prairie was the site of giant works and a population of over eight thousand people. While this growth was remarkable, prompting one reporter to suggest that the builders must have had the help of Aladdin's genie of the lamp, it was not unique in a rapidly growing nation which had seen many a boom town come and go. What attracted world attention to Pullman, Illinois, was the sight of a town being built out of whole cloth in which "everything fits." America's "first all-brick city," Pullman was intended as an example of how forethought and planning could solve community problems. The experience and intelligence of American business would demonstrate how industrialization could resound to the mutual benefit of employer and employee.

The charter of the Pullman Palace Car Company only allowed the company to "purchase . . . and hold such real estate as may be deemed necessary for the successful prosecution of their business." [2] Eager to avoid legal difficulties, George Pullman consulted his company's attorneys concerning the four thousand acres Bowen had purchased. On their advice, he kept about five hundred acres for the car company, and turned the remainder over to a corporation, the Pullman Land Association, formed in the spring of 1880, but which was never anything other than a legal fiction.[3] It was on the P.P.C.C.'s holding that factory and town were to be built.

From early January 1880, an architect and a landscape designer were hard at work in an office set aside for them in the company's building on Michigan Avenue. Solon Spenser Beman and Nathan F. Barrett had been recently commissioned to plan and supervise the construction of the model community. For perhaps the first time in America, an architect and landscape designer were to collaborate on the aesthetic and functional form of an entire town. The *Boston Herald* (August 1, 1881) described their assignment as a "professional dream come true."

Barrett had landscaped estates on his native Staten Island and in fashionable Tuxedo, New York, and Long Branch, New Jersey. In the spring of 1879, when George Pullman wanted to improve his New Jersey estate, "Fairlawn," a neighbor recommended Barrett, who in turn introduced Beman to the sleeping-car king. Pullman, dissatisfied with his Chicago architect, invited Beman in the fall of 1879 to remodel the Prairie Avenue mansion. Pleased with his work and liking Beman's personality, the businessman asked him to submit sketches of buildings for the proposed factory.

Though only twenty-seven S. S. Beman was already an experienced architect. At the age of fourteen, he had started an apprenticeship with the celebrated Richard Upjohn, and remained with him for eleven years. In his last two years he had worked on the state capital building in Hartford, Connecticut. In 1877, Beman established a practice and met Barrett, with whom he collaborated on several estates in the New York vicinity.

In 1880, it was still unusual for architects to design industrial buildings. Though experienced in large buildings, Beman had never designed a factory. In mid-November 1879, he visited the Detroit yard and then went to New York, stopping at several car shops along the way. A fast draftsman, he completed the drawings by the year's end and brought them to Pullman, who was then consulting with Bowen in Long Branch. Pullman needed only a few days' consideration before hiring Beman to design factory and homes, while Barrett was engaged to lay the buildings out and to landscape them. The architect was also placed in complete charge of construction.

Nathan F. Barrett, thirty-seven and a family man, was to commute periodically between Chicago and his practice in New York, but the bachelor Beman would remain west until the town was completed. For the first few months, they consulted company officers, hired assistants, visited the site, and prepared plans. Both men were enthusiastic about the unprecedented opportunity offered them. Pullman wanted an attractive and functional town built with due consideration for minimizing the costs of construction, operation, and maintenance. A harmonious and enduring relationship developed among the three. When the town had become famous, Pullman rendered them full credit always expressing complete satisfaction with their performance. In September 1897, nearly twenty years after their first meeting and only one month before Pullman's death, Barrett and Beman were again commissioned to work on the Long Branch estate.[4]

Pullman wanted the car works in operation by the spring of 1881, and groundbreaking was scheduled initially for April 20, 1880. Complications caused postponement for several days, but finally on April 24 the surveyors began their work. Quickly, streets and blocks were platted and building foundations staked out. The town site was a two-mile long and half-mile wide strip of land lying between Lake Calumet and the Illinois Central tracks. The lowness of the land meant that drainage and grading had to precede construction. The former Chicago superintendent of sewage, Benzette Williams, was responsible for raising the area and installing pipes to run excess water into the Lake. He also laid water, sewer, and gas mains, while a spur-line was brought down from the Rock Island Railroad, a mile north of the site, to facilitate hauling construction material. On May 25, the ground was broken for the Allen Paper Wheel factory, the first building scheduled for completion.

Work once started moved quickly and smoothly. By July, over one hundred freight cars of supplies were unloaded weekly. In August, machinery for the works began arriving, and the number of cars coming weekly approached two hundred. October saw the

shops' foundations all laid, their walls going up, and the exterior of
the Allen works nearly complete. Attention could now be given to
non-industrial buildings, and digging began on the foundation of
the first of these: a hotel. Labor started on one hundred dwelling
units in November. The sight of a town being built so rapidly on
such a grand scale and according to a preconceived plan proved
exciting. The Chicago press frequently reported on its progress,
and their stories were occasionally used by other American and
even foreign newspapers. An unemployed Englishman in Surrey,
reading of the town, wrote George Pullman asking for passage fare
and a job on the construction gang.[5]

Pullman wanted to accrue every possible advantage from the
magnitude of the undertaking. This was done in several ways. Supplies were purchased at bulk rates and as much as possible in an
unfinished state. Techniques of mass production, used extensively
in car manufacturing but skimpily in building construction, were
adopted when feasible. Wood, for example, was bought at wholesale prices as green timber and dried and cut for use at the site.
Then window sashes, doors, and other standard wooden parts were
prefabricated for later installation. To expedite matters, the first
departments set up in the shops were those, such as painting, iron,
and woodworking, which would be useful in the ongoing construction. In many such ways, operations were co-ordinated to save time
and money,[6] the results being proudly displayed to the press as
examples of industrial ingenuity and efficiency.

Early in May, temporary shacks were thrown up to provide quarters for the architect's staff and the construction gang. One large
building, humorously named "Hotel de Grub," served as a mess
hall. Between July and January, 1881, two thousand men worked
on the town. Aside from a few hundred living in neighboring communities, most of these workers commuted from Chicago. The Illinois Central ran trains at 6:30 A.M. and 7:00 P.M. that used a new
"double ender" engine which could move the cars forward or backward with equal facility. Commuter tickets were a dollar a week,
and the "Pullman Specials" were always overcrowded, only a fortunate few finding seats for the forty-minute trip.

Several hundred men began bunking in old palace cars placed at a siding near the town of Kensington. This town was only a half mile from the main shop sites and experienced a boom. Hotels, boardinghouses, and saloons doubled within a year. Payday night on Saturday was known as the "busy season" in Kensington, with an average of twenty arrests for drunkenness and brawling. In several instances, intoxicated and over-exuberant construction workers were blamed for starting fires in and around the site.

Most of the construction crew were what a company official referred to as a "floating class of unskilled workers." Many were immigrants, with the Irish predominating. Unskilled men, such as lumber carriers and pilers, received one dollar a day for an eleven-hour, six-day week. Organized in craft unions, skilled workers averaged $2.50 to $3.00 a day, while stonemasons, the highest paid trade, got $3.75 daily. When the shops opened, many of the construction workers, desiring steadier employment, found jobs in them.

Winter arrived early in 1880. By mid-November frozen ground, cruel winds, and dropping temperatures slowed the work. Chicago builders, concerned with speeding up construction after the fire of 1871, had learned to add salt to mortar to permit brick-laying in freezing weather. Canvas was placed on the ground and buildings to keep them dry and warm, and artificial lighting allowed men to labor after early nightfall. Though workingmen needed fires to keep themselves from freezing and "stone and brick had to be picked out from the drifts of snow," outdoor work continued until January. Then activity was restricted to interiors, and several hundred men were laid off.

By now, the town was ready for its first resident. On January 1, a foreman from the Detroit shop, Lee Benson, moved his wife, child, and spinster sister into Pullman. Within the next few months, several hundred men from Detroit came with their families. By June 1881, the town had a population of 654. To take care of immediate needs, wells were dug, but this water was unsatisfactory and a better source was sought after an outbreak of typhoid occurred in September.

Beman took advantage of the lull in work to go east on January 7, 1881. He was reported "tired under the strain." Construction had progressed so rapidly that the architectural staff had been sorely pressed to keep ahead. As one draftsman, Irving Pond, later described it: "full size details were often laid on the rough floors of a building under construction." [7] On the way to his home in New York City, Beman visited Rochester, New York, to examine an arcade building. According to the widely read syndicated columnist, "Gath," George Pullman had much admired this building in his youth and wanted Beman to use it as the model for the town's civic center.[8]

As Pullman had wished, in March 1881 car repair work began in the shops, and an advertisement appeared in Chicago newspapers: "Wanted 150 car-builders, cabinet makers and coach painters." April saw several important occurrences. On the first day of the month, the Illinois Central passenger depot at Pullman, "prettiest on the line," was opened, and a day later George M. Pullman brought fifty visitors in his private car to watch eleven-year-old Florence Pullman push a button sending power through a 2400 horsepower motor, the Corliss engine, to begin the manufacture of new cars. The Corliss was the world's most powerful engine. Built by a Rhode Island firm, it had supplied the power for the Philadelphia Centennial of 1876, whose theme was the coming of age of our native industry. The size, power, and design of the Corliss had been considered visible proof of American mechanical ingenuity. Pullman, impressed, purchased it for $130,000. The 350-ton engine required thirty-five cars to carry it to Illinois.

The Corliss was to be a showpiece. Placed near the I.C. tracks and behind plate glass windows, it was clearly visible from passing cars. The engine, however, was more than ornamental; it powered machinery in all the car shops. Woodscrapings from the carpentry shop, a health hazard, were dragged by powerful fan-drafts to twelve boilers which fed steam to the powerful engine. Exhaust water from the Corliss filled an artificial lake, Lake Vista, which had been dug in front of the engine building. The area about the lake and building was carefully seeded with flowers and shrubbery to give the appearance of a park. A reporter viewing the scene noted: "There is a purpose evident that the various [industrial] structures shall express to the eye an adoption of artistic means to utilitarian ends." [9]

The coming of warm weather in March saw a resumption of outdoor work, and the construction crew returned to full strength. By now, greater attention could be given the residential area. Summer saw one hundred homes complete and four hundred more under way. As much as possible, the construction was finished as it went along, leaving few rough edges to the casual eye. The first residences built were the more expensive, intended for company officers and others able to pay high rents. These were erected on a wide boulevard, Florence Avenue, and near the Illinois Central tracks.

The I.C. began to run special weekend excursion trains to Pullman for the curious. Businessmen and prominent people were brought to the rapidly emerging town in George Pullman's private car and given guided tours. It was soon said of visitors to Chicago that they insisted on seeing two things, the stockyards and the model town.[10] By the fall of 1881, Henry Demarest Lloyd could write: "one of the shrewd ideas that built Pullman is beginning to do its work. The town is advertising itself and everything connected with it. Its short but remarkable history is becoming a household word. It is famous though not yet finished." [11]

There can be no question that Pullman was pleased. He visited the town frequently in the summer months of 1881 and wrote to his wife, then away from Chicago:

> The place has improved wonderfully since June and I am sure you would be delighted to see it. Florence Avenue and all the little parks are now quite complete. There are great quantities of flowers which with the trees, shrubbery, and fresh green lawns makes a beautiful picture. If the Hotel was ready for occupancy I think I would prefer to stay there instead of Chicago.[12]

In September 1881, the hotel was completed and named Florence, after the car magnate's favorite child. Work moved swiftly on several buildings—market house, livery stable, and multi-purpose arcade—which would meet community needs. Imitation-bronze gas street lamps with cone-shaped gloves and white porcelain shades were installed. I.C. ticket agents reported people asking for evening trains because the brilliantly lighted streets of Pullman made a "particularly pretty sight at night." When a train passed the town, passengers rushed to the windows.

By November 1881, 1,725 people lived in the town. *The Union Stock Yards and South Chicago Weekly* reported that "in former times when a man moved away it was said of him, G.T.T., gone to Texas. Now it is G.T.P., gone to live at Pullman." The number of men employed by the town's industry reached two thousand. The spring of 1882 saw this number nearly doubled and the work on the factories all but complete; the car company announced its facilities could produce two coaches and twenty-five freight cars daily.

George Pullman was eager to attract outside businesses, which would protect the community from dependence on the well-being of one company and profit its landlord. In this he was disappointed. Several large firms examined the site and expressed interest, but none located there. The only businesses moving to Pullman, with minor exceptions, were those connected in one way or another with the sleeping-car company. Of these, several were controlled by George Pullman, and the others depended on him for purchase of their products.

Industry and community were kept physically apart, separated by Florence Boulevard. Along its northern side ran an attractive stone and brick wall, and behind in a park-like setting were the several shops of Pullman Palace Car Company, the Allen Paper Wheel Company, the Union Foundry, a massive water tower, a lumberyard, and a gas works. The sleeping-car company's shops consisted of nine buildings grouped over thirty acres stretching back from the I.C. tracks. Between them and the lake were the lumberyard and gas works. The Pullman office and main construction shop fronted the tracks for seven hundred feet, or more than the combined length of two football fields. Its center section, containing offices, rose to a height of one hundred feet above the two flanking wings and was topped by a 40-foot tower which held a large illuminated clock. Behind the main building was an elongated structure which housed an erecting shop, a woodmachine shop, and an engine room. In its rear were two freight shops, a lumber storehouse, and a lumber dry-house. Off to the side were hammer and blacksmith shops. Several of these smaller shops had been grouped about a 190-foot water tower, the first five stories of which were used for industry and the remaining five to house a five hundred thousand gallon tank.

Separated by a distance of several hundred feet, the Allen Paper Wheel Company's building adjoined the palace company's shops on the north. Facing the I.C. tracks, it was a two-story building, 368 feet by 140, which a writer described as "immensity roofed in." The two large buildings of the Union Foundry were a quarter-mile north of the car works and closer to the lake. This company's main product was a cast iron wheel for freight cars, while the more expensive paper wheel was used exclusively on passenger coaches. Both companies would normally employ a total of three hundred men and were controlled by the Pullman Palace Car Company.

The dominant architectural features of this industrial area were the vertical thrust of the two towers balanced by the strong horizontal lines of the steel roof trusses used in the larger shops. All structures were of red brick, with limestone frequently used for the trim, as in the Romanesque window arches in the car construction shops. Detailing was kept simple and intended to blend the buildings with the nearby residences, while Lake Vista and careful landscaping gave the grounds the appearance of a park. At a time when factories were built for the "sole view of providing a shelter for their men," [13] industrial buildings which actually enhanced a town's appearance drew comment and praise.

Equal care was devoted to the buildings' interiors. Most rooms were high-ceilinged with large windows. They were deliberately painted in light colors to give a cheerful appearance, while machinery was carefully placed to allow maximum room for movement. All this was done because Pullman believed that the "factory is practically the home of the operatives," and that healthy and happy workers would mean greater productivity.[14]

But other ways were sought to maximize production and profit. The various buildings and departments were laid out with due consideration to saving time, motion, and money in the production and servicing of cars. Bridges connected second and third stories of buildings to spare men the need of descending to street level. Over twenty miles of company-owned rails were put down in the town, principally in the area of the shops, to move cars quickly.[15] The French economist de Roussiers reported with unstinting admiration:

> The planning of these workshops is remarkable, and every detail seems to have been considered. To cite one point, the buildings in which freight-cars are built are a series of vast sheds as broad as the cars are long. Opposite each car a large bay opens on the iron way and a car, as soon as it is finished, runs along the rails and leaves the shop. All the timber that forms a car is cut to the required size and is got ready for fitting together in a special department, whence it is brought along the same rails to the sheds where the car is built. Tiny little locomotives are running along the lines which are built in the spaces between the various workshops. . . . Everything is done in order and with precision; one feels that each effort is calculated to yield its maximum effect, that no blow of a hammer, no turn of a wheel is made without cause. One feels that some brain of superior intelligence, backed by a long technical experience, has thought out every possible detail.[16]

Separated from the remainder of the town by empty lots were a few small shops on the southern end. Directly across the tracks from Kensington was the Chicago Horseshoe Company and to the east a coalyard. These together employed fewer than a hundred men. Farther south a brickyard with seven kilns was built in April 1882. One hundred and fifty French-Canadians were imported to work for wages of thirty to forty-five dollars a month. Clay for the operation was obtained from dredging Lake Calumet. In winter, the men from the brickyards "harvested ice" from the Lake's frozen surface, storing it in an ice house with a capacity of 6,000 tons for use by the town and in Pullman dining cars. Both the brick and ice works proved profitable and durable, soon employing an average of two hundred and fifty men. The southern industrial area was not considered an integral part of the town, and visitors were rarely brought here.[17] The brick workers, mainly unskilled and poorly paid laborers, were housed in wood frame dwellings which were distinctly inferior to the accommodations offered the other residents.

George Pullman had built all else in the town of brick and stone. He justified the expense by pointing to their greater permanence and safety. This was to be a community which would wear well. By April 1882, two years after surveying had begun, over $5,000,000 had gone into the town, three million bricks had been laid, and the works were nearly complete. What remained to be erected were more dwellings for the workers and buildings for civic needs. Industry had preceded community, but the latter was now to be provided.

6

Physical Planning and Social Control

Pullman would not be a Stoke Poges. A writer of 1881 described "ordinary towns [as] a growth; their commencement is an accident, and house is added to house, and store to factory, when the necessity for them arises." In Pullman, all needs were considered from the start. The town was a physical reality before becoming a community, and arriving residents found their wants had been anticipated. A "plan" accommodated the "desirable" and excluded the "baneful." As the prominent Chicago minister, Reverend David Swing, stated: "The town of Pullman possesses an interest above and beyond that of railcars and wheels. It stands related to the question how cities should be built and, in general, how man should live." [1] The most recent developments in engineering skills supplied the homes with "conveniences and luxuries." But beyond mere attendance to physical needs, George Pullman wanted to help the inhabitants improve themselves. The town was to have the best in "uplifting facilities." Commenting that only in America was it realistic to offer the worker hope, a French visitor reported that George Pullman "has supplied the necessary steps for those who wish to climb higher." [2]

It was expected that the town would engender values which

Pullman referred to as "habits of respectability." By this, he meant "propriety and good manners," cleanliness and neatness of appearance, industriousness and sobriety, and self-improvement through education and savings/ He believed the community would develop a superior type of American workingman. A company officer confidently told a reporter, "the building of Pullman is very likely to be the beginning of a new era for labor."

To visit the town from Chicago, one bought a fifty-cent round-trip ticket at the I. C.'s Central Depot, Michigan and Twelfth Street. Trains left at regular intervals between 5:30 A.M. and 11:30 P.M., and the journey of forty minutes was by all accounts pleasant. For several miles the train skirted the lake shore. On the west was Grant Park, soon followed by fashionable Prairie Avenue. Visible from the train was Pullman's mansion on Eighteenth Street. The homes gradually became farther apart, and then the tracks left the lakefront and entered the open prairie. Fourteen miles out was the town. As the train passed the shops, the passenger saw the Corliss engine and the lofty clock tower—two obvious symbols of the industrial order.

> The train halts at a station which is a gem of architecture and the conductor calls out "Pullman." As you face the town there is a broad stretch of closely shaven lawn, acres of flower beds, and to the left, along the great shop front the green carpet extends and borders a beautiful lake [Vista]. On your right as you face the east is the Arcade.[3]

The Arcade Building, a block long and ninety feet high, was the most impressive building in the town and a center of community life. Its central section, flanked by two symmetrical wings, reflected the building's interior arrangement. A huge glass and iron arcade ran from front to back. Along the sides of the ground floor were shops and a staircase which led to a gallery overlooking the activity below. It was in the Arcade that "people congregated to shop [and] make use of the various conditions contained in the great building, and the animated scene of dozens of people occupied in their pursuits or gathering in groups to talk in friendly gossip cannot fail to impress the observer." Pullman's arcade, supposedly modeled on one in Rochester, New York, was said to be the first in the Midwest. A fascinated reporter found it a roofed-in American "Oriental bazaar." Arcades represented an interesting effort by nineteenth-century architects to develop a multi-purpose commercial building which would relieve the problems of disorder and congestion in transportation. However, as a serious building type, the arcade barely survived the century.

Even before the Arcade's completion in June 1882, newspapers reported over seven hundred applicants for its thirty-odd shops. The company made a deliberate effort to include essential services, and when feasible two or more of the same type were selected to insure competition.[4] The ground floor contained "dry grocers," dry goods, furniture, tailor, a stationery store that sold books, tobacco, and newspapers, and a pharmacy with an ice cream parlor. On the next floor was a billiard parlor, barber shop, meeting rooms, library, theater, and offices rented to doctors and lawyers. Several offices were kept for use by the town's officials, and there were even plans for an art gallery, but this never materialized. In 1883, a bank and post office were added.

The library and theater, rarely found in small towns, provoked considerable attention. Consisting of five rooms, the library was located in the northeast corner of the second floor. All but one of the rooms were decorated "to convey an air of 'richness and comfort.'" Stained glass windows, chandeliers, Wilton carpets, and upholstered chairs gave the impression of a gentleman's club. The fifth room, the Men's Reading Room, was relatively austere. It was simply furnished with cane-bottom chairs and floor matting, and had a separate entrance. As one writer explained, the company had "thoughtfully" provided for the men coming from the works, who "could not be tempted into the main rooms . . . with soiled hands and faces [but] readily go into this private reading room."[5]

The library's facilities were also used for adult evening classes. Courses ranged from the practical, such as stenography, to art, language, and literature. Moreover, education was not restricted to the class. A newspaperman who visited the library with his bowler on was firmly told by an "old maid" librarian that "no gentleman ever enters . . . except with uncovered head, or sits in a library with his hat on." The bowler was quickly removed.

The library was not to be a place of casual perusal and idle relaxation. As Pullman stated in the document conveying his personal gift of 5,100 books to start the library, it was intended to promote the "moral and intellectual growth" of the community. The company's annual statement for the fiscal year 1887-88, proudly reported that most of the library's collection was on serious subjects, with "only 31 per cent of the books . . . classed as fiction and juvenile." By 1894, the library had well over six thousand volumes and subscribed to the leading scientific and mechanical journals. At this time, the town's librarian was Miss Bertha Ludlam, a cousin of George Pullman and a woman active in many of the town's educational and cultural organizations.

The Reverend David Swing, in his dedication on April 11, 1883, contrasted Pullman's generosity toward the library with the flamboyant self-indulgence of William K. Vanderbilt, whose $100,000 fancy ball several months before had scandalized the country. Pullman's library was not free; membership was three dollars a year for adults and one dollar for children. As this only met part of the cost, the company donated the remainder, including space. It was explained that no one respected gratuitous gifts. A fee made people feel that the library was theirs and, therefore, caused them to be more interested and appreciative.[6]

Membership in the library never exceeded two hundred. Some believed it too expensive, while others found its luxuriousness forbidding or the librarians overbearing. On the other hand, the company claimed that for every member several others would use his card. A five-fold increase in circulation between 1884 and 1894 was pointed to as proof that the library had been successful in encouraging reading.

The Arcade theater, "the pride of Pullman," was considered by many to be the finest one west of the Hudson until Sullivan's and Adler's Auditorium was built. A *Chicago Tribune* reporter found the "arrangement of seats and aisles . . . admirable . . . with a full view of the stage obtained from every seat." Hughson Hawley, a friend of Beman and a stage designer for New York's Madison Square Theatre, was brought to Pullman in June 1882 and remained about six months to paint scenery sets and drop curtain and attend to the theater's appointments. The recently published *Arabian Nights* had stirred the public's imagination, and Hawley decorated the theater in a "persian motif." Ticket prices were thirty-five, fifty, and seventy-five cents, this being considerably less than prices charged by Chicago theaters. The most expensive seats were in ten side boxes that projected from a horseshoe balcony.

Several offers to lease the theater were rejected out of hand. George Pullman wanted the right to pick "only such [plays] as he could invite his family to enjoy with the utmost propriety." [7] In this he was successful, for he and his family with their guests usually attended several performances each year. The theater drew its acts from Chicago theatrical groups and touring players. Its repertoire included melodramas of the period, black-face minstrel troupes, and variety shows which inevitably featured dialect comedians. Several amateur theater clubs were formed in Pullman, and one which lasted well into the 1890's attempted such ambitious undertakings as Du Maurier's *Trilby* and the prohibition potboiler *Ten Nights in a Bar Room*.

The company claimed that, financially, it broke even on the theater, but many doubted this. Its one thousand seats seemed too large for the small community and surrounding areas. An Englishman who attended on a Saturday night found an audience of seven hundred, which he was told was an exceptionally good crowd. The box office yield, however, was only "seventy pounds." When he suggested raising prices, he was told that it was the policy to keep them as low as possible.

South of the Arcade and roughly parallel to the I.C. tracks were the school, a stable, and a long, low building known as the Casino. The latter housed the town's maintenance department on the ground floor, while a large lodge hall was on the second. The stable was a neat, attractive building leased to a concessionaire, except for space reserved for the volunteer fire companies. By George Pullman's fiat, all horses in the town had to be kept here. These included the dray horses used for the delivery trucks, as well as carriage teams and riding horses owned by wealthier citizens. Those who owned neither horse nor carriage could rent them for three dollars a day, and a favorite treat for a family was a fast drive on a clear Sunday afternoon. The school was considered a "model" by a state investigating committee who visited it in 1885. The three-story brick structure had thirteen classrooms, praised as "light and cheerful," [8] which could accommodate over eight hundred pupils, sixty children to a classroom not being considered too many by the standards of the day. A playground, still a rarity, adjoined the school. The basement also served as a play area until 1888, when enrollment exceeded thirteen hundred and all spare space had to be used for classrooms.

The Florence Hotel, south of the railroad station on 111th Street, or Florence Boulevard, was a two-story red brick building skirted by a broad white veranda and with a roof elaborately laced with gables and dormers. It had the appearance of a "large gingerbread country villa." The ground floor consisted of a lobby, public parlor, restaurant, and bar. Above were seventy rooms renting for three to four dollars a day, twice the daily pay of an unskilled worker. A Chicago hotel trade paper, however, found the rates "very reasonable in view of the excellence of the accommodations." A suite—parlor, bedroom, bathroom, and a butler's closet—was kept at George Pullman's disposal.

The building cost $100,000, and furniture totaled another $30,-000. During its first year, there were 8,875 transient guests, who, with the small number of permanent residents, turned a profit for the hotel. A professional manager was hired to maintain service at a high level. However, as the town lost its novelty, the number of visitors declined and the hotel began operating at a loss. This was patiently borne by the company, which insisted on maintaining top quality and high prices. The hotel had simply been built on too large and elegant a scale for the town's needs.

By deliberate design the hotel's bar was the single place in town where liquor could be purchased. The dining room, according to one reporter, offered excellent food in attractive surroundings and "only charged seventy-five cents." It seated 145 at one time and, with other public rooms, could be rented for special occasions, such as wedding receptions and formal parties. Offering more than mere lodging for the wayfarer, the hotel was an important part of the social life of the community.

A workingman wrote in 1893 that he frequently walked by and "looked at but dared not enter Pullman's hotel with its private bar." [9] As far as can be determined, the hotel was open to all. Yet, men lived in the town who could count their visits to the Florence on a single hand. Many of the workers must have found its prices prohibitive, while others were intimidated by the hotel's decor. Its public facilities were apparently used primarily by the town's shopkeepers and professionals and the company's officers and clerks. That George Pullman intended the hotel to have "class" appears definite, and in the 1890's he hired a Baron von Fritsch as its "titled boniface."

No American community could be complete without one church and usually more. Daniel Burnham, in his *Chicago Plan*, published in 1909, observed: "So numerous are the sects into which Christianity has divided itself and so diverse are the nationalities to be provided for that the suburban church building rarely offers to the eye any relief from the monotonous ugliness of the . . . street which it helps to frame." [10] Anticipating Burnham, Pullman thought it more rational to build one edifice for all. A large church could afford a size and beauty which would enhance the town's architecture just as consolidation gave strength and order to business. Accordingly the large Greenstone Church was erected one block south of the hotel, on 112th Street. Constructed with the straight, simple lines of the American Protestant Church, its massive serpentine stone, roseate stained windows, and belfry gave a Gothic appearance. It seated six hundred, and on December 11, 1882, the Reverend Dr. James Pullman of the Universalist Church of Our Savior in New York City dedicated the church, as reported the next day in the *Chicago Times*, with a sermon on the need for a practical religion for all mankind. Among those present were his brother,

George, and over one hundred prominent members of the Chicago business community.

George Pullman regularly attended weekly services, but at several different churches. He went to the Reverend David Swing's non-denominational Central Church, his wife's church, the Second Presbyterian, and to the First Universalist. Pullman considered religion important, but was more concerned with practical ethics than with mystery or ritual. He apparently did not realize that others viewed these as essential.

The town's first settlers soon organized congregations and improvised accommodations. By 1882, the Roman Catholics, Methodists, Episcopalians, and Presbyterians were holding Sunday services. An attempt to gather these deonominations into one Union Church was unsuccessful; they preferred to cling to tradition and go their own separate ways. This presented George Pullman with a serious problem.

Like all else in Pullman, the Greenstone Church was expected to repay the company a 6 per cent profit on its cost. The rent had been set at $3,600 annually with an additional charge for its parsonage. No single denomination had a congregation large enough to afford the church's spaciousness and beauty. While George Pullman was pointing out to visitors how well the Greenstone Church complemented the town's appearance, its doors remained locked except for rare occasions. Not until 1885, when the rent was reduced by two-thirds, did the Presbyterians occupy it. The other denominations in the meanwhile met in rented rooms in the Arcade and Casino. The Catholics and Swedish Lutherans entreated Pullman for permission to build their own edifices. Although for years he resisted their efforts to deviate from the original plan, he finally consented to lease them land for their own churches, but only outside the town proper.[11]

Pullman's interest in consolidation was further demonstrated by the Market Hall, where all stores not found in the Arcade were located. The ground floor held a "lunch counter" and stalls which sold fresh meats and vegetables. These were inspected daily by a company employee hired to insure the cleanliness of the stores and freshness of their produce. On a second floor was a large empty room which could accommodate six hundred folding chairs. Several times a year this hall was used for revival meetings, sometimes featuring the famous team of Dwight L. Moody and Ira D. Sankey. On one occasion in 1891 the young Clarence Darrow spoke on "The Eight Hour Day: How to Obtain It."

The builders of Pullman never gave their reasons for avoiding the ubiquitous business street. Nor can any prior precedent for the centralization of commercial activity be found. It was possibly inspired by the example of the department store, which grouped what had been diverse stores under one roof. Or, as with other innovations in the town, it may have been prompted by the belief that bigness allowed for efficiency and planning.

All reports suggest that people found it convenient and pleasant to shop in the Arcade and Market Hall. One outsider described shopping in Pullman as "saving time and strength." During inclement weather, buyers could move from store to store without being exposed to the elements. Chairs and tables allowing relaxation and refreshments were always close at hand. By leasing the shop, Pullman deliberately avoided the practice of the company store, or "truck system," where workers were paid in chits redeemable for provisions.[12] In addition to the company's efforts to foster competition within the town, consumers could go to nearby neighborhoods for their shopping. As indicated by the Arcade Mercantile Company's signs claiming that its prices were as low as in the Loop, people from Pullman made some of their purchases in Chicago. There seems to have been a general conviction that Pullman stores were more expensive than elsewhere. A partial explanation for this might have been the high rents paid in the Arcade and Market buildings.

Much of the produce sold in the Market Hall came from a "sewage farm" three miles south of the town. Vitrified pipes carried the human waste from the residences of Pullman to a tank at the base of the water tower. From there it was pumped to the farm, treated, and sprayed over the fields. Potatoes, corn, onions, and cabbage were grown and sold in Pullman and Chicago. In 1885, the company reported an 8 per cent return on its investment, and the farm was widely hailed as an example of how scientific planning could produce a profit even from human waste. A herd of cattle was also acquired and dairy farming complemented the produce growing.

In their search for the functional, the builders were equally aware of the ornamental and recreational. A large park was placed at Florence Avenue and the lake front. From there, a wooden bridge led to an artificial island a hundred feet off shore. On the two-acre island were a spacious, ornately designed boathouse and several race tracks which in winter were flooded to make ice rinks. In the summer, there were regattas and boating. The park was laid out with baseball, cricket, and football fields, tennis courts, and a grandstand to accommodate spectators. Looping about the park was a long, winding roadway, called Pullman Drive, which went nowhere in particular, but offered a scenic Sunday drive.

The town was planned not only for what it would include but also for what it would omit. As *Appleton's Railway Guide* (1883) noted, "Pullman contains most of the characteristics of a great city —and yet it lacks certain things which hitherto have everywhere been accompaniments of city life. Pullman has no saloons or brothels. Except for the bar in the Hotel Florence, George Pullman proscribed the sale of liquor in his town. He was not a prohibitionist, but he believed his men and his company would be better off if the supply of alcohol was limited. His people could and did get drink elsewhere, but not in Pullman. In an interview with the *Ottawa Daily Free Press*, which appeared September 9, 1882, he commented:

> We allow no liquor in the city; now take strong drink away from men who have been accustomed to it, and not furnish something to fill the gap is all wrong—there is a want felt, a vacuum created and it must be filled; to do this we have provided a theatre, a reading room, billiard room, and all sorts of outdoor sports, and by this means our people soon forget all about drink, they find they are better off without it, and we have an assurance of our work being done with greater accuracy and skill.

The physical planning of the town was for social ends. Not only were the needs of the inhabitants to be anticipated and met, but they were to be directed and shaped. The wherewithal for self-improvement and advancement were supplied, and it was hoped the self-impediments removed. Much of the land around the town was owned by the Pullman Land Company, which retained it as a buffer between the controlled environment of the town and the outside world with its temptations. "With such surroundings and such human regard for the needs of the body as well as the soul . . . the disturbing conditions of strikes and other troubles that periodically convulse the world of labor would not need to be feared here." [13] George Pullman, knowing what kind of community he wanted, thought he knew how to get it.

Originally, the residences were to be built between the industries on the northern and southern ends of the town. A complaint of many urban dwellers was the casual interspersal of homes and factories which led to health hazards and eyesores. In Pullman, workshops and residences were to be kept clearly separate, and the residential area would contain the various public buildings. Barrett's and Beman's specialized handling of land use proved well ahead of the times.

By the fall of 1882, the community had already outgrown the original residential site, and it became necessary to build dwellings north of the works, close to the Union Foundry. Six hundred units were constructed in an area of fourteen blocks (104th to 108th Streets) soon to be called North Pullman.[14] Most of the people who lived there worked at the Union Foundry or the Allen Paper Car Wheel Company. These companies hired primarily unskilled workers, and the homes in North Pullman were generally of a more humble kind than those in Pullman proper. No stores or community facilities were ever erected in North Pullman, which meant that its inhabitants had to walk ten or twenty minutes to the Arcade.

The streets in Pullman were broad and had wide cobblestone gutters. Both they and the town's alleys were completely macadamized. Sidewalks usually measured an adequate eight to ten feet from curbing to lawn, but the front yards were only twenty feet deep. Numerous elm, maple, and linden shade trees lined the avenues, and in late spring and summer, the town was ablaze with strong colors. To provide adequately and inexpensively for the town's landscaping needs of trees, bushes, flowers, and grass, the company devoted six acres of land between 113th Street and 114th Street on the lake shore to a nursery and greenhouse.

Rents in Pullman started at four and a half dollars a month and went as high as seventy-five dollars. Despite its sobriquet as a "model worker's town," the community contained a socially and economically heterogeneous population. The most expensive dwellings were found on Florence Boulevard and adjoining streets, where there were a dozen and a half detached and semi-detached homes. But most of the town's housing were row on row of two- to five-family buildings, built of the same brick and of approximately the same size. Efforts were made to offset this "mechanical regularity" by an imaginative treatment of skylines and the use of various facades. However, when winter stripped the town of its greenery, the row houses seemed monotonous. On the eastern-most street of Pullman, Fulton Street, were ten "large" tenements, three stories high and three to a block.

The residences were arranged in a gridiron street pattern. Rectangular blocks, neatly paralleled, had become a distinguishing feature of the American community. As the London *Pall Mall Gazette* (February 7, 1884) pointed out concerning Pullman, "one would expect . . . an American utopia should be regularly laid out, with streets appointed and set forth very commodious and handsome." New York's well-known designer of Central Park, Frederick Law Olmsted, however, was critical of the gridiron, which, in his view, imposed ugly and monotonous geometric patterns on nature. He urged his colleagues to avoid artificial regularity in their work and to heed the contour of hill and river. Pullman's topography made any alternative to the grid implausible. Nevertheless, Barrett, through informal treatment of the open spaces adjacent to public buildings, interrupted the severe order of his physical plan to introduce variety. The most important grouping of public buildings centered about kidney-shaped Arcade Park, across from the railroad station. East of park and station was the Florence Hotel, to the south was the Arcade; between them, but at a further distance, was the church. Here was the focal point of community activity, and a "smiling face for visitors."

By September 1884, over fourteen hundred dwelling units had been built. The company's investment in town and factory neared $8,000,000, and Pullman's population rose to over 8,500. In less than five years, a city stood where once had been only swamp. Soon Chicago newspapers boasted: "As all the world knows, [Pullman] is an industrial hive of many thousand busy workers, all placed in an environment unique and unmatched the world over for solid comfort and luxuriousness." [15]

Most visitors during the early years sang its praises. Nor was its founder ignored. The *Chicago Times* (October 23, 1881), in a special supplement devoted to the Calumet area, called the town a "living monument to the culture, philanthropy, enterprise and business capacity of [George Pullman] . . . and future generations will bless his memory." Though Pullman always insisted that his reason for building the town was strictly business self-interest, others doubted his statements as too modest or otherwise unfair to himself. The industry's most prestigious publication, *Appleton's Railway Guide,* in 1883 observed: "Mr. Pullman has established a world-wide reputation as a benefactor of the general public by the now indispensable system for the comfort of railway travelers. . . . His greatest work, however, as will be better realized hereafter, is embodied in the beautiful manufacturing city bearing his name."

The relationship between town and car company was not forgotten. It was pointed out by the *Boston World* (August 1, 1881) that the "same thoroughness and perfect taste," the same careful concern with beauty and comfort were present in sleeping coach and community. But the usual standard of comparison was between the town of Pullman and the slums of Chicago. Numerous writers dwelt on the model town's order, contrasted to the city's social and physical chaos. Richard Ely wrote in *Harper's Monthly* that Pullman was as handsome to the eye as any "wealthy suburban town" that had sprung up as a sanctuary for the middle class from the problems of the city, and Ely added: "It is avowedly part of the design of Pullman to surround laborers as far as possible with all the privileges of wealth."

Pullman built the "Pioneer" in 1864 in the belief that enough Americans could and would pay for the best. In the model town, he assumed that carefully planned, large-scale construction would provide superior residential and social facilities which the ordinary worker could afford. The extra cost of a sleeping car was a sometime occurrence, and the traveler could always select a regular coach instead. Rents in Pullman, with their surcharge for beauty, were an economic constant, and the resident, unlike the traveler, had no simple alternative. Ely, in his *Autobiography*, written fifty years after his article on the town, commented: "In ways of material comforts and beautiful surroundings Pullman probably offered to the majority of its residents quite as much as they were in a position to enjoy, and in many cases, even more." [16] If Pullman was the "most perfect city in the world," [17] as one London newspaper maintained, its costs were borne by the inhabitants. The company did not intend to subsidize the town beyond an initial investment which would be repaid with interest. For its "practical philanthropy" was to be limited to helping the men to help themselves.

In 1883, Barrett went home to New York, but Beman, who had married during the construction of the town, remained in Chicago until his death in 1914. By 1883, he was at work on a building for the Pullman Palace Car Company's national offices on Michigan and Adams Avenues. When it was completed in the summer of 1884, he moved his office there and resumed private practice. His personal and professional relations with Pullman and his family remained close. Pullman found him assignments with other businessmen, and gave him company work, including the task—unusual for an architect—of designing interiors and exteriors of railroad cars. In 1892, the company put Beman on an annual retainer of five hundred dollars a month.[18]

Beman's professional interest in the town continued after his departure to Chicago. From 1884 to 1887, he supervised the erection of three hundred dwelling units, and as late as 1891, another one hundred were added. Most of this later construction was tenement row houses erected in North Pullman. In 1892 when a fire destroyed the Market Building, Beman considerably altered the architecture of the new building, and added a Romanesque arcade to the surrounding square.

Contemporaries frequently referred to the town's public buildings as "secular Gothic," and the homes and hotel as "Queen Ann." According to Irving Pond, an architect who learned his trade working on Pullman, no consistency of style was sought by Beman, who wanted only to design attractive and functional buildings.[19] To do this, he eclectically selected from the wide variety offered the Victorian architect and tried no innovations. Beman's work was competent and creditable. Of the many aspects of the town of Pullman, few would receive less criticism and more praise than his buildings and Barrett's plan. As the *Chicago Journal of Commerce* (January 3, 1883) described the town, "the aesthetics of architecture and landscaping are made prominent features. The grouping of buildings and trees to produce a pleasing effect is studied as diligently as the arrangement of machines in the shop."

Figure 1. Southern Suburbs of Chicago. Kensington, or "bum town," is west of the Illinois Central tracks at 115th Street. Roseland starts at Thornton Road (later renamed Michigan Avenue) and 111th Street. The old village of Hyde Park, which gave its name to the entire township, is along the lakefront at the northern end of the map. (Illustration from Richard T. Ely's article on Pullman in *Harper's Monthly*, 1885.)

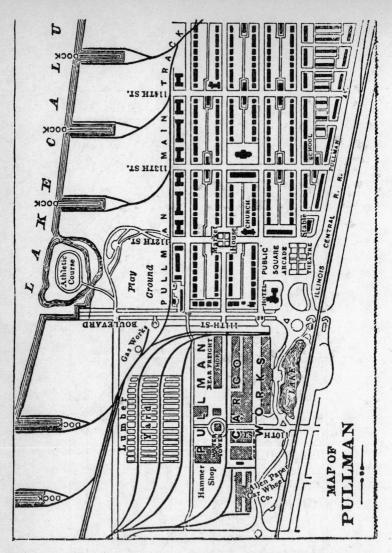

Figure 2. Map of Central Industrial Area and South Pullman. Industry and homes are separated by Florence Boulevard (111th Street). The residential area's grid layout is interrupted by the informal treatment of the public area. Arcade Building, hotel, and Market House provide a commercial and social focus for the community. The location of the school in proximity to the ungraded railroad tracks was an error in the plan which escaped early notice. (Illustration from Richard T. Ely's article on Pullman in *Harper's Monthly*, 1885.)

7

Social Characteristics
of Workers and Residents

In the summer of 1882, George M. Pullman told a reporter from the *Cincinnati Enquirer* that he was "paying more attention to the Town of Pullman than anything I have on hand. I am studying the effect of improved homes upon the laboring society." His faith in the town had been strong enough for him to risk his professional reputation and his company's money. Now he waited to see himself proved right. Believing that "everything depends upon surroundings," Pullman anticipated that the removal of people from the city to his town would bring about a transformation in their values and ways. But, as he admitted, the first sight of some of the families moving into the "nice new cottages with their old dirty traps made me feel a little discouraged."

Pullman and others frequently spoke of the "poor and improvident families" coming to the model town from Chicago's slums. There were such people in Pullman, but they were a distinct minority. The town was not to be populated by residents who represented a random selection from the worst urban neighborhoods. A set of circumstances guaranteed from the first that the average workingman in Pullman would be well above what was considered typical. Observers coming to the town, however, believed the peo-

77

ple "superior" because of their homes and schools and libraries. Almost forgotten was that Pullman had built the town to attract and
hold a better type of employee.

Most of the town's residents worked in the factories, and of these
about two-thirds were employed in the repair and manufacturing
shops of the Pullman Palace Car Company. Because of the nature
of the work, three-fourths of the men hired were considered skilled
"mechanics," and only the remainder unskilled laborers.[1] This was a
much greater percentage of trained people than most industries
and explains why average salaries in Pullman were higher than
elsewhere. Furthermore, at a time when employment practices
were generally loose, the company made an effort to be selective.

> In making application for a position in the employ of the Pullman
> Company, a man must face a formidable written examination in-
> volving a great deal of personal history. Among other things he
> must tell whether or not he has ever been married or divorced,
> whether he is in debt, and if so to whom, and how much, how
> long he went to school, whether he has any physical deformities,
> why he was discharged from or voluntarily left his last position
> . . . whether he uses intoxicating liquors, [or] plays games of
> chance.[2]

One indication of the company's interest in the residents was the
ten censuses taken in the town's first four years. By July 1885 its
population was 8,603, of which 3,752 were men and only 1,945
were women, the balance being children under sixteen. The dispro-
portionate number of men was explained as a temporary situation
due to the town's youth. The company made a special effort to
provide employment for women, but males continued to greatly
outnumber females well past the end of the century. Single men
took rooms with a family or lived in the twenty boarding houses
managed by private parties who rented them from the company. In
1894, there were still 1,100 boarders in Pullman. Strangers living
with families were viewed by critics as an undesirable situation
which invited immorality, and this was a feature of the "model
town" that would one day come in for criticism, for "a roomer can

not go to his own room without going through the private rooms of the family, which breaks into the sanctity of the family." [3]

Another way in which Pullman's population differed from that of the ordinary town was youth. As a community where people came looking for work, it attracted men in their prime of life; the average age of males in Pullman in 1885 was given as twenty-nine. Not until the town grew older did it begin to have the elderly and retired. Once in the early years, George Pullman "was expiating [to a group of visiting businessmen] on the very low death-rate of Pullman as compared with Chicago or New York. An Englishman interrupted, 'But y'know there has been no time for anyone to die, yet.' " What seemed obvious to the layman, however, eluded the experts. In November 1883, Oscar De Wolf, M.D., Commissioner of Health for Chicago, read a paper on the model town before the American Public Health Association meeting in Detroit. He reported: "during the two years of its existence 69 persons died, its death-rate being . . . 6.9 per thousand. The death rate of Hyde Park . . . is 15 per thousand." [4]

In 1884, a three-day convention of the "chiefs and commissioners of the various bureaus of statistics of labor in the United States" met in Pullman to study the "economic, sanitary, industrial, moral, and social conditions of the city." They found that from November 1, 1883, to November 1, 1884, there had been fifty-three deaths, or 7.599 per thousand. Though only two deaths were of people over fifty and twenty-eight were of infants under one, the statisticians never considered Pullman's age distribution in explaining why its death rate was a third of the average for American cities. Instead, they attributed this to the town's excellent sanitation, and soon Pullman would be called the "world's healthiest city." By 1893, however, its death rate had already risen to nearly 15 per thousand. [5]

The sight of immigrants arriving with "wooden shoes on their feet and all they had in the world bundled in a red bandana handkerchief" was common on Chicago's streets and even more so on Pullman's. While in 1880 59.3 per cent of the city residents were native-born, in 1885 only 46.6 per cent of the town population were of American stock, and by 1892 this figure had probably dropped. At this time only 28 per cent of the men working for the company were born in the United States. One observer, commenting on the increase of foreign-born, noted that those already here helped to bring relatives over. No other information to explain the increase can be found except that immigrants from certain countries had the skills needed in car building. The little biographical information available suggests that most immigrated to this country from an urban background, were skilled workers, and usually arrived in Pullman only after having lived in the United States for several years.

The ethnic profile of Pullman in 1885 generally resembled that of Chicago in 1880 and 1890, except for the Dutch and Swedes who were more numerous proportionately in the model town. Roseland, a community on high ground a half-mile due west of Pullman, was an old Dutch community whose residents soon sought livelihoods, though rarely homes, in the factory town, working usually as laborers. By 1892, 10 per cent of the work force of Pullman had been born in the Netherlands. The probable explanation for the large number of Swedes is that they were generally disproportionately represented in industries requiring skilled mechanics. Germans, Englishmen, and Scandinavians were viewed by a company executive as industrious and intelligent workingmen who made good citizens, but were inferior to American born in "executive ability." On the other hand, he considered the Irish to be undesirable and more inclined to politics than "honest work." [6]

Nationalities did form social and religious groups, such as the Swedish Methodists and Lutherans, but the smallness of Pullman apparently made ethnic neighborhoods unnecessary. In at least one instance, however, workingmen from an "old country" were concentrated in a particular shop; twenty-two Bohemians in 1891 made up nearly the whole "glass department." If there were ethnic tensions during the first two decades, they have left few traces. It was said of the Germans that they liked their beer, and with the Swedes they tended to purchase homes in the surrounding communities. On the other hand, remarks in a more critical vein were made by Edward F. Bryant, the manager of the Pullman bank, who told a reporter from the *Chicago Inter Ocean* (September 6, 1888) that foreigners "expected to find gold in the street." According to Bryant, they came to Pullman, acquired the necessities and some luxuries, and "every year their comforts increased, their indulgences increased and they wanted more." For Bryant, it was those "who became thoroughly Americanized who find the least fault." The others tended to be improvident, discontented, and socialists.

One of the town's doctors, John McLean, thought the foreign workers were ambivalent about America in general and Pullman in particular. He believed that they recognized and appreciated the higher wages and better living standards, but strongly resented their lack of free time and energy to enjoy these. To illustrate his point, McLean recounted a conversation with an English carpenter who was earning three dollars and twenty-five cents a day in the Pullman shops, and who told McLean: "I could only get a dollar twenty-five [in England] . . . I could not save money; it was impossible to get any ahead. I could work for that, and of course get my clothes cheap and lived cheap, and went in to get all the little fun possible. . . . Now I can hardly take off the Fourth of July and Christmas." When McLean asked what he thought of this country, the man replied: "Well, this is my home now. I have come to stay! I believe it is the only place in the world a laboringman can get up and get ahead in the world." Many of his countrymen, though, were reluctant to become citizens, and on October 6, 1887, the British Naturalization Society held a meeting in Pullman to induce over eight hundred British subjects there to take out papers.

A feature of the town which soon became apparent was the instability of its population. The average length of residence in 1892 was four and a quarter years.[7] This was partly due to the company's rapid turnover rate in both men and officers. Others, however, quickly took the place of those who left, and the company had little anxiety over vacancies. By 1888, Pullman had grown to 10,000, and by the summer of 1893 had swelled to 12,600. As long as the shops offered work, the residences remained occupied even if the tenants charged. But already in October 1884, Richard Ely on assignment for *Harper's Monthly* had found that the town's transiency was affecting the community:

> Nobody regards Pullman as a real home, and, in fact, it can scarcely be said that there are more than temporary residents at Pullman. One woman told the writer that she had been in Pullman two years, and that there were only three families among her acquaintances who were there when she came. Her reply to the question, "It is like living in a great hotel, is it not?" was, "We call it camping out."

A reason for the town's instability was that a man could not own his home. From the first, George Pullman let it be known that he "would not sell an acre under any circumstance," a policy believed necessary to maintain the harmony of the town's design. The company, through its sole ownership of the town, administered it like any other piece of real property. Exclusion of bar and brothel were law in Pullman as company policy in the role of landlord. George M. Pullman was convinced that his desires for the town could not survive sale to the inhabitants and feared loss of control would mean the introduction of what he referred to as "baneful influences." As long as Pullman governed through ownership, he could proscribe sinner and troublemaker.

Inquiries about buying homes in Pullman were quickly and quietly rejected. There was, however, frequent mention during the first few years of the possibility of laying out land west of the town for sale as home sites. In late 1883 George Pullman told a reporter for the *New York Sun* (December 9, 1883) of an ambitious plan he soon expected to put into effect. Lots would be sold for three hundred dollars. "When paid for, the company would put up a house and sell it to the employees at actual cost on easy monthly payments, amounting to very little more than the ordinary rent. It is expected that many outsiders will take advantage of this offer, and that the number of houses built under such circumstances will be large. This suburb of Pullman, as it is called, will be supplied with all the conveniences to be found in the parent town, and will be connected with Chicago by means of a railroad to be owned and operated by the company."

The railroad was soon forgotten, but the housing development was considered as late as 1890, when George Pullman gave his reason for deferring action to a visitor:

> It is truly my intention to form another town, near this one, where each resident will build a cottage after his own inclination, suited to his own needs, and which will be his own. . . . I do not think the time has yet come for beginning this enterprise. If I had sold the sites to my workmen at the beginning of the experiment, I should have run the risk of seeing families settle who are not sufficiently accustomed to the habits I wish to develop in the inhabitants of Pullman city, and all the good of my work would have been compromised by their presence. But to-day, after ten year's apprenticeship, several families . . . recognize the advantages of them and will see that they are observed, wherever they may settle. Such families form the pick, and I hope to sell the building lands near the workshops to some of them, little by little.[9]

By 1894, however, only the preliminary surveying of one hundred acres had occurred.

Many of Pullman's men lacked the patience to wait until he thought them ready. They purchased homes in the surrounding communities of Grand Crossing, Wildwood, Fernwood, and Gano, but principally in nearby Kensington and Roseland. By September 1892, of Pullman's 6,324 "operatives," about 850 (13%) owned their homes, while still another 1,397 (22%) rented outside the town.[10] Some of the men had lived nearby before they were employed in the carworks and for their own reasons had remained, but others moved there from Pullman. Living in these outside communities meant certain disadvantages. The longer walk made it impossible to return for lunch as did the men living in the town. The homes outside of Pullman were usually in unimproved areas which lacked the grading, sewage, and paved streets of the model town. Commonly frame rather than brick, they were distinctly inferior in facilities to Pullman's houses.

Asked why he had bought a home, an ex-resident answered laconically that he felt a greater freedom in his own place. "I own this little patch of ground and the house, and this is how it comes that I live outside of Pullman." It was generally accepted that the better workers were buying homes, and this was taken to reflect the fact that "a self-respecting man wanted his own castle." Some moved from the town because they could get more space for less money. Rents in Kensington and Roseland averaged at least 10 to 20 per cent less than in Pullman between 1881 and 1893, and the homes had larger rooms and yards.

In 1884, the state labor commissioners were told: "If one or two men must be discharged, and each has a family, and one resides away from Pullman, and the other at Pullman, the resident is to be preferred." This rule, however, was probably never observed, despite claims to the contrary during the strike of 1894.[11] Until the middle of 1893, the company had no reason to practice such a policy. Except for a brief period in the early years, business had been good and demand for dwellings exceeded the supply. The company not only made no effort to prevent its people from leaving the town, but in ways encouraged them to buy homes. Statistics on home ownership were even cited as proof that the town's moral environment had prepared the men for this symbol of middle-class respectability.

In September 1888 a free weekly with ample advertisements from Pullman, Kensington, and Roseland merchants began publication. By 1891, it had reached a circulation of two thousand and changed its name to the *Pullman Journal,* with a sale price of two cents. Recognizing that the Chicago papers were widely read in Pullman, the *Journal*'s stated policy was to feature only local news, and general stories "which endeavor to convey entertainment and instruction and to keep fully abreast with new phases of the application of modern science to modern industry." Its masthead listed the publisher as the Arcade Mercantile Store, "Pullman's largest drygood emporium," but omitted the editor, known to be Duane Doty. Doty was the company's senior town officer and an enthusiastic admirer of the "Pullman experiment." Despite its pledge of impartiality the paper, until Doty's illness caused its demise in 1898, never wavered in its support of George Pullman's policies. For these reasons, it is significant that the *Journal* gave full coverage to the real estate market in the Calumet area, accepted ads from builders and realtors, and carried stories advising on home ownership. Typical of these was one in January 3, 1891 which contained plans for a two-story frame cottage to be built for $640 above the cost of the lot, and instructed the reader:

> Nearly every man receiving fair wages can save something if he fully determines to do so. Do not use tobacco nor drink beer. Do not imitate the rich in dress nor table. Do not say yes to thriftless fellows who ask for loans. . . . Pay cash for everything and see that the dealer gives full weight.

On May 7, 1883, the Pullman Loan and Savings Bank was incorporated with capital of $100,000 and offices in the northeast corner of the Arcade. Controlled by the company, the bank encouraged savings among workers by offering a handsome 4 per cent interest and aided home ownership through extending loans at reasonable rates. As it deposits grew, George Pullman proudly cited them as evidence that his people were being taught the value of thrift. The *Chicago Inter Ocean* reported on October 16, 1885: "It is fair to assume that the gradual increase in savings [in Pullman] is in some degree attributable to the absence of saloons and other debasing influences and the general healthful and moral surroundings of the place."

Only a few months later, a scandal made it painfully obvious that not everyone in Pullman had learned to be frugal. It was discovered that John Myers, an Englishman and the bank's bookkeeper, had embezzled $5,500. He and his family lived in the Florence Hotel for a hundred dollars a month rent, exactly his monthly earnings. Myers received three years in jail amid reports that George Pullman had refused to ask the judge for leniency. In 1887, the *Chicago Inter Ocean* (September 6) carried an interview with Dr. John McLean, who said that "a good many people [in Pullman] are a little afraid to deposit money here—they are a little superstitious [*sic*]—they have an idea that if they are making a little too much money the company would cut them down a peg, and so they make deposits elsewhere."

Edward F. Bryant, who had come to Chicago from Massachusetts in 1885, was made manager of the bank in 1886. One of his
principal functions was to act as paymaster for the company and to
collect its local debts. Until 1892 these two services could be performed almost simultaneously. The workers went to the bank every
two weeks to collect paychecks from which half their rent had already been deducted. The state commissioners of labor had found
in September 1884 that "this . . . caused some complaint, but the
system is now generally liked, for when wages are paid there is no
bother about rent bills, and the wife and children know that the
home is secure." In May 1891 the Illinois Legislature passed a
"Truck Law" which prohibited this practice. Instead the worker on
payday received two checks: one in the amount of his rent and the
other for the balance of his wages. Pressure was placed on him to
immediately endorse the rent check and apply it to his debt, but he
could convert it to cash there or elsewhere.[12]

In his 1879 pamphlet on "model tenements," Alfred White had
cautioned that "any rental above $10 [a month] is beyond the
reach of the majority of the working class." Yet many of Pullman's
workers paid considerably more than White's maximum: sixty-five
per cent of the town's 1,753 dwelling units charged more than this,
while the average rent for all homes was $14.00.[13] Pullman's belief
that his way of constructing the town would mean superior housing
at reasonable cost for the worker proved only partly correct. The
town's rents were moderate only when considered in terms of the
facilities. The *St. Louis Spectator* (September 30, 1882) asserted
that "rents are cheaper in Pullman than in St. Louis for comparable
homes. But there are few in St. Louis which can compare." Similar
comments were frequently made about Chicago. Middle-class observers who came to Pullman and compared the homes and rents to
their own viewed them as a bargain. But for some of the workers
the rents in terms of their means were high and excessive.

About two-thirds of the families in Pullman lived in so-called
tenements, buildings with more than one apartment, of two general
types. The first resembled a single family dwelling except for its
several entrances and multiple dwelling units. The other was the

"block houses" on Fulton Street which were three stories high and contained twelve to forty-eight apartments. One of the latter was carefully evaluated in the spring of 1893 by representatives of the United States Labor Commission.[14] They were critical of the building's wooden staircases and lack of fire exits from apartments. A comment less understandable to the modern reader was the fault finding in "that there are no arrangements to prevent the promiscuous mingling of occupants upon landings, stairways and corridors."

In general, though, the report was favorable. The building was well built, adequately equipped, and in pleasant surroundings. The Labor Commission representatives were particularly impressed by its location on a large lot of which only a third was covered, leaving ample space for children's play and facilities for drying clothes. Four apartments were on a floor, each having its own watercloset on the landing. All apartments had a pantry, a gas cooking stove, gas fixtures for lighting, a sink, and a water tap. The rooms were small and low-ceilinged, but each had at least one window.

The building studied had eight three-room apartments, renting for $8.00 and $8.50, depending on the floor, and four apartments with four rooms at $9.00. They were occupied by cabinetmakers, carbuilders, and laborers who spent an average of 20 per cent of their salaries on rent. Costing $13,050 to erect, the building brought the company $1,224 annually. The report found that because of their low rent, tenements were popular and usually occupied. In particular, the smaller tenements that offered the appearance of a family home at low rent found favor with the men.

The investigators also described a representative single-family house which contained five rooms and a basement that could be used as a kitchen-dining room. This home rented for $18.00 and cost $1,580 to build. It occupied one-fourth of a 17 by 100 foot lot in the rear of which stood a coal shed. Inside the house there was one bathroom and a water faucet on each of the two floors. Rooms were considerably higher and roomier than in the tenement, and certain extra fixtures, such as chandeliers and fireplaces, were provided.

A third of Pullman's dwelling units were single-family homes, costing between $15.00 and $25.00 per month, and primarily occupied by skilled workingmen. Homes for more than $25.00 were usually rented by the town's merchants, professionals, and company officers, including some foremen. Stephenson Avenue, between 114th Street and 115th Street, was known as "Foreman's Row." It was the mechanics in private homes, who paid from $15.00 to $25.00 a month who could least afford Pullman's surcharge on beauty. In the spring of 1893, a time when paychecks were fattened by overtime, they paid a third of their salaries in rent —as compared to a fifth paid by those in the tenements—and many had to take in boarders to meet expenses.[15] When the company, affected by the depression of 1893, began a policy of cutting salaries and holding rents constant, the workers living in Pullman's single-family houses were the hardest hit of any group within the town.

Anyone wanting to live in the community applied at the agent's office on the second floor of the Arcade. If found of "good character," the person would sign a one-year lease and keep a copy. This lease had been carefully drawn by company lawyers in November 1880 to circumscribe tenants so as to prevent their damaging property or annoying neighbors. Proscriptions were spelled out in exasperating detail which left the tenant with little freedom to decorate his home without written approval.

Two clauses in the lease attracted particular attention in August 1894, when a presidential commission was examining this document as part of its investigation of the recent strike. The first was a highly unusual stipulation that either party could terminate the lease by simply giving ten days' notice. George Pullman and Duane Doty explained that the provision had been added as an afterthought by lawyers seeking further protection from the use of homes for "improper purposes."[16] While this feature of the lease obviously did not add to the tenant's sense of security, it was rarely employed. In thirteen years, 1881 to 1894, only twenty-five evictions occurred in Pullman.[17]

The commissioners were also critical of the "ironclad" requirements concerning repairs. According to the lease, the tenant was responsible for all damages, including those due to ordinary use. But as Almont Lindsey in a study generally critical of the company has written, "in practice . . . this particular clause was greatly softened; and, as far as can be determined, no renter was ever charged for repairs except those due to gross carelessness or malicious breakage." [18] Periodically, the company's town officers advertised in the *Pullman Journal,* requesting tenants to notify them of things to be done. Repair and painting were regularly performed and annually cost over $40,000 for the residences alone. The company also attended to lawns and yards, collected garbage and ashes from barrels specially provided, and maintained the halls of tenements.

A 6 per cent return on the investment in the residences and public facilities was expected. With this in mind, Duane Doty established rental rates in late 1880, but explaining that his calculations were too conservative, raised them nearly 20 per cent one year later. Individual buildings were assessed according to their cost and street frontage, with apartments then pro-rated according to size and location. The company did not let the real estate market influence its rents. With minor changes, the charges fixed in 1881 remained constant until 1894, through flush times as well as bust.

The company never realized its goal. After deductions for taxes

Table 1
CENSUS OF PULLMAN, 1881-85

	Families and Households	No. of Men	No. of Women	No. of Children	Total Population
January 1, 1881	1 Family	1	2	1	4
March 1, 1881	8 Families	31	14	12	57
June 1, 1881	102 Families	357	119	178	654
February 1, 1882	321 Households	1,168	445	471	2,084
March 8, 1883	705 Households	1,956	984	1,572	4,512
August 15, 1883	910 Households	2,878	1,039	1,906	5,823
November 20, 1883	1,048 Households	3,128	1,388	2,169	6,685
September 4, 1884	1,295 Households	3,817	1,773	2,613	8,203
September 30, 1884	1,361 Households	3,945	1,845	2,723	8,513
July 28, 1885	1,381 Households	3,752	1,945	2,906	8,603

Table 2

ETHNICITY OF RESIDENTS OF PULLMAN (1885) AND CHICAGO (1880 AND 1890) AND OF WORKERS IN PULLMAN SHOPS (1892)

Birthplace	Pullman 1885 Number	Per Cent	Chicago, 1880 Per Cent of Population	Chicago, 1890 Per Cent of Population	Pullman Employees 1892 Number	Per Cent
United States	4,013	46.6	59.3	52.5	1,796	28.4
Germany	1,088	12.6	15.2	15.2	732	11.5
Sweden	1,024	11.9	2.6	4.0	1,163	18.4
Ireland	563	6.5	8.9	6.4	402	6.4
Canada	557	6.5	2.6	—	264	4.1
England	406	4.7	2.7	2.7	365	5.7
Holland	271	3.2	0.4	0.5	753	11.9
Norway	267	3.1	1.9	2.0	169	2.7
Scotland	144	1.7	0.8	0.8	131	2.1
Denmark	75	0.8	0.5	0.6	89	1.4
Switzerland	63	0.7	0.3	0.2	28	0.4
France	36	0.4	0.3	0.2	26	0.4
Italy	33	0.4	0.3	0.5	99	1.6
South America	6	0.1	—	—	—	—
Greece, Poland, Bohemia	57	0.7	1.6	3.0	—	—

Table 3

RENTAL AND TYPE OF DWELLING UNITS

Rent	Number of Dwellings	Per Cent	Type of Dwelling
$10.00 or less	618	35.6	Tenement
$14.00 or less	558	32.1	Tenement
$17.00 or less	353	20.3	Single family
$20.00 or less	85	4.9	Single family
$25.00 or less	61	3.5	Single family
Over $25.00	61	3.5	Single family
Total	1,736	99.9	

and maintenance, the $291,846 grossed on the homes brought a return of only about 4.5 per cent. In 1892 and 1893, increases in both taxes and cost of repairs reduced profits to 3.82 per cent.[19] For reasons that will be discussed later, the company did not make these facts public until forced to do so by the United States Strike Commission. It preferred to give the impression that the town paid neither more nor less than called for by the plan. According to Pullman, he had proved that business methods and management could provide adequate housing that the laboring classes could afford. It was only a question of time before the beneficial effects of the environment would be apparent in the residents.

8

Public Opinion and the Town

The town of Pullman was intended to propagate middle-class values of frugality, industry, and morality. By demonstrating that capital and labor could co-operate, it would affirm not challenge national orthodoxy. Visitors came to Pullman eager to discover that it worked, and no scoffing circle of outsiders erected walls of suspicion to isolate the town from its neighbors. Here was an American utopia that people wanted to succeed.

The Reverend David Swing, in dedicating the library, compared Pullman with Brook Farm and New Harmony. The two earlier communities were based upon "abstract principle," while "industry and economy . . . are the foundation stones of the latest and wisest experiment." [1] Although Swing mentioned that the company town had been built by a businessman to meet business, as well as social, needs, he neglected other distinctions between it and the earlier, ill-fated settlements. No one was required to subscribe to any set of ideals before moving to the Chicago suburb. Prior conversion was unnecessary; one only had to want to live in the town. Changes in the individual would come once he was there and was influenced by its environment. Above all, Pullman was expected to show that man could be improved by proper surroundings and that

American industry could provide this without sacrificing profit. Brook Farm, New Harmony, and Pullman all differed from the ordinary American community, but only the last was not viewed as alien or peculiar.

From 1880 to 1893, the town was intensely surveilled. Hundreds of thousands saw this most modern and novel of communities and an overwhelming majority left impressed. An Englishman touring this country in 1887 reported to the (London) *Times:* "No place in the United States has attracted more attention or has been more closely watched." On a pleasantly warm and sunny Saturday in June 1882, two thousand people came to spend the day. For several summers, the company encouraged visitors by placing a steamer, the *Calumet*, at a pier below 111th Street, charging a small fee for a tour of the lake. A fleet of fast phaetons was rented to those who wanted their sight-seeing along with a pleasant ride. Conventions held in Chicago were often invited to this "wonder of the world," and businessmen and dignitaries were guided through the town and entertained by the charming Duane Doty. As a showplace for the company, the town of Pullman was an unqualified success. A professor, M. Loudelet, was specially sent by the French Ministry of Commerce to inspect the town and report on its success for possible imitation. By October 1882 it became necessary to place the industrial area off-limits:

> Several hundred daily visit the town and throng in the shops, plying the workingmen with questions, and causing serious interruptions in the work. Visitors will have free access to the various points of interest in the city, and will be excluded from the shops alone.

Among the curious were serious observers, such as journalists and government officials, who came to see if Pullman offered a lesson to others. Their numerous stories and reports give glowing descriptions of the town's charm and offer an abundance of facts on construction materials used, type and size of buildings, and even on such aspects of the plan as sewerage and schools. But on the important question of how the people felt about their model town, there is relatively little information.

Surprisingly few of Pullman's observers solicited opinions from its residents. They usually spoke to co-operative company officers and then spent a day or more inspecting the town's buildings. For the most part, the people were condescendingly dismissed with a casual glance or a cursory question. On the surface nothing appeared amiss, and certain signs that the environment was achieving its expected results could be easily detected:

> The scenes which the streets and public resorts of the village present after nightfall are entertaining in the extreme and prove perhaps more conclusively than anything else the fact that Mr. Pullman's estimate of human nature is far from wrong. After the evening meal the people made their appearance on the streets. They are presentable almost without exception and most of them are surprisingly neat in their dress and circumspect in their manners. The women and children in clothing and deportment present such a striking contrast to the people of their class in the noisy and dirty city that having seen the two modes of life, an observer may be pardoned for doubting that Pullman is made up almost exclusively of mechanics and laborers and their families. In gay groups they assemble on the streets, or promenade, visiting the Arcade.[2]

Many commented that the residents appeared well dressed, well behaved, and generally prosperous and busy. It was even noted— as evidence of the lack of absenteeism and unemployment—that men were not to be seen on the streets during working hours. Happy and clean children were found at play in parks and yards "in marked contrast to the children of the gutters and alleys . . . in Chicago." To Pullman, the difference between his town's appearance and that of the usual city neighborhood had to be credited to the planned environment. He told a New York reporter: "I have not been disappointed in [the town] in any respect. It is a beautiful place, and even on the hardest the effect of the handsome surroundings has been beneficial. On a broad avenue lined with cozy houses, with flowers and lawns on every hand, and scrupulous neatness everywhere maintained, a man of the dullest mind would feel ashamed to appear in public in his shirtsleeves or barefooted."[3]

Duane Doty confided to Helen Starrett, authoress and charity worker, that frequently families moved to Pullman who lacked a decent concern for appearance. In the evening they would be seen lounging on their doorsteps, the husband in his shirtsleeves, smoking a pipe, his untidy wife darning, and half-dressed children playing about them. They were soon made aware that they were expected to appear in public properly attired and that the park, not their stoops, was the place for relaxation. Nor was sloth tolerated in the homes. When it was discovered that families "accustomed to filth and squalor" would not mend their ways, company inspectors visited to threaten fines unless proper care was taken. In many ways the people of Pullman were made to feel that they were on public display and must act so as not to shame the company.

A few interviews with residents did appear in the papers. A worker of thirty spoke of his boyhood on a farm where there was "always plenty of good wholesome food, pure water, clean clothes and fresh air." At fourteen he had gone to Chicago, learned a trade, and obtained a job at good wages. He liked the city while single but after marriage he found it difficult to live there, giving the following description of his circumstances:

> We had a little cottage on the west side but there was mud on all sides of us, two beer saloons within a block, clouds of soft coal, poor sewerage, villainous water, and everything else that was bad and disagreeable. After our little girls were born I began to feel uncomfortable. . . . There were many deaths daily in our section of the city from diphtheria and scarlet fever, and we found it next to impossible to keep everything clean. . . . I found I could work here at wages fully equal to those paid in the city, and that I could rent a whole brick house with water and drainage . . . for $15 a month. . . . We have a clean and comfortable house and plenty of pure air. My children are healthy and, as far as my wife, she has seemed like a different woman.

The wife of one worker told a reporter that until she came to Pullman her life had been filled with "anxiety and foreboding." Her husband, as a skilled mechanic, had always earned a decent salary, but spent most of this in saloons, leaving little for necessities. The

company had employed him on the understanding that he would
stop drinking.

> With the terrible temptations of the open saloon gone he did, and
> now we have a beautiful home with comforts and luxuries. . . .
> After . . . work my husband comes home, takes a bath, puts on
> his good clothes, enjoys dinner with the children and me, and
> then sits down at home or strolls . . . along the pretty streets
> sometimes to the library and theatre. . . . We have money in
> the savings bank, our children are getting a good education, ev-
> erything is peaceful and hopeful . . . we are very happy.

It was often said that women were particularly happy with the
new town. According to the state commissioners of labor, there was
a consensus that housekeeping was easier and life more varied. The
commissioners indeed believed that Pullman "has really wrought a
greater change for the women than for any other class of its dwellers." Above all, they were supposed to be enjoying a novel sense of
security. Their husbands earned a full paycheck with no bar to pass
on the way home. Children had a healthful surrounding and a good
school. As the rent was paid automatically and in advance, there
was no fear of seeing the furniture put out in the street as commonly occurred on Chicago's west side.

Until 1885 few reports critical of the town had appeared, with
the possible exception of the labor press. At least two workingmen's
organs, Chicago's *Arbeiter Zeitung* and the *Progressive Age* of Philadelphia, attacked the town as a capitalist's scheme to snare his
workers in a "gigantic monopoly of labor." [4] But such papers, with
their limited circulation and marginal audience, did not reach the
people whose opinion George Pullman valued. And the "respectable" papers accepted the company's position that its action benefited both worker and society. To the *St. Louis Railway Register*
(December 15, 1882) and others, "Pullman was a city on a hill."

The town's appeal was as a unique and tangible effort to solve
significant social problems. Presumed a success from the start, Pullman was hailed by journalists as clearly showing that planned communities were superior to the ordinary ones built helter-skelter by

speculators. Before it was more than a few years old, the model town was credited with having produced a new type of dependable and ambitious workingman. Pullman's community was widely cited as evidence that a rationally ordered environment was the key to reducing the alcoholism, crime, and other disorders usually associated with the laboring classes and their neighborhoods.

To many, the town's charm was that its homes and factories were in a park-like setting. It showed that industry could be located at a distance from the city and its workers housed elsewhere than a slum. In the late 1880's, Henry Demarest Lloyd wrote that "every American laborer had the right to get the clean dirt of soil on his hands, as well as the filth of machines." [5] Surrounded as it was by thousands of acres of unused land, the model town offered men this opportunity. To many observers the workers in Pullman did not live in squalor "amidst temptation to vice and disorder," but in a community whose scale was considered proper for social control and yet large enough to contain desirable institutions usually associated with the city. At a time of widespread concern over the rapid growth of cities, other industrialists were urged to follow this example and take their men to the country. According to the *St. Louis Railway Register* of November 4, 1882: "The experiment has shown that there is a practical and profitable method to remove a large class of working people from their unhealthful homes in the cities and their families from various associations. . . . There is no reason why all other large and prosperous manufacturing establishments that need not by nature of their business be situated in the middle of a city should not follow the profitable and beneficial example of the Pullman company."

However, even favorable accounts indicated, often inadvertently, that there were dissatisfied people in the town. A reporter mentioned several instances where residents "fond of city life and attached to friends who lived in Chicago complained of the dullness." But when he tried to inquire further people were reluctant to talk. Helen Starrett found "that to a great many [of the townsfolk] the neat and commodious and beautiful appointments of the place are a painful restraint. They feel at first as strange and unfamiliar and uncomfortable as they would if suddenly transported to heaven. There are no saloons . . . and many are lonesome and homesick for places where they can drink and rowdy after working hours." It was assumed that with time Pullman's improving and educating influences would become apparent and its residents adjusted. But when an element in the town remained critical, they were dismissed as social incorrigibles of little intelligence and no importance. A reporter for the *St. Louis Spectator* (September 30, 1882) thought one resident's remarks worthy only of heavy-handed humor:

> I found one Irish policeman with the choicest brogue, and he had as lively an appreciation of the meaning of this latest and most wonderful flower of civilization as a hog wallowing in a mud hole. He was disgusted with the decency and quiet of the place. Doubtless born in a bog and raised upon a diet of sour milk and potatoes, he had as little enjoyment of the comfortable dwellings, the green clover-carpeted and flower scented lawns, the general air of thrift as the Digger Indian. He was growling at the small wages and high cost of living of the men; life to him was a bore, he was without occupation, his club was so useless an appendage that he had ceased to wear it, and not a drop of whiskey was obtainable within the limits of the town.

When, in the fall of 1884, the state commissioners of labor visited Pullman, the question of whether the town was a gilded cage had already risen. They shrugged this off with an easy answer: "If the workman at Pullman lives in a 'gilded cage,' we must congratulate him on its being so handsomely gilded; the average workman does not have his cage gilded." [6] Others, however, and not necessarily in criticism, referred to the ubiquitous presence of the company. It was virtually impossible to come there without constant reminder that this was a company town, and if the casual visitor was highly conscious of this fact, one can imagine the resident's awareness. The journalist from the *New York Sun* (December 9, 1883) who had noted with pleasure Pullman's street scenes also reported:

> A stranger arriving at Pullman puts up at a hotel managed by one of Mr. Pullman's employees, visits a theatre where all the attend-

ants are in Mr. Pullman's service, drinks water and burns gas which Mr. Pullman's water and gas works supply, hires one of his outfits from the manager of Mr. Pullman's livery stable, visits a school in which the children of Mr. Pullman's employees are taught by other employees, gets a bill charged at Mr. Pullman's bank, is unable to make a purchase of any kind save from some tenant of Mr. Pullman's, and at night he is guarded by a fire department every member of which from the chief down is in Mr. Pullman's service.

Starting in 1885 as its novelty passed, the model town was criticized frequently in certain Chicago papers associated with the Democratic party and occasionally elsewhere. The *Cleveland Post* on March 2, 1885, quoted a resident of Pullman who called the town an "exaggeration of the store-order system," and said, "the company owns everything and it exercises a surveillance over the movement and habits of the people in a way to lead one to suppose that it has a proprietary interest in [their] souls and bodies." A few months later the *New York Sun* (October 11, 1885) observed, "The people of Pullman are not happy and grumble at their situation. . . . They say that all this perfection costs too much in money and imposes upon them an untolerable [*sic*] constraint. . . . They secretly rebel because the Pullman company continues its watch and authority over them after working hours. They declare they are bound hand and foot by a philanthropic monopoly."

Of the more important Chicago papers, the *Tribune* and *Inter Ocean* sustained their faith in the experiment until the strike of 1894. But the *Herald* and *News* were consistently critical after 1885. Most others, including the widely read *Times,* had no firm editorial or news policy. By 1885, the initial unquestioning acclaim for Pullman had worn off, but not until 1894 did the town receive more censure than praise from the news publications. It continued through the eighties and early nineties to receive a generally favorable press and a good public image. After 1885, however, naïve assumptions were tempered though not abandoned, and its friends were forced to meet the issues raised by its critics.

The question of paternalism in the model town was given a national audience when *Harper's Monthly* published an article in

February 1885.[7] "Pullman: A Social Study," was significant because
of the peridical's prestige and circulation and also for the author's
penetrating criticism. Richard T. Ely, thirty-year-old assistant professor of economics at Johns Hopkins University, had only indi-
rectly received the assignment. *Harper's* editor, Henry Mills Alden,
became interested in doing a story of Pullman in 1881 and arranged
for Henry Demarest Lloyd, chief editorial and financial editor of
the *Chicago Tribune* who had recently become prominent by an
attack on Standard Oil, to do the writing. Lloyd had long been
interested in the town and knew its background well. In October
1881 he visited the community and spoke to Doty and Pullman.

Lloyd found the town a place where "brains have been mixed
with the mortar from the foundations to the roofs, and where the
self-interest of the capitalist has been something shrewder than
selfishness of the ordinary type." There was no question in his mind
that the company was right in assuming that the town's "beauty
and convenience" would banish troublesome disputes between capital and labor.[8] The article generally read like a promotional puff
for the Pullman company as well as Chicago's industry and the
potential of the Calumet region.

Unhappy with Lloyd's work, Alden asked that it be rewritten,
but when he was still dissatisfied with the second effort, he altered
it substantially. On receiving the galley proofs, Lloyd found he had
no by-line, and indignant, he refused to permit publication.[9] *Harper's* now went ahead to make other arrangements for its story.

In January 1883 Stewart Woodford, a prominent Republican politician and United States attorney for southern New York who later
was our ambassador to Madrid at the outbreak of the Spanish-
American War, delivered a speech at the opening of the Arcade
theater. At this time he discovered George Pullman eager for further publicity and especially interested in *Harper's*, the nation's
best-known magazine. On Woodford's return to New York, he contacted Alden and learned of Lloyd's work. To Woodford, "the
scope of the experiment [was] too broad and its possibilities too far-
reaching to have [*Harper's*] presentation made by one who is

merely a newspaper-man or even magazinist." He wrote Andrew White, President of Cornell University: "I want you who have travelled much and thought much on social problems, who are yourself a rich man and yet have all the sympathy of a working publicist with labor and its aspirations to go out to Pullman." Woodford added that he desired Pullman and White "to know each other, for I am sure that each will become heartily interested in the work of the other." [10]

Giving the press of work as reason, President White at first declined. Woodford, a University trustee, remained adamant; and in February 1884 White traveled to Chicago. He spoke at a Commercial Club dinner as George Pullman's guest and the two discovered that White on his first visit to Chicago had been a visitor at the Tremont Hotel on the same day that the then unknown businessman had raised it.[11] The academician promised Pullman, whom he liked and respected, to return in April and write about the town. But on his return to Ithaca, he found himself unable to keep this arrangement and suggested his friend Richard Ely as a substitute.

On May 28, Ely wrote White that he had signed a contract with *Harper's* to visit Pullman during the summer.[12] Ely, however, had previously committed himself to teaching summer school at Chatauqua, and was forced to postpone the trip. He waited until after his marriage in September, and on October 1 arrived with his bride at the Hotel Florence. His payment of $175.00 for the article defrayed the honeymoon's cost.

Ely had been interested in the problem of the working class since his graduate studies at the University of Heidelberg in the late 1870's. There he had rejected classical economics, with its apotheosis of the laissez-faire state, as neither correct nor moral. On his return to the United States, he wrote a comparative study of the French and German laboring classes. At the time of his trip to Pullman, Ely was gathering similarly minded young academicians into the American Economic Society, which was formally founded the following year. He intended to develop a group who would forcefully present a Christian and "scientific" critique of social problems.

With a broad knowledge of urban and industrial conditions in Europe and in this country, Ely was an excellent, though roundabout, choice to write a serious study of Pullman.

His initial reaction to the town was one of approval. A favorable impression was made by the appearance of buildings and parks and "by the all-pervading air of thrift and providence . . . of general well being," which he believed resulted from a whole town being "systematically [constructed] upon scientific principles." To Ely the town illustrated and proved "both the advantages of enterprises on a large scale and the benefits of unified and intelligent municipal administration." As a young man confident that science provided the means for a rational ordering of life, Ely saw in the town a gratifying example of how planning and industrial power could be woven together to provide a beneficial environment.

Ely endorsed not only George Pullman's conception and execution of the town but also his motives. The effort expended was taken as adequate evidence that "his heart must be warm toward his poorer brother." And more important Ely believed that "Mr. Pullman ha[d] partially solved one of the great problems of the immediate present, which is a diffusion of the benefits of concentrated wealth among wealth-creators." To the writer the town was in many ways a step in the right direction, and he found no fault with the intention of converting the residents to middle-class standards of respectability. After the first few days, however, his enthusiasm began to wane with the realization that he could not agree with all that went on. Conversations with company officials made him aware that the town's affairs were "conducted with what seems . . . a needless air of secrecy. When he wanted to interview residents, a minister advised him against carrying a notebook, for people believed the company hired "spotters" who reported criticisms. Determined to examine these "unpleasant features of social life," Ely attended a picnic and frequented the same shops in an effort to win confidence. A disgruntled company officer, Walter E. Barrows, secretly agreed to provide him inside information.[13]

The town's weakness, according to Ely, was the total power of the company and the absence of self-government. In consequence, the resident had "everything done for him, nothing by him." This led to a lack of real concern with the town or commitment to its future. The knowledge that home ownership was impossible also prevented many from putting down roots. For Ely the important fact was not that the company had used its great power injudiciously, but that it could. He presented some hearsay reports of abuse, but did not necessarily assume their veracity. He simply thought that the company's authority, likened to that of the German Kaiser and Russian Tsar, made residents feel insecure and helpless before a "monopoly" which hemmed them in by "constant restraint and restriction." Believing that actions in their homes affected their jobs and vice versa, the residents responded, according to Ely, with a sullen servility. Outwardly, they conformed to the rules, but inwardly resolved "to beat the company." No one publicly criticized the town, but many moved elsewhere.

The writer's "unavoidable conclusion" was that the "idea of Pullman is un-American. . . . It is benevolent, well-wishing feudalism, which desires the happiness of the people, but in such way as shall please the authorities." He clearly approved of planned and ordered communities, including a prohibition on saloons, but only if it could be controlled by the citizens. As it was, the benefits resulting from Pullman's superior environment would be more than nullified by its lack of democracy. For "if free American institutions are to be preserved, we want no race reared as underlings." Implicit in the article is Ely's hope that the industrial advances made by the application of science to technology could be matched by an equal application and gain in social organization. As for the town of Pullman, he limited himself to the vague suggestion that, perhaps, it should include "cooperative features" to "awaken in the residents an interest and pride in Pullman."

Ely remained in Pullman ten days, and by October 14, 1884, Alden had received the article, which he found "entirely satisfactory." [14] Three months later it was published and, according to Ely, received "an immense amount of attention." [15] Alden later told him that in his opinion the article was the best published in any American magazine for 1885. One less than enthusiastic reader was George M. Pullman. Barrows, having left the company's employ, wrote Ely that "Mr. Pullman says you were unfair and that he is to employ someone to answer you." And he reported that "heads have been chopped" in an effort to discover Ely's source of information.[16]

"Pullman: A Social Study" was a milestone in Ely's career. *Harper's* quickly gave him a follow-up assignment to do several articles on railroad companies, and he soon gained prominence as a social critic. For the model town, Ely's article was also pivotal, and the community never lived it down. Defenders rose to point out that nothing could be more American than a town dedicated to preparing workers for self-improvement and a more comfortable life. But Ely had raised questions that could not easily be answered. Was the community "a model in the present and a pattern for the future," or merely an echo of the feudalism so carefully banished from this country? Charles Dudley Warner, co-author with Mark Twain of the well-known novel *The Gilded Age*, probably spoke for many when almost as in reply to Ely's questions he wrote: "It may be worth some sacrifice to teach people that it is better for them morally and pecuniarily, to live cleanly and under educational influences that increase their self-respect. No doubt it is best that people should own their homes, and that they should assume all the responsibilities of citizenship. But let us wait the full evolution of the idea."[17]

III

THE COMMUNITY AND THE COMPANY

9

Democratic Government and the Business Ethic

The [town of Pullman] is and will become a model community. It is a community, and yet it is not, in the understood sense of the word. It will be managed for the best interests of the whole community.[1]

Joseph Brown

George Pullman assumed that the company's interests were identical with those of the residents and could best be served by running the town in a business-like way. When a reporter asked him: "How in the world do you govern these people?" he replied, "We govern them in the same way a man governs his house, his store, or his workshop. It is all simple enough." On another occasion the same question was answered somewhat differently: "As long as the town of Pullman is owned by one association there is little necessity of agitating the subject of its control by any municipal government." Many of the problems usually handled by town government were not present in Pullman. Public services had been provided in advance and were sustained by the company in its capacity as landlord. For some, however, an American town without the democratic institutions of self-rule was a travesty.

The company officer in charge of the residential area was the town agent, who supervised the several departments that maintained streets and buildings, operated gas and water works, and offered fire protection. The town agent was also responsible for various business enterprises, such as the hotel, sewage farm, and nursery and greenhouse. In all, there were nine department heads and nearly three hundred men under him. Appointed by George Pullman, the agent's duty was to provide efficient, economical direction of the town. He was a businessman rather than politician, and his client was the company not the community.

From 1881 until the position was terminated in 1902, Pullman had six town agents. One, Duane Doty, held the job twice, 1881-83 and 1901-02. All were men of considerable experience and broad backgrounds, several being university graduates. While the importance of the town agent probably depended upon his ability and personality, his role was essentially administrative rather than policy making. This may partially explain why town agents never became involved in controversy. Though nominally in charge of the residential areas, the town agent was responsible to the superintendent of the shops, the company's general manager, and most importantly George Pullman.

The relative unimportance of the job was underlined by the resignations of its two best-known and most capable occupants. Edward Henricks, graduate of the United States Naval Academy and chief clerk at Pullman, became town agent in 1883 but in 1888 he was promoted to the superintendency of the brickyards. Duane Doty had a varied career before moving to the town. Graduated as an engineer from the University of Michigan, he was an officer and war correspondent in the 1860's and returned to civilian life as assistant editor of the *Detroit Free Press*. After this he was superintendent of the Detroit schools until 1877 when he assumed the same position in Chicago. A Republican, Doty resigned in late 1879 during a dispute with a Democratic mayor. This controversy brought him to Pullman's attention and he was appointed the first town agent. In 1883 he resigned to become the community's civil engineer and statistician.

Doty's official position belied his continuing importance. Using the statistics he had collected, Doty wrote articles demonstrating the town's success, and also acted as cicerone for important visitors. A friendly and well-liked man, Doty played an active role in community life. Particularly interested in efforts to improve educational opportunities for workers, he was a prominent member of many organizations. Next to George Pullman, whose complete confidence he always enjoyed, Doty, rather than the town agents who followed him, was the most important man in the model community.

American towns are not political islands, and Pullman was no exception. It was part of the township of Hyde Park, which in turn was a subdivision of Cook County. The township, covering more than forty-eight square miles, had authority over such local matters as sewerage, roads, schools, and licensing, but permitted considerable freedom to its constituent communities. Until late in the century, it was a sparsely settled rural area with a few pockets of population. In consequence a loose form of government sufficed.

Hyde Park Township swelled from 16,000 people in 1880 to 85,000 in 1889 and was expected to triple again in the following decade. Its southern part, the Calumet region, suddenly became a center of heavy industry, while its northern area—35th Street to 71st Street—became a favorite residential area for Chicago commuters. The rapid transformation of the huge township into a patchwork of rural, residential, and industrial communities placed great strain on its crude government. After 1880, Chicago newspapers stridently insisted that the township must be annexed to the city.

From 1880 to 1885 the number of distinct communities in Hyde Park Township increased from fourteen to twenty-three including several incorporated as towns. Among the more important were the industrial villages of South Chicago, Colehour, Grand Crossing, Pullman, and the residential towns of Woodlawn, Kenwood, and Hyde Park, from which the township derived its name. Pullman, second only to South Chicago in population, was joined with neighboring Kensington for purposes of township voting. It was widely believed that George Pullman controlled his town's votes, and Ely noted that its representatives in the township were company officers.[2] These obviously could not have served without Pullman's permission or encouragement.

Hyde Park was governed by a six-member Board of Trustees, half of whom were elected annually for a two-year term. Other officers were a prosecuting attorney, collector, village clerk, supervisor, and assessor. Of these, the last was most important, for he

estimated property value and established tax rates. A citizen, however, had recourse to a Board of Review, consisting of the assessor,
village clerk, and supervisor. No issue in his relationship to the
township was more important to George Pullman than that of
taxation, and he always acted vigorously to protect his interests.

By and large the township left the model town alone, which was
exactly what George Pullman wanted. It provided the use of Hyde
Park's courts and jailhouse and the service of two policemen, one
working the day shift, the other the night. In August 1882 an agreement was reached for selling township water to the company, but
only after Pullman had threatened to lay his own pipes to Lake
Michigan. Water rates were reduced in 1885 and again in 1886
amidst complaints that George Pullman now paid considerably less
than anyone else. The trustees defended their action by stating that
Pullman was the township's largest user and spent enough to warrant special consideration.

In 1882, the assessor valued the Pullman property, including residential and industrial buildings, at $550,000, which would substan-
tially increase taxes. Pullman protested, asserting that the township
had few expenses in his town since many usually incurred were
borne by the company. He also argued that industry should be favored with low taxes to attract others. The board of review reduced
the assessment to $350,000, but Pullman remained dissatisfied.
Present on the board in his capacity as village clerk was Edward
Henricks, Pullman's town agent, who thought $264,000 reasonable.

Pullman's unhappiness with the township's policies led him in
1883 to aid the newly formed Taxpayer's party in gaining control of
the board of trustees. He supported them again in the election of
1884, but by 1885 a break occurred and he threw his weight behind
the Republicans. The latter won a majority of the seats on the
board, but Henricks, now a Republican, was defeated and as conso-
lation appointed village treasurer. He promptly placed the township's funds in the Pullman Loan and Savings Bank.

The Hyde Park Republican party although not affiliated with the
national party, did contain many people who were. Limiting itself
to local issues, it stressed fiscal conservatism and low taxes on in-

dustry. For these reasons the Republicans were generally supported by business, and their opponents charged them with serving the interests of the Pullman Palace Car Company, the Union Stockyard, and the several Calumet steel mills. The party retained control of township government in the hard-fought election of February 1887, the *Chicago Herald* reporting wholesale coercion of voters by the large employers of the area. In particular, the paper demanded an investigation of the polling in the model town of Pullman.

Those who believed Hyde Park could be freed from domination by its industrialists only through annexation to Chicago joined with others to force a vote on this issue in April 1887. Annexation was carried, but George Pullman, who was adamantly opposed, managed to get his town exempted from the area under consideration. The annexation vote was later voided for technical reasons by the Illinois Court, with another election being scheduled for June 1889. This time, the town of Pullman was to be included.

In a village election in April 1889 township control was finally wrested from the Republicans by the pro-Chicago Citizens' party. Credit for this upset victory was generally given to John Patrick Hopkins, a former Pullman officer who, by bolting the Republicans, had broken with his employer. Ironically, Hopkins was mayor of Chicago during the strike of 1894, and for this reason his early association with Pullman warrants attention.

Hopkins, born in Buffalo, New York, to Irish Catholic immigrant parents, was twenty-one when he came to Chicago in December 1879. Finding work on the construction crew in Pullman, he quickly demonstrated unusual ability and began a rapid rise from the ranks. By August 1881 Hopkins was head timekeeper for the car shops. A bachelor, he moved with his widowed mother and unmarried sister into a home on Watts Avenue. Convivial and of unfailing good humor, Hopkins was generally respected and liked. A Chicago reporter described him as "of rather noticeable physique . . . of the Apollo figure; his hair is glossy black, with a tendency to break out in ringlets; and his eyes are brown and kindly . . . fascinating smile which plays under the drooping mustache." [3]

Hopkins possessed a remarkable memory, a useful skill for a politician, and knew most of the workers by their first names. In 1884, he was the principal force in organizing the Democrats of Pullman for Cleveland's election, but in township affairs Hopkins followed George Pullman's lead and was first a member of the taxpayer's party and then a Republican. During 1886 he became township treasurer, while also forming a business partnership with a Calumet merchant, Frederick Secord. The two capitalized the Arcade Trading Company at $10,000 and rented four stores in Pullman's Arcade building for general retail merchandising. It seems Hopkins was firmly entrenched in his employer's good graces, for he not only retained his job as timekeeper, but also secured a secret agreement to have a portion of his rental remitted.

Sometime in 1888, however, a falling out occurred between the two men. Pullman reneged on his promised rebate and the Secord-Hopkins firm moved to Kensington;[4] Hopkins, however, continued to reside in the model town. He intimated the rift was caused by his activity in the Democratic presidential campaign of 1888, but most probably the reason was Hopkins's switch to the Citizens' party and his enthusiasm for annexation.

George Pullman contributed heavily to the Republicans, and made facilities in the town available for anti-annexation meetings. The biggest, held two weeks before the election, was in the Arcade theater. Over a thousand people heard speakers charge that Pullman's superior facilities, in particular its schools, would be shortchanged and damaged by city officials. On other occasions, George Pullman himself insisted that annexation would undo all that had been accomplished. It would mean that ignorant and corrupt politicians, rather than competent businessmen, would administer the model town, and the plan for built-in order and moral upgrading would disintegrate.

According to Hopkins, Pullman opposed annexation because he feared that his taxes would rise and his one-man rule of the town would end.[5] Hopkins charged the company with exceeding the accepted limits of partisan politics to influence its employees' votes. He claimed that several men had been fired for signing annexation

petitions, while others had been threatened with dismissal for expressing support.

Hopkins's allegations were widely trumpeted by Chicago newspapers, most of which viewed their city's expansion as manifest
destiny. The *Chicago Times*, for example, waged a lively campaign
for annexation. It contended that Hyde Parkers stood to gain more
competent and honest officials who would provide better civic services for lower taxes. But most took this with a grain of salt. Chicago's recurrent political scandals were too well known for all but
the most naïve to think that its rule would bring the blessing of
good government.

When the polls closed on June 29, 1889, 62 per cent of the township's 8,366 voters supported annexation.[6] In Pullman, however,
76.5 per cent of 1,631 ballots were against. The triumphant Hopkins assumed these "lopsided" returns proved that George Pullman
had intimidated his men, for otherwise why would they vote differently from other Hyde Parkers. Specifically, he charged several
company foremen with violating the privacy of polling places, and
threatened suit against one. An angry Hopkins called the company's action "the biggest outrage on American freedom ever perpetrated."

The accuracy of these charges is difficult to determine. In general, the skewed pattern of the township's vote suggests that purely
local issues, such as schools and sanitation, decided the election
differently in Hyde Park's various communities. The one-sided vote
of Pullman was the rule, not the exception. Kenwood and Woodlawn were nearly as strongly against annexation, while Colehour,
South Chicago, and Hegewisch were over 90 per cent in favor.

The Pullman Palace Car Company no doubt abused its power by
interfering in this election as well as in others. There is support for
the assertion that its opponents had difficulty in leasing meeting
halls within the town. On the other hand, many of the accusations
against the company are vague and less creditable. The view that
George Pullman controlled the Hyde Park government, in particular, seems erroneous. There were too many wrangles with the trustees in which he did not get his way. His influence, though strong,

was not decisive, and both in public and in private he expressed displeasure with township government,[7] though preferring it to Chicago's rule.

Ely, in conversation with a company executive, gained the impression that George Pullman believed his interests necessitated active involvement in local politics, but that he limited his actions in national elections to contributions to the Pullman Republicans and occasional attendance at their rallies.[8] One reason for this moderation may have been that his close friend, Marshall Field, a member of the company's board of directors, was an ardent Democrat. Ely, who was in Pullman during the campaign of 1884, attended a rally of Cleveland supporters and found it well organized and heavily attended. Blaine won the town, however, but four years later Cleveland carried it by a narrow margin.

President Harrison was a personal friend of Pullman, who was said to have contributed $50,000 to help Harrison's try for reelection in 1892.[9] During this campaign he drew the ire of Democratic newspapers by warning his workers that Cleveland's victory would mean tariff reductions and a depression. Despite this remark, the Democratic candidate got 986 votes in Pullman to the Republican's 843. In July 1894, at the time of the strike, a *New York Herald* reporter interviewed the car magnate and inferred from his remarks that he had deliberately cut his workers' wages—the action which led to the walkout—to punish them for disobeying his instructions to vote for Harrison. The *Chicago Sun* (August 27, 1894) dismissed the charge as nonsense, but the *Chicago Evening Post* found it plausible. In 1896 and again in 1900, McKinley ran against Bryan, and the Republican easily carried the town.

⌊Despite his misgivings, there is no indication that annexation weakened George Pullman's control of the town. The city retained the township's loose relationship with the model town. As part of the thirty-fourth ward its residents voted for Chicago office-holders, including two aldermen who represented the thirty-fourth in the city council. The company's policy of encouraging its executives to run for political positions was continued.⌋

In the ward's first aldermanic contest, a special election on September 10, 1889, Dr. James Chasey, the town's agent, won a seat as a Republican. In the regular election that quickly followed in April 1890, Chasey retained his office after a controversial campaign. Two prominent company officials, General Superintendent H. H. Sessions and General Manager G. F. Brown, had canvassed the shops seeking votes. Later a discharged workingman protested to the Chicago Board of Election Commissioners that he was fired because he had refused to support Chasey. The commissioners, however, accepted the manager's explanation that the man had been guilty of general insubordination and was simply trying to cause trouble.[10]

Hyde Park's entry into Chicago made John Hopkins a power in the city's Democratic organization. In 1890, he lost the nomination for sheriff of Cook County, but did become chairman of the party's campaign committee for three years. He was also made president of the Cook County Democracy, a marching society, which reportedly "electrified Springfield" at Governor Altgeld's inauguration. In January 1893 Hopkins broke with the regular Democrats who supported Carter Harrison for the mayoralty nomination. When Harrison won not only the nomination but the election, Hopkins suffered a temporary political decline. In July 1893 he received the first federal appointment of President Cleveland's second term in Chicago, that of receiver for the Chemical National Bank.

Mayor Harrison was assassinated on October 29, 1893, by a disappointed office seeker. The stunned city council appointed a Republican alderman as mayor protem with a special election set for mid-December. Hopkins, supported by Altgeld and an anti-city hall faction, won the Democratic nomination and ran on a platform which emphasized clean government and such particulars as the "speedy solution of the garbage problem." Backed vigorously by the *Chicago Times* and waging an active campaign, Hopkins squeezed through a narrow victory to become at thirty-five Chicago's youngest mayor.

The city had the previous summer experienced the grandeur of the Columbian Exposition. Now it began to reel before the impact of the Panic of 1893 which the unusual activity generated by the

Fair had delayed. Hopkins's brief administration was beset by troubles from the beginning. Among these would be the Pullman or Chicago Strike of 1894 and a head-on confrontation with his former patron and employer.

It is difficult to give an over-all evaluation of the relationship between the company and the politics of the town. Much of the truth has been blurred beyond comprehension by the complexity of local issues, the loss of important documents, and the partisanship of the participants. A few generalizations, however, may be in order. At a time when businessmen commonly influenced votes, the Pullman Palace Car Company, because of the peculiar nature of the town, had more reason and opportunity to do this than most. How far it went and with what success elude precise statement.

The answers probably lie somewhere between the accusations of its critics and the denials of its defenders. George Pullman always insisted that his people had complete freedom of choice. His friend the Reverend Eaton, however, admitted that there might be instances where foremen had tried "to curry favor with the management by unduly crowding workingmen and controlling political action," but, he added, "such action is contrary to the desire and policy of the president and superior officers of the company."[11] Despite his public statements, George Pullman never forcefully acted to convince the workers that they were free to vote as they pleased; nor is there indication that officials who transgressed this principle were punished. At least in local politics, a widespread belief existed that a man opposed Pullman's candidate only at the risk of his future with the company. This alone hampered the opposition.

The charges against Pullman were exaggerated for political purposes. Hopkins, for one, kept careful watch over the town's political life, intent on finding abuses which the Democratic newspapers of Chicago were eager to print. Many people in Chicago began to believe George Pullman a ruthless autocrat who crushed his opponents and cast them from the community. The town was frequently described as a feudal barony whose residents lived with their master's yoke set firmly in place. The *Arcade Journal* furiously denied dictatorial rule, pointing to several elections that had gone contrary to Pullman's wishes.[12]

On one thing both sides agreed. There was little opportunity for political expression on town matters, and the only community election was for the school board. The town's supporters made no effort to conceal this because they viewed the absence of local rule as a virtue rather than a vice. The *Arcade Journal* in an editorial in 1890, two years after Lord Bryce's *American Commonwealth* called attention to the "conspicuous failure" of city governments, quoted with approval Andrew White's statement that "under our theory that a city is a political body a crowd of illiterate peasants, freshly raked in from Irish bogs, or Bohemian mines, or Italian robbernests, may exercise virtual control. How such men govern we know too well." To Duane Doty municipal problems, by and large, were not proper questions for political consideration, but rather, as they concerned property and money, should be handled by a businessman trained in the rational ways of the market. In Pullman it was the executive not the "boss" who made decisions. If detractors lamented the exclusion of the "town meeting," defenders rejoiced in the absence of the "political machine."

10

Company Community and City Satellite

The conviction that the city was a repository of vice, disorder, and ugliness had prompted George Pullman to locate his town at a distance from Chicago. Business considerations, however, had necessitated proximity, which combined with good transportation formed firm connections between city and model town. Pullman, designed as an independent and intact community, was never more than a satellite of its neighbor. Powerful currents of urban life from the north always flowed through the small town. As a result, George Pullman soon discovered that he had not succeeded in building a town isolated from Chicago or apart from its problems.

From 5:30 A.M. to midnight, trains stopped at least every half hour at Pullman's station. Chicagoans visited the model town on occasion and out of curiosity, but the residents had need for frequent excursions to the city. Some of the men in the shops lived in the metropolis and commuted nightly or weekly, and many people in Pullman had left friends and relatives in the old neighborhoods. Those who had no personal connections with Chicago went there for its theaters, restaurants, and elegant department stores. The *Pullman Journal* always carried a full listing of Chicago's theater fare, and Chicago restaurants and department stores advertised in the town paper. Even Pullman, with its unusual opportunities for shopping and recreation, could not match the excitement and variety of the Loop.

Chicago's newspapers were widely read in the town, and the next day's papers were brought daily by the evening train. The desire to increase this circulation, as well as the interest provoked by a novel experiment, explain the town's extensive coverage in the metropolitan papers. The *Inter Ocean, Times,* and *Herald,* in an effort to capture readers, often ran columns of items about Pullman and other Calumet towns, including notice of visitors, parties, and sporting events. The *Pullman Journal* never attempted to compete with the urban dailies but acted only to complement their information. Its primary function was not that of a small-town newspaper but only of a neighborhood journal.

Although Pullman's principal industry, the manufacturing and servicing of cars, was directed toward the national market, much of the town's other business was Chicago-oriented. The produce and products of truck and dairy farms were daily delivered to the city's South Water Street Market, and the town's ice house provided the means to keep these fresh. More important, once Pullman was complete all the brick from the yards and much of the cast iron made by the Union Foundry were sold to Chicago's construction industry. This relationship was reciprocal, for Pullman storekeepers bought from Chicago merchants, while the company depended upon the city for its supplies and replenishment of its work force.

The most obvious impingement upon Pullman's isolation, however, came not from the city but from the nearby communities of Kensington and Roseland. The car manufacturer had deliberately selected a sparsely settled area as his site. Within a radius of a mile and a half, there had not been more than several hundred people, mainly farm families in 1880. The coming of the Pullman shops and other industries into the area triggered a chain reaction of real estate speculation and rapid home building by developers.

Kensington, a mile west of Lake Calumet at 115th Street, lay directly across the I.C. tracks from the southern industries of Pullman. It came into existence in the 1850's at the junction point of the

Michigan Central and Illinois Central Railroads. In 1880, Kensington had a population of 250, a railroad yard, several boarding houses, and two saloons. The arrival of the construction crews to build Pullman created a boom, and by October 1881, a new affluence—and an estimated twenty saloons—were found in Kensington. But the price paid was the town's reputation. As early as the fall of 1880, the Hyde Park Trustees considered the need for a jailhouse in Kensington to accommodate drunken brawlers. Before long, the village was familiarly known throughout the Calumet region and as far north as Chicago as "bumtown." Throughout the 1880's, "bumtown" usually had a police detachment of five men headed by a sergeant and including two jailkeepers. Pullman had two, augmented by a company force of thirty nightwatchmen, and the neighboring community of Roseland averaged only a one-and-a-half man force.[1]

Once the model town was completed, Kensington's prosperity continued. Some of its men found jobs in the shops, while other people, attracted by the nearness of the car works, settled there. By 1883, the population had increased to about 1,300. When John Hopkins angrily left the planned community, he moved his business to Kensington and along with its other merchants profited from trade with Pullman residents. During the 1880's, the railroads enlarged their yards, and a few small manufacturers located in Kensington. The town's real moneymakers, however, were believed to be businesses engaged in the "commercialized vice" forbidden in Pullman.

The contrast between "model town" and "bumtown" was striking. The Reverend Charles Eaton suggested that anyone who would appreciate the advantages of planning should visit the two and compare them:

> Leave the well-paved, well-sewered, and well-cleaned streets of [Pullman], with its neat and convenient houses, and walk for five minutes along the half-hid-out streets of Kensington with its open sewers, its piles of decaying vegetation, its pools of stagnant water, its ill-ventilated and tumble down tenements, its scores of liquor shops and houses of doubtful character.[2]

⌊In 1894 the main street of Kensington had over forty bars, including several with gaming tables. What Eaton neglected in his eagerness to lavish praise on the model town was that "Red" Bockmann, John Malone, and other Kensington saloonkeepers were getting rich from a Pullman clientele.⌋

The workers of Pullman were frequent, though not always conspicuous, visitors to "bumtown." When the shops closed, especially on a Saturday or payday night, many of the men made their way to Kensington's long row of saloons. Some came by a direct route, but others used the alleys and side streets to avoid detection, and it was not altogether unknown for a man to leave Pullman walking in another direction, only to arrive ultimately at Downey's on 115th Street. Nor was it a rare spectacle to see a delivery cart from Kensington on a Pullman street, or a car shop employee walking home with a pail of beer purchased across the tracks.

William Stead, the English evangelist and social reformer, whose *If Christ Came to Chicago!* shocked the city in 1893 with its scathing indictment, found Kensington a town "given over to disorder." Unlike Eaton, he attributed the cause to the effect of Pullman's plan rather than to the unplanned nature of Kensington. According to Stead, it was the enforced absence of the grog shop in the model town which explained the plenitude on 115th Street. For, just as the sewage farm received Pullman's physical waste, so did its "moral and spiritual disorder" empty into Kensington.[3]

There is no indication, however, that drinking or alcoholism were more common in Pullman than might be expected. Ely thought it much less than in other industrial towns due to the exclusion of saloons. "The temptation 'to drink' does not constantly stare one in the face, and this restriction has not entirely failed to accomplish its end, the promotion of temperance." [4] By and large, the company's work force had a reputation for being temperate in an age known for its excess. Kensington only illustrated the recurrent phenomenon of "dry" communities, a portion of whose citizens invariably frequented the nearest "wet" town. Every army post has its "boom town" and every city a "bohemia," and, perhaps, every planned community must have a nearby area which offers services not socially acceptable enough to have been included in the plan but for which a demand exists. Thus, Pullman's prohibition did not solve the problem of drinking in the community, but probably did not add to it and, if anything, made it less visible. Both citizen and visitor to the model town seldom saw a drunk staggering the streets. The Pullman resident who wanted to "raise hell" had to cross the tracks to escape the social restrictions of his own town.

On a high ridge a mile west of Florence Avenue was the town of Roseland. The land between them was owned by the Pullman Land Association, which left it undeveloped. Roseland had been founded in the 1840's by a small group of Dutch farmers and was called for many years the Holland Settlement. By 1880, there were 1,000 residents who prided themselves on "pretty homes and well kept lawns." The coming of the Pullman shops brought an increase in population with land values soaring. Many of the car workers, especially among the skilled and thrifty Swedes and Germans, settled in the community, and by 1883 its population rose to about 2,000. Because of the distance from the railroads, no industry located in Roseland, but its men found employment in nearby shops. The dairy and truck farms which had surrounded the community were forced to the south and west. One Hundred and Eleventh Street and Ridge Road, later Michigan Avenue, developed as a shopping area which also served surrounding communities, including Pullman and Kensington.

Unlike Kensington, Roseland, despite many changes, maintained a continuity with its past. The Dutch Reformed Church and the original families remained influential, and the town, expanding into unimproved areas, still sustained an attractive appearance. Its reputation continued good, though it was now known as a residential area for skilled and respectable workingmen. Roseland had saloons but these were neither numerous—only nine in 1889 as composed to Kensington's twenty-nine—nor boisterous and many a Pullman matron shopped here rather than in "bumtown" because of the greater propriety.

These three very different Calumet towns had one important

thing in common—their prosperity depended on the Pullman Palace Car Company. Perhaps a third to a half of the men of Kensington and Roseland worked in the model town,[5] and naturally, their associations with colleagues did not end at the factory gate. They participated in Pullman's social clubs, and as company employees, were eligible to use the town's special facilities. On the other hand, the social halls of Kensington and Roseland often played host to workers' groups which could not or would not meet in Pullman. More than once labor unrest spread from Chicago to the three towns, resulting in packed meetings in Kensington's Turner Hall to hear Chicago speakers call for a union.

In the 1880's as farm land was profitably abandoned to industry, the area about Pullman lost its rural appearance and became suburban. By 1892, Roseland's and Kensington's combined population was 12,000, while within a four-mile radius of the model town's Arcade, there were over 60,000 people. The increases in the Calumet region were reflected in the census of 1890 which showed Chicago to be America's second city, with 1,098,570 residents; the following decade, this figure rose to over 1,698,575, despite several years of depression.

An important reason for the south side of the city's continuous growth during the 1890's was the Columbian Exposition. Located on the lake front in the old village of Hyde Park, the Fair encouraged the development of transportation throughout the former township. In 1893, the I.C. expanded suburban service until sixty-two trains a day stopped at Pullman. The same year also witnessed the extension of streetcar service southward, mainly along Stony Island, from 71st Street to 111th Street. It was now possible to travel from Pullman to the Loop for a nickel. Added convenience and lower cost in transportation between the city's outskirts and center naturally attracted new residents and hastened settlement. According to *The Calumet Region: An Industrial Supplement to the Chicago Telegram*, October 24, 1904, the aggregate population gain for the United States in the years 1890-1900 was 20 per cent, for Chicago, 54 per cent, and for the Calumet region, 148 per cent.

It was only a question of time before sparsely inhabited areas would be filled, causing the old towns to lose their distinctions and blur into the urban panorama.

De Tocqueville had been fascinated by the tendency of Americans to come together in voluntary associations. In 1893, Pullman, only twelve years a community, had forty social organizations. The number, variety, and strength of these groups was partly due to the role of the company in the town's life. Officers and clerks of the Pullman Palace Car Company and its related enterprises assumed positions of leadership in all social activity, while its president encouraged these organizations in a number of informal ways.

Of the forty organizations, about one-third were local chapters of national fraternal orders, such as the Odd Fellows and Masons, but the others ranged from the purely pleasure-seeking to those actively engaged in educational, cultural, and philanthropic work. A reporter reading notices tacked on the huge bulletin board that stood outside the factory's main gate was surprised to see weekly meetings of a chess and whist club, practice sessions of a choral society and string band, and advertisements for a performance of the Pullman Thespian Social Club. He looked about him at the men re-entering the factory grounds after a noon-hour break with assurance that at least one group of American workingmen had opportunities for a better way of life.[6]

Three of the town's organizations warrant special notice because of the interest they generated. The Pullman Athletic Club was incorporated in the fall of 1881 with a capitalization of $10,000. Its first president was E. W. Henricks, then chief clerk of the works, and Dr. John McLean, company physician, was vice-president. By 1883, its membership was 125, including every chief of a department.

The club sponsored sporting events, the proceeds of which were used to maintain the athletic facilities of the artificial island and park and to purchase equipment for the town's various teams. Several major contests were held each year, large prize awards attracting top contestants from all over the country along with thousands of spectators. On Decoration Day, May 31, track and field contests culminated in a long-distance road race from the Wilton Hotel in Chicago's Loop to the Florence Hotel—sixteen miles. During July and August, sculling and sailing regattas focused national attention on the town. The Pullman Athletic Club always entered a team in the race and hired a trainer to ensure a good showing. The day's events were climaxed by a large banquet at the hotel where Pullman's notables rubbed elbows with important Chicagoans such as Joseph Medill and Marshall Field, who had come down for the day by private car. When possible, George Pullman attended with members of his family, for he shared the then prevalent view that athletics served a useful purpose in enhancing character development as well as health. Because of his views on charity, he did not give money outright to any community organization, but extended low interest loans to the P.A.C. and others.[7] It was well known that athletes found it easy to obtain employment in the town. Until George Pullman's death near the turn of the century, his community was famous throughout the Midwest for fielding crack teams in a number of sports.

Less famous but also important in the town's life was the Pullman Military Band. Started in 1881, by 1893 it numbered forty musicians, all of whom were employees of the shops. During warm weather, it played concerts in Arcade Park, while the theater was used for special money-raising concerts in winter. It regularly participated in the parades which were so common in Chicago and neighboring towns, and its natty grey uniforms, precise military formation, and spirited renditions drew many accolades and prizes. The company's contribution to the band was free use of a practice room, and on occasions when the men participated in a program scheduled during working hours, they continued to receive pay.

The P.A.C. and band not only added variety to the town's life, but their publicity enhanced Pullman's reputation and contributed to civic pride. The Woman's Union, on the other hand, worked exclusively within the community, attracting little attention elsewhere. Aside from the charitable activities, the club was principally devoted to raising the town's educational and cultural level. In these efforts, the women—often the wives of officers and foremen—could depend on company support.

The Woman's Union welcomed newcomers to Pullman, taking special pains with the families of the unskilled living in the tenements, who were viewed as backward in regard to taste and values. The clubwomen attempted to instruct the wives in the art of home decoration by guiding them through the better cottages, which one visitor described as "very cozy, and homelike, and comfortable. There will be books, and plants . . . bright warm colors in carpet and papering with perhaps a piano." [8] Classes were organized in domestic skills, such as sewing, and the company did its part by selling plants and flowers at cost. On at least one occasion it purchased a large quantity of wallpaper at wholesale prices. A man was sent to the "poorer houses with a number of varieties, from which the tenant was requested to select one, the company offering the paper at the very low figure at which they purchased it, and agreeing to hang it without charge." [9] E. W. Henricks, as town agent, customarily sent letters of appreciation or potted plants to the lady of a particularly attractive house.

George M. Pullman, who at first had misgivings about the earliest tenants and their furnishings, soon expressed satisfaction that the laboring class in the tenements was now emulating the home style of the middle class in the cottages. Richard Ely was one of the few disinterested observers to visit tenement apartments before 1894, and he found that:

> Everywhere even in a flat of two rooms in the third story, one sees prints and engravings on the walls, Christmas and other cards, with cheap "bric-a-brac" on brackets in the corner, or on some inexpensive ornamental table, and growing plants in the windows. It is comparatively a small matter that a highly developed aestheticism could not approve of much that is seen, for it is only the beginning of an education of the highest faculties, and better things will be seen in the children.[10]

The Woman's Union collaborated closely with the school board and the library in developing a strong program of special educational courses and lectures in the town. Teachers, often of university level, were brought to Pullman to offer evening adult classes in foreign languages, art appreciation, and history and political theory. A free kindergarten was provided for preschool children, and for the three hundred boys between the ages of fifteen and eighteen who worked in the shops, a special apprenticeship was arranged by which they could take courses in industrial skills, or, for the more ambitious, bookkeeping, stenography, and mechanical drawing.

The Pullman elementary school included Grades 1 to 8 and was generally considered among the best in the state. A principal and twenty-four teachers (supported by the highest school tax in Hyde Park Township)[11] administered to a student body of over one thousand. Two of these teachers were special instructors for art and music. It was obvious that the educational programs of the model town were well in advance of the times, and Chicago reformers throughout the 1890's tried to convince the city's board of education to adopt them generally. The school was controlled by an elected school board whose president was Dr. John McLean (1883-89), and whose other members were usually company officers. On one occasion, the Cook County superintendent of schools asked for the removal of Daniel R. Martin, the Pullman principal, as not qualified for his position, but this was resisted by McLean, who insisted on the board's autonomy in Pullman affairs even after it became part of Chicago.

The number and vigor of social organizations, however, may not be indicative of their true relations with the community. No matter the scope of their purpose, Pullman's clubs were run by a small segment of the town's population. Unskilled workers, who made up 22 per cent and 21 per cent of the town's work force in 1883 and 1889, respectively, were eligible for membership in the clubs, but were virtually unrepresented on lists of officers for these years.[12] But upper-level management—assistant superintendents and above—comprised 20 per cent of organizational officers in 1883 and 16 per cent in 1889, although constituting only 1 per cent of the population. Skilled "mechanics" always were in a majority among breadwinners in the "model workingman's town," but the managerial, professional, and commercial classes which composed 16 per cent of the town's labor force in 1889 held 57 per cent of club offices. On the other hand, one large group, no matter their occupation, was badly under-represented in town organizations, and that was boarders who, mainly single men, seem not to have concerned themselves in community organizations with the exception of the athletic teams.

Community leaders appeared with remarkable rapidity. In 1883, less than two years after arrival, McLean, Henricks, and Eli C. Tourtelot, a company clerk who by 1889 was chief clerk, had each been elected not only to the board of education, but also as officers in two social organizations. The names of these three and certain others—Major Joseph L. Woods, Duane Doty, E. T. Martin, N. F. van Winkle, and Edward F. Bryant—reappear in club lists throughout the years, and they and their wives dominated the social news of the town as reported in the *Pullman Journal*.

In addition to the obvious—talent, temperament, interest—there were other explanations for this. These leaders held jobs which were flexible, while most other men in the town were confined to long arduous hours which left little time or energy for civic participation. Their backgrounds reveal certain similarities which contributed to close personal ties that enhanced their professional and civic contacts. All were native Americans in a town where aliens were in a majority, and they had fathers who were farmers, small merchants, or skilled mechanics. Their education level was high for the times, and many of the older men had participated in the Civil War as army officers. Most were ardent Republicans and strong admirers of George Pullman. When the strike of 1894 threatened their community, they proudly wore miniature American flags in their lapels to demonstrate visible support for the company.

Thus, a well-knit and influential group supported Pullman's policy toward the town, but he also had his critics among the residents. These until 1894 did not form a distinct and recognizable element, and little can be said about who they were. As already mentioned, early writers viewed malcontents as longing for the sordid excitement of the city slum. Even Richard Ely commented "that there are those who do not feel it a hardship to live in a dark alley of a great city, and there are men and women at Pullman incapable of appreciating its advantages." [13]

It was generally assumed that those unhappy with the model town had been scarred by their earlier background and would adjust in time. As the years passed and criticisms of the town continued, at least some people began to consider them more than a passing phase. Reporters for the *Herald* and other papers which printed negative remarks often mentioned that their informants were respectable, skilled workingmen, to establish their credentials as responsible critics, but omitted names to avoid reprisal.

By 1893, it was generally accepted in Chicago that many men in Pullman had honest grievances. These fell into two broad categories. One concerned what was believed to be the company's efforts to exploit its tenants through overcharging them for rents and utilities. The other was the fact that the company deliberately interfered with private life by ringing the residents in red tape and hiring "spotters" to spy on men after working hours. Just how widely these views were held by the town's residents in whole or in part and with what intensity cannot be ascertained. Anyone who felt very strongly, of course, could leave the town, but human nature being what it is, this may not always have happened, and it should be remembered that some believed residence in the town was security against lay-offs.

The Presidential Strike Commission of 1894 found the workers of Pullman to be of "comparatively excellent character and skill, but without local attachments or any interested responsibility in the town, its business, tenements, or surroundings." [14] A townsman told a journalist that "the people of Pullman are like the Chinese in America. They come here thinking to make what money they [can]. For most of the town's population, Pullman was viewed primarily as a place to work rather than to live. As long as employment was steady in the shops, no major trouble erupted in the community. But it was only natural that irritations incurred during working hours would be brought home and nurtured against the town, for both factory and home were owned and managed by the same company. George Pullman had once said it was easy "to fathom the Pullman scheme." We are "landlord and employers. That is all there is of it." He would soon have reason to rue these words.

11

Innovation and Employee Dissatisfaction

William Vanderbilt of the New York Central and Wagner Sleeping Car Company on a trip to the mid-west in the fall of 1882 publicly ridiculed the new town. A group of reporters boarded his train at Detroit in the hope of obtaining an interview before arrival in Chicago. About an hour away from the city, Vanderbilt consented, and as the cars passed Pullman on Chicago's outskirts, they asked him for an opinion. "He expressed great admiration for the beauty and substantial appearance of the place," but added, "when the Wagner Company builds a place like that and call [sic] it 'Wagner' you'll know it. The Wagner Company puts its profits in the pockets of its stockholders." A short time later the New York Central erected new car works in Buffalo, New York. Freely admitting that the factories were to be modeled after Pullman's, Vanderbilt firmly stated:

> It is not the intention of the company to rival . . . [the] model town, as experience has demonstrated that the Illinois experiment smacks too much of the old-country landlord system. Land in the vicinity of the [Buffalo] shops is cheap and the workmen are being encouraged to buy.

The town of Pullman had the good wishes of many, but some business and labor leaders were skeptical from the beginning. Certain industrialists viewed it as an impractical venture which invited trouble. Charles Elliot Perkins, president of the Chicago, Burlington, and Quincy Railroad and Pullman's friend, thought he had turned his company "into an eleemosynary institution," and forecast a harvest of bitter fruit from his action for "he has got to keep doing more and more, or else there is bound to be discontent." [1] Some labor leaders, on the other hand, assumed that any action by a capitalist must be contrary to his men's interests, and regarded the model town's apparent benevolence as only a snare.

When the company's board of directors found it necessary to vote a stock issue to pay for the town's construction, their action was greeted with derision. "The Pullman stock [in late 1881] was sometimes called out on the New York Exchange: 'How much for flower-beds and fountains?' " [2] Addressing a group of visiting businessmen, George Pullman commented that he intended to make his town permanent and self-supporting. When he pointed out that even the church and theater were expected to bring 6 per cent, this "raised a laugh among [those] who saw something funny in the thought of building houses of worship as one would a storeroom."

These reflections on the business perspicacity of its president embarrassed the company. George Pullman countered by sarcastically remarking that his critics were as shortsighted as those who many years before had scoffed at the "Pioneer." Statements were issued that the town's rents more than met its expenses. When a journalist interviewing him asked whether the town paid, the reply, "while not explicit as might have been wished was . . . 'the aim was to realize 6 per cent on the investment. We have done that and are satisfied.' " But Judge A. O. Lochrane, company counsel, admitted that "people imagine that the town of Pullman is a white elephant to the company; that it is an onus that eats up the earnings."

A bold face was always maintained before others. There are indications, however, that even George Pullman had second thoughts about his social experiment. In 1883, the Cincinnati soap firm of Procter and Gamble was planning a new factory for the city's suburbs. One of the young partners, Harley Procter, was also interested in building homes for the workers. Melville Ingalls, a railroad executive, suggested he speak to Pullman, who advised against the idea.[3] Procter was told there would be unforeseeable complications: the tenants would abuse the property and fall behind in their rents, and when it was necessary to evict someone, their wives always fell conveniently ill. Returning to Ohio with Pullman's architect, S. S. Beman, Procter built a factory which had an "eye for beauty as well as utility. . . . A broad lawn separated the factory from the street, trees were planted, flower beds set."[4] A playing field even adjoined the works—but no model town.

Pullman, in late 1881, announced plans for a new office building at Michigan and Adams. Only its first three stories were intended for company use, with the remaining six floors to be divided into apartments for the office staff: a white-collar model tenement. But when the Pullman building was opened for occupancy in the fall of 1884, the residential units had been leased at large sums to "prominent society people and substantial citizens." Perhaps valuable urban property did not permit moderate rentals, or this may have been another reflection of George Pullman's dissatisfaction with his model town. His own presidential suite—waiting room, secretary's office through which all visitors passed, Pullman's own office, and that of his assistants and the company's second vice-president—occupied the entire northwest corner of the first floor, and was the center of the company's far-flung operations.

Although many of his peers thought Pullman had made a mistake in building the town, they continued to respect his business acumen. Concerned with the permanent value of his company's property, he avoided the common practices of watering and speculation. His goal was a financially sound structure, adequately buttressed by undivided profits to withstand the cyclical swings of the business pendulum. During hard times the company loaned money on interest to railroads wanting to contract for its car. Regularly paying a handsome 2 per cent quarterly dividend, the Pullman Palace Car Company dominated one lucrative field—car operation—and had a leading position in another—car production—throughout the 1880's.

In its financial report for 1881, the company stated that it had

30,209 shares outstanding, with a face value of $100.00 each; assets exceeded $16,000,000, and yearly revenue approached $3,000,000. By 1893, 4,000 stockholders, including Queen Victoria, owned stock valued at $26,000,000. Yearly earnings had risen to $11,000,000, and assets now totaled $62,000,000. Of the company's two primary enterprises, the operation of the cars was far and away more important than their manufacture. In 1893, it accounted for more than $9,000,000 of the company's earnings. Over 2,000 parlor, sleeper, and dining cars carried the company's name on 125,000 miles of the country's railroads. It was generally viewed as one of the nation's more impressive monopolies.

George Pullman bested his rivals by convincing public and railroads that he offered them more. The company remained eager for new ideas and inventions to improve cars and services. To a large extent, however, innovations in the 1880's were more technical and less dramatic than those so successfully publicized earlier. Still, they contributed in no small way to passenger comfort and safety. Pullman pioneered the "Baker system" of heating cars by means of steam or hot water circulating in coils located under the floor. In 1883, his sleepers began replacing the picturesque but dangerous Hicks and Smith brass oil lamps with the "Pintch system" of gas lighting, and in the next decade introduced Edison's electric light. In passenger service, the company strongly supported the industry-wide movement to facilitate travel by means of a "coupon ticket." These covered trips over several roads, saving the bother of buying separate tickets from the individual companies.

At this time, Pullman's most important innovation was the vestibule car, which culminated a twenty-year effort by railroads to find a way for passengers to move freely through a train. Elastic diaphragms at the end of two cars were firmly joined together by means of powerful spiral springs. This not only ended open-platform accidents, but also the rocking motion of the cars in movement. In the event of derailment or other railroad accidents, the vestibule often prevented the dual threat of "riding" and "telescoping," which occurred when cars were forced into each other.

Patented by George M. Pullman but invented by H. H. Sessions, a company employee, the vestibule was introduced on the Pennsylvania railroad in June 1887 amidst wide interest. The innovation was quickly adopted by the industry.

> . . . several sleeping cars, a dining car, and a car fitted up with a smoking saloon, a library with books, desks and writing material, a bathroom and a barber shop. With a free circulation of air throughout the train, the cars opening into each other, the electric light, the many other increased comforts and conveniences introduced, the steam heating apparatus avoiding the necessity of using fires, the fast speed, and absence of stops at meal stations, this train is the acme of safe and luxurious travel. An ordinary passenger travels in as princely a style . . . as any crowned head in Europe.[5]

The financial strength and strong leadership of the Pullman Palace Car Company enabled it mercilessly to batter competitors. Throughout the 1880's there were three principal rivals: the Wagner Palace Company, the Woodruff Sleeping Car Company, and the recently established Mann Boudoir Car Company. The vestibule car administered the "coup de grace" to the latter two, who, in 1888, were consolidated to form the Union Palace Company. Within a month the new company was absorbed by Pullman's, adding 15,000 miles to its already extensive network. Only the Wagner Company, strongly supported by the New York Central was able to withstand the pressure. But when it introduced its own version of the vestibule car, Pullman immediately tied it up in litigation. In April 1889 a United States Circuit Court vindicated his contention that Wagner's vestibule infringed on Sessions's invention. By 1893, three out of every four miles of the nation's rails were included in the Pullman system. On these the passenger had no choice but to use the company's services or none at all.

As early as the 1870's several state legislatures had considered policing Pullman car rates. The company bitterly fought this practice, arguing that as an interstate company it could not be regulated by one state.[6] When necessary, its large legal staff effectively used the courts to thwart the Texas and Iowa efforts to set rates. In 1886, the company's position was upheld by the Supreme Court's decision in Wabash vs. Illinois. Now impervious to state action, the Pullman Palace Car Company also managed to be excluded from the Interstate Commerce Commission's supervision of railroads. For several years the company enjoyed freedom of action, but there were numerous complaints of high fares and arrogance toward the public. By 1893, interest had been aroused among some congressmen, including the influential Senator John Sherman, to bring the company under the I.C.C. The unfavorable attention brought to the company by the strike the following year strengthened this effort.[7]

In the early 1880's, George Pullman participated in two transactions long legendary in early railroad history. He had been an important officer of Henry Villard's Oregon Railroad and Navigation Company, and participated in Villard's famous "blind pool" which raised $8,000,000 to take over the Northern Pacific. Older historians have usually presented Villard as systematically milking this railroad until he left it in 1884, ravaged and broken. More recent studies, however, suggest that Villard, brilliant as an organizer of capital and highly successful as a promoter, lacked the business foresight to prepare his road for the depression which began in August 1883. Pullman's involvement in the Northern Pacific's debacle seriously affected the Palace Car Company. Its stock dropped seven and one-half points in one day on February 15, 1884; Pullman and his associates only prevented a panic by buying shares as quickly as they were offered for sale. At this time he made an interesting but enigmatic statement. He told reporters that he was not the company's largest stockholder.[8] Whether this only meant that he did not own a controlling interest, or that some one else—perhaps Marshall Field—had more stock than he, is not altogether clear.

The other incident involved the West Shore Line principally owned by Pullman and officers of the Pennsylvania Railroad and of which Horace Porter was nominal head. This road was to be constructed between Buffalo, New York, and Weehawken, New Jersey —the point of entry for New York City. The route closely paralleled the New York Central's line, which ran on the opposite bank of the Hudson. William Vanderbilt, furious at this action by his two powerful foes, charged "blackmail." Defending himself by rate-slashing, he looked about for a counterattack, and persuaded Carnegie, William Whitney, and William Rockefeller to back his scheme of developing a rival line to break the Pennsylvania's monopoly of Pittsburgh's lucrative carrying trade.

By 1885 this "conflict of the titans" was worrying the nation's financiers. The West Shore—intent upon building a double track over the 400-mile route, and using the finest rolling stock—was experiencing financial difficulties in completing construction. Hard hit by Vanderbilt's actions, it also had to combat a business decline. At this point, J. P. Morgan intervened to arrange a settlement between the warring parties, and the West Shore was sold to the New York Central.

Those who knew Pullman well never doubted that of his many interests, the model town was closest to his heart. After the removal of the company's offices to the new building, however, his visits became increasingly infrequent. During the winter and spring of 1893-94, when conditions within the town were known to be critical and needing unusual attention, he went there only six times.[9] Periodically throughout the decade Pullman complained of fatigue and nervousness, and his doctors cautioned against overwork, advising programs of fresh air and exercise. In 1880, he was a vigorous forty-nine, with an appearance deceptive of his years. Ten years later he had aged considerably; his hair had greyed and deep lines had been firmly etched about his eyes and forehead. Still he retained firm hold of his company, and there can be no question that whatever his financial position within the company, he kept the confidence of his colleagues. Often important meetings of the board took place without a quorum being present. For all apparent purposes, the president was identical with the company.

By 1893, the Pullman Palace Car Company was one of the giants of American industry, with over 14,000 employees of which 5,500 worked in the model town. Along with shops scattered across the country (St. Louis; Omaha; Detroit; Elmira, New York; and Wilmington, Delaware), those in Pullman serviced the cars contracted to railroads. The town, along with Detroit, also engaged in car manufacturing, and between 1891 and 1892 its work force produced a weekly average of 3 sleepers, 10 coaches, and 240 various types of freight cars. Of this total, about 70 per cent was built for sale to the industry, and it was this aspect of the town's economy that was most precarious. The servicing of cars remained relatively stable no matter the state of business conditions, and the building of the company's new cars could usually be planned ahead to moderate the highs and lows of demand, but "outside orders" ebbed and flowed with the cyclical rhythm of the economy.

During the business recession from 1883 to mid-1886 car production dropped throughout the country. In October 1884 the cancellation of an order for two hundred cars from the West Shore required a lay-off of several hundred men in the town, and like others the company began tightening its belt and lowering bids in order to get work. When business conditions worsened, competitors often found it expedient to shut down and wait for better times. George Pullman, however, had to eschew this alternative.[10] Realizing how disastrous closing the shops would be to the model town—and the company investment of money and prestige—he tried to keep his men employed by taking contracts at a loss. This practice drew the ire of other manufacturers. John Jackson, head of the large Wilmington Car Company, complained bitterly to the press:

> To be plain, the Pullman Company has inaugurated an unjust, unfair, and disastrous competition. The company having built up a large town . . . in order to maintain this it must keep its shops filled, regardless of price, and contracts have been and are still being taken from cost to 25 per cent below cost.[11]

The company always insisted that its relationship to its employees living and working within the town was in no way different from that of any other hirer of labor. It firmly announced that it did not pay its men any more than the market rates for their skill, and their hours were the same as those of others in the industry. The company of necessity had to discredit the idea of some businessmen that in building a town it assumed a charitable stance toward labor that would require other concessions not in its interests. Yet, when the panic of 1893 again caused a shortage of work, the Pullman Palace Car Company closed the manufacturing department of the Detroit shops to provide jobs in Pullman. By erecting the town and making it a show place, the company had invested pride and money which forced it to assume a special responsibility. At the time of the strike, observers were quick to point out that residency in the town had made the workers more dependent on the company, but in less obvious ways ownership of the town made the car company more responsible for its employees. When, during the heat of battle, George Pullman announced that he and his men had no other obligation to each other than that stated in the work contract, public opinion would disagree. He found himself unable to evict men for non-payment of rent, though this meant that the company in effect subsidized a strike directed against itself.

The model town established a relationship between management and labor different from that which generally prevailed. George Pullman never appreciated this. He had originally thought that the model town would be a simple solution to his labor problem, and when this proved untrue, he could not understand the complex situation that had been created by his search for lucid answers and firm control.

From the company's point of view, the most important objective in erecting the town had been to provide itself with a stable work force free of discontent and disturbances. But the model town never did provide this. Before it was very old, its history was marred by strike; on February 14, 1882, one thousand construction workers stopped their labors to protest a change in company policy. For several months their employer had paid half the I.C. commuter rate between Pullman and Chicago, but now ended its contribution. The men demanded a restoration of the half-fare and several other concessions. The company conceded the minor points but refused to pay the half-fare, and after being out for two days most of the men returned to work. Two hundred, however, left the town rather than agree to what amounted to a sizable wage cut.

The depression years of the early 1880's brought labor unrest to the nation and saw a remarkable growth of that first major effort to unite all American workingmen, the Knights of Labor. In Pullman, wage slashes prompted several small strikes in various departments, and by late 1885, there was talk of a plant-wide walkout. In early 1886, the Knights began recruiting in the town as part of their plan to call a national strike on May 1 to force the eight-hour day standard for all industrial workers. In March 1886 George Schelling, a prominent Chicago labor leader, "denounced the [model town] as a slave pen without an equal in the United States." [12] In April, Schelling and the more radical Albert Parsons, who later was executed for alleged responsibility in the Haymarket Riot, held meetings in Kensington's Turner Hall after being refused use of Pullman's facilities. Denounced by the town's Catholic priest as "outside agitators" bent on provoking trouble, they reportedly signed up four hundred car workers.

On May 1, 1886, a Saturday, over 60,000 Chicago workers remained away from their jobs. Violence at the McCormick reaper plant caused a mass protest meeting to be held on May 3 at Haymarket Square. Here, a bomb tossed at a policeman led to a clash which resulted in several deaths and many injured. A wave of horror and fear spread from the city to the remainder of the nation. George Pullman's reaction was expressed in a letter to Andrew Carnegie that wondered whether the democratic system could survive the "excesses of our turbulent population." [13] Ironically, this letter was an acknowledgment for Carnegie's sending him a copy of his recently published *Triumphant Democracy*. Pullman's remarks no doubt reflect the fact that his men had struck on that day, and also a sermon delivered that Sunday by his friend, Rev. David Swing, which stated that the purpose of government was the prevention of violence and the protection of life and property. According to Swing, if a democratic government couldn't assure these, it should be replaced by a monarchy.

On May 5, the Pullman workers went out, but they did not limit themselves to the eight-hour day. Though business conditions had recently improved, the company, rather than restore the old wage rates, had instead placed many of the men on a piece-work scale.

To President Pullman, this was viewed as a means of increasing production, and also an "educational tool in that it offered incentive to the worker to improve his skill." [14] For the workers, however, piece work was but a whip to spur them on for the stockholders' profits. There were complaints then, and later, that not only were rates generally low but through lack of knowledge they were inequitably set, favoring some trades and departments at the expense of others.

Until early 1886, the company had assumed responsibility for all injuries incurred on the job. Dr. John McLean had been appointed company physician in 1881 and a clinic had been installed in his home, which faced the main gate. Injured men were immediately brought here for care at company expense and, if need be, transported to Chicago's St. Luke's Hospital. When H. H. Sessions, the inventor of the vestibule car, was made general manager of the shops early in 1886, he discontinued the general practice of paying everyone for the days they had lost. Sessions—fearing that malingerers were exploiting this policy, whose generosity was highly unusual—declared that only men who proved that their accidents had not been due to personal negligence could receive a per diem. Industrial injuries, which could cripple a man for life and leave him dependent on inadequate private charities, were the scourge of all workingmen. Such a possibility was not remote; in the years between 1884 and 1894, McLean had attended 4,155 cases of men injured on the job.[15] Of these, the majority were serious enough to warrant the loss of at least two days of employment.

Before the May 5 strike, an executive committee appointed by the workers presented a demand for a 10 per cent salary increase, changes in piece work, and a return to compensation for all industrial injuries. George Pullman replied that he could not permit employees to control his policies, but did offer to allow the committee to examine the books for proof that circumstances did not warrant wage raises. This was declined, and the men stayed away from the shops. As the days went on, Pullman became apprehensive; he wrote his wife early on Monday, May 10: "My anxiety is very great although it is said that I appear very cool and unconcerned about it.

Some change must occur very soon now, but I cannot yet predict what it will be." A few days later he opened the shops under police protection, and the men began returning. Perkins, of the Burlington, confided to a friend: "Pullman's experience turns out to be just what I have always prophesied. He thought he was doing a great deal for his employees and would never have strikes, but the fact is, the more you do for your men . . . the more they want." [16]

From 1887 to 1893, there were only a few isolated incidents. On these occasions, skilled workingmen of a particular trade and department walked out. But never numbering more than a handful, their morale was quickly broken by the company's ultimatum: return to work or face discharge. Most of these disputes involved wages, and George Pullman remained consistent in his belief that the managers of capital must set salaries to protect investments. The workers' right was one of choice—to labor for those wages or not. To prevent the development of unions which would impinge upon his managerial prerogatives, he used strikebreakers, the black list, and company spies.

In early 1891, the company became aware that men in the iron foundry were organizing. A "special agent" was sent with a letter of recommendation to Superintendent Sessions who hired him without knowledge of his real purpose.[17] This man—identified only as "W. W. C."—worked and lived in the town from March 16 to April 8, when his fellows in the blacksmith department became suspicious. By constant inquiries, he discovered the names of the officers of the union and which men had joined. His report was considered important enough to send to George Pullman vacationing in Hot Springs, Arkansas, while copies were given to various officials in the town. E. F. Doran, Superintendent of the Iron Works, commented: "There are some good points in Agent's report of which I am glad to receive. He names several who he says are agitators, whose names I did not have, and I have some he does not mention in his report."

While the agent's chief purpose was to supply intelligence on union activity, he also provided considerable information on working conditions in the shops and on the men's attitudes toward individual foremen. The issue of despotic foremen had a long and deep

George M. Pullman at sixty years of age in 1891. The fastidious appearance and conservative dress apparent in this portrait were characteristic of the man. (Courtesy of the Chicago Historical Society.)

PLATE I

This drawing of the town of Pullman was done in 1881, before construction was completed, and used frequently to illustrate early articles on the community. The artist has emphasized the park-like setting, and the possibility of harmony between industry and nature.

Pullman's home on Prairie Avenue. Built in 1873 it was frequently altered and added to until newspapers estimated its value at well over $300,000. (Courtesy of the Chicago Historical Society.)

PLATE II

Rear of the Prairie Avenue mansion. Conservatory, fountain, and formal garden were designed in 1879 by S. S. Beman. George Pullman's satisfaction with this work explains the young architect's commission for the model town. (Courtesy of the Chicago Historical Society.)

The Pullman main factory building, looking north from the Arcade Building. Chicago is on the horizon. On the left is the Illinois Central Railroad station and a small park. Left of center is the artificial Lake Vista. The vacant land west of the railroad, owned by the company, preserved the town's isolation and its rural appearance.

Looking directly south from the car shop toward the central area of town. Hotel and Arcade are at right center, the old Market Hall at left center.

PLATE III

Looking from the Arcade Building east to Lake Calumet, on the left is the Market Hall as it appeared before it was destroyed by a fire in 1892 and rebuilt in Romanesque style. This picture clearly shows the variety of housing offered in Pullman. In the rear are the barrack tenements.

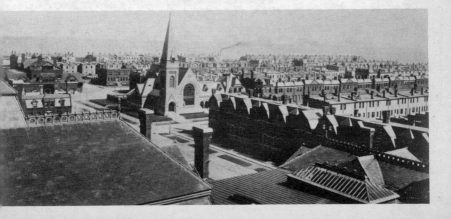

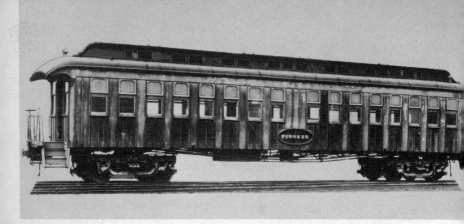

The classic "Pioneer," the first sleeping car with a folding upper berth. This photograph (c.1900) was taken several years after retirement from service when the car was placed on permanent display at the model town. (Courtesy of Pullman, Inc.)

PLATE IV

Use of a turntable suggests the industrial forethought that went into car production. "In building a car as the work progresses it is passed from one shop to another until it is ready for the road." One may wonder whether this early example of moving a product to the worker influenced the later development of the assembly line in the automobile industry. (Courtesy of Pullman, Inc.)

PLATE V

The opulence and luxury associated with the name Pullman in railroad travel is demonstrated by the parlor car "Santa Maria," built in 1893 and part of the company's exhibit at the World's Columbian Exposition. (Courtesy of Pullman, Inc.)

Lake Vista (artificial) is the setting for the main building of the car works. Behind the glass windows to the left of the entrance and clearly visible to passersby was the Corliss engine, the world's largest and the principal attraction of the Philadelphia Centennial of 1876. Its energy supplied the motive force for the works, and the exhaust emptied into Lake Vista. Clock tower and engine were obvious symbols of an industrial society.

PLATE VI

Looking eastward along 111 Street is the wide boulevard separating factory and community. In the foreground is the Hotel Florence which contained the town's only bar. The hotel became a social center for community leaders. Workingmen, though not specifically forbidden, avoided it because of the prices and its ornateness.

The center of community life was the Arcade Building, ninety feet high and a block long. One reporter described it as a roofed-in American "oriental bazaar."

PLATE VII

Interior of the Arcade Building. The first floor consisted of stores and the Pullman bank and post office. The second contained the town agent's office and a theater and library.

Main reading room of the Pullman Public Library, which despite its name charged a membership fee. Giving the general impression of a gentlemen's club, the library was intended to promote the community's "moral and intellectual growth."

PLATE VIII

Men of the Illinois First Regiment and their command post on the lawn of the Florence Hotel, July 1894. The Pullman strike was a decisive experience which began the community's transition from model town to an urban, industrial neighborhood. (Courtesy of the Chicago Historical Society.)

history in the model town. Ely, in *Harper's,* had felt obliged to dwell on it at length,[18] and woodcarvers in the cabinet department had once struck for the removal of a foreman they accused of arbitrariness in assigning work. Of eight strikers who testified before the Presidential Strike Commission of August 1894, five mentioned abuses by foremen as being a major complaint. This is all the more important as the men were queried primarily on rents and wages, not conditions in the shops, and offered their comments gratuitously. Of five letters by workingmen quoted in Carwardine's *The Pullman Strike,* four referred to trouble with foremen. One had written: "The treatment we have received from the foreman of the company has been worse than the slaves ever received in the South." The men were generally concerned with nepotism, favoritism, and obnoxious behavior by some placed over them. But when they protested to management, the company invariably supported the foreman. He was its direct representative to the men and on his authority depended industrial discipline. No adequate structure for the expression of grievances was ever apparently considered. The company was determined not to share power with the employees, and, in consequence, few opportunities for meaningful communications between labor and management were developed.

Many of the town's employees were long-time car workers. From prior experience, they knew that "in a large establishment like the Pullman shops there must necessarily be a large force of foremen, under foremen, sub-bosses, as well as heads of departments and higher officials," and that in such a system inequities and unpleasantnesses were inevitable. Until the summer of 1893, grievances felt by the men, which of course varied with their own particular circumstances, were generally held in check by respect for the general manager, H. H. Sessions, a firm but competent man who was considered interested in the employee's welfare despite his earlier action in ending the company's payment for lost work for all industrial accidents. When Sessions was transferred, however, he was replaced by a man without his experience or tact, who was no sooner on the job than a business recession caused the company to engage in necessarily unpopular actions. The souring of relations between the men and the local management of the shops quickly caused an estrangement between them and George Pullman, who had been heretofore highly regarded. According to Thomas Heathcoate, the leader of the Pullman strikers of 1894: "The employees were very well disposed toward Mr. Pullman until the actions of the last management seemed to estrange the men . . . from Mr. Pullman." [19]

A leading advocate of the efficiencies of planning and bigness in business, George Pullman was to fall victim to the problems of industrial management. As the Palace Car Company grew larger it necessarily became more complex and diverse. Despite this, every effort was made to keep the reins tightly held by officers located at Michigan and Adams in the Loop. A close check on all the many-faceted operations required an incessant flow of information from the extended parts to the center, which created complaints about the innumerable reports that had to be written and filed. Everyone above foreman's rank in the Pullman shops was required to write a weekly report, and this with a summary of the high points was sent to the company's uptown office. According to Carwardine, officers sometimes disturbed the workers in evening hours at home to ask for information needed in their reports. Officials in the field were irritated by "red tape" and lack of opportunity for personal initiative.[20] Many even said that these were the principal reasons for the high turnover in management, which in itself was disquieting. The modern American business structure was taking shape and then, as now, it sometimes proved abrasive to the human element. Nowhere could this have been more salient than in the model town, where the company as employer and landlord was ubiquitous, and opportunities for errors became magnified. Even if George Pullman remembered Charles Reade's advice—"put yourself in his place"—it could not have helped him to understand the needs and problems of his many employees. His company had grown too large for such a simple, personal touch.

IV

IMPACT OF STRIKE AND BOYCOTT
ON THE COMMUNITY

12

The Walkout

With typical American "hoopla" the World's Columbian Exposition opened on May 1, 1893. Advertised as "the biggest and best Fair ever," it offered attractions ranging from Mr. Ferris's Wheel to the "White City's" remarkable industrial and scientific exhibits. Chicago's leaders had given generously of time and money to guarantee success. George Pullman, a member of the fair's Executive Committee, was one of several to subscribe $100,000, and he was determine that his company make a good showing.

The Pullman exhibits were in Louis Sullivan's simply designed Transportation Building. Near the entrance was a large plaster of Paris model of the town—scaled an eighth of an inch to the foot—and in an adjoining annex were two tracks of Pullman cars. One carried an "exact counterpart of a New York to Chicago limited express," while on the other stood examples of the various types of cars manufactured in the model town. A specially prepared illustrated pamplet telling the story of the sleeping car and the town was distributed free of charge.[1]

Many visitors, their curiosity whetted, journeyed to the real town. In the four months of the fair, over 10,000 foreign tourists alone visited the model community. Their reaction was generally favorable. In summer the town was at its prettiest, with its many trees and flowers in deep, rich color. The workers were earning good salaries and appeared content. Few fair-goers found reason to doubt the company's claim that "[Pullman is] a town . . . where all that is ugly, and discordant and demoralizing, is eliminated, and all that inspires to self-respect, to thrift and to cleanliness of thought is generously provided." [2]

In early October the company's annual financial statement was released. A record four million dollar surplus remained after payment of the usual dividend. Fifty-five hundred men had been employed in the model town, averaging an unprecedented annual wage of $613. The fair's stimulus to passenger travel strained to capacity the town's shops. They built over three hundred cars for the company use alone, and still it was necessary to buy others elsewhere. The freight and other contract departments received so many orders from railroads that soliciting was suspended.

Railroads, including suburban lines, "miraculously" carried over 35,000,000 passengers to Chicago during the 184 days of the fair. Yet, this temporary increase in business could not save the railroad industry from running aground on the reefs of over-expansion and mismanagement. The consequence was a national depression that severely reduced manufacturing in general and car production in particular. Paradoxically, this situation threatened Pullman's livelihood at the very time visitors were commenting on its prosperity. The summer of 1893 introduced a year of trial for George Pullman and his employees. By causing an extraordinary demand for cars in the winter and spring of 1893, the Columbian Exposition postponed the depression for the model town, but when it came the drop was all the more severe because of recent glutting.

In early June 1893, a journalist, acting on reports of lay-offs in other car plants, sought an interview with George Pullman to find how his company was being affected. [3] Pullman told him that the company was "having some trouble in collecting money . . . owed us" and predicted "Jacksonian hard times." He believed that businessmen needed to act vigorously if a severe depression was to be avoided. The currency was essentially sound and, therefore, if the bigger companies maintained production while cutting costs, they could operate profitably. After a while general confidence would be restored, leading to an upturn. Only the inefficient lacking the stamina to adjust need be hurt.

The trade newspapers reported in July that railroads had a three-year supply of cars on hand. The worried Pullman Company began a reorganization. It closed the Detroit plant to bring all construction to Chicago, and the Detroit manager, A. M. Parent, was transferred to Pullman as assistant to Harvey Middleton, who now replaced Sessions in charge of the Pullman shops. Unlike his predecessor, Middleton was primarily a businessman rather than a car builder, and his selection was intended to result in cost reductions.

For several months the company's bidding had been too high, and no orders were acquired. In every possible way it sought to lower them. Starting in August, wage reductions occurred in various departments. Lack of work also required drastic paring of the labor force. From July to November 1893 the number of employees in Pullman dropped from 4,500 to 1,100. To make matters worse the company took several hundred of its own cars off the roads and placed them in storage while construction of new palace cars was halted.

By November, George Pullman had decided to acquire contracts even at a loss. Another series of wage cuts took place at the month's end. In December, a large order was received from the Long Island Railroad, and in the next few months, several smaller contracts followed. According to the P.P.C.C., from August 1, 1893, to May 1, 1894, it bid on $2,775,481.81 worth of contracts, and received $1,421,205.75 of this, upon which cost exceeded price by $52,-069.03.[4] The company also brought in as many of its own cars for servicing or repair as possible and undertook an extensive program of plant improvement. By spreading this work, it was able to employ 3,100 men by April 1894.

Decline in real earnings during the fall of 1893 was severe for most of the town's employees. Lay-offs and loss of time had considerably magnified the wage cuts. Resentment at decreases in earnings was compounded in some instances by inequities in their distribution. As mentioned in the last chapter, a piece-work system had been adopted as a more scientific method of production control. Due to the diversity of work performed in the shops, however, it presented difficulties for management which were probably insurmountable. Paradoxically, the piece-work system gave more *de facto* authority to the weakest link in management's chain, the foreman, at the same time that efforts were being made to develop centralized control from the top.

The company had instituted a cost-accounting department to determine proper piece rates. At least in theory the rates were set on the basis of an average workingman's performance of an assigned task.[5] This assumed a repetition which usually did not exist in the shops. Car repair and service entailed an amount of skill and time varying in each instance. Car production tended to more regularity, but ranged from refrigerator to palace sleeper, with each railroad wanting its own specifications. Rates could not be reduced to a simple and uniform system, but always had to be adjusted to fit a particular job by foreman and shop manager. Even the company realized limitations. Mechanics were assigned an hourly scale for doing jobs which could not be prorated, and unskilled labor almost always worked for day wages. Furthermore, in the winter of 1893-94 the workers began to complain that the company was using the performance of experts to establish piece rates.

A description of the Pullman system of manufacturing which underscored its potential for friction and confusion was given the *Chicago Tribune* (May 14, 1894) by one experienced car builder. Most cars were made in sixteen steps or "jobs" each requiring a crew of four or five skilled workers with a "straw boss"—assistant foreman—in charge. The company assigned a "price" for a "job," and on completion the straw boss had to divide this among the men. He was to consider the skill and performance of each, and the general going rates, but much had to be left to his discretion. The "job," however, was not officially ended until approved by an inspector. The whole "gang" remained idle until his arrival, sometimes a wait of several hours. The inspectors or foremen "being ambitious to advance themselves [tried] to improve on the specifications by making changes

. . . and compel [the men] to do the extra work for nothing."

According to this Pullman worker, there was widespread dissatisfaction among his fellows that the "job's price" was not always divided fairly. Many also believed that they were being penalized by the ambition or incompetency of their immediate superiors. Trouble between the workers and lower management seems to have been a fairly common theme in much of American industry of the time.[6] The ability of a foreman to get along with his subordinates was not a factor in his selection and he received no training in human relations. In the Pullman shops, the use of the piece-work system heightened the friction by giving foremen a power over the worker's purse.

In normal times a man made more money on piece-work than on day wages, but after the cuts the opposite became true. Foremen were charged with showing favoritism in sending friends to the better paid day work. Harvey Middleton—an abrupt and sometimes short-tempered man—began to be held personally responsible for the failings of his foremen. On taking over he had replaced many of Sessions's people with his own. Before long, the men's attitude toward him and his staff had hardened into hostility. A letter signed "Employees" appeared in the *Chicago Times* of December 10, 1893:

> The Pullman car works is at present a mere plaything, and its masters don't know how to keep the children quiet. At one time it was a carworks. That was sometime ago, however, when we had a competent car builder managing it. His name was H. H. Sessions. Well-known it is that George Pullman had things misrepresented to him. Mr. Pullman is a fine fellow and what he wants is fine fellows to work for him. . . . Give Mr. Sessions charge of us and the workers will go smoothly. He is the boy who we can help to estimate low enough to catch every car order in the market, and when we bid too low we will work for lower wages to help him, but we can't help the present management. No, not a bit of it.

Middleton was retained, however, even after a short-lived strike started among the steamfitters and blacksmiths on December 9,

1893. They demanded higher wages, but after a few days most returned to work. Those who would not return were blacklisted.[7]
The difficulty of fighting a powerful company, especially at a time
of depressed conditions, became evident. No one department or
trade was important enough to stand alone. A strike to be effective
had to close the shops. Several craft unions looked about for a
means of alliance. The difficult times and the uncertainty of the
future made the workers more conscious than ever that only
through combination could they guarantee a voice for themselves in
the company's decisions.

Under the auspices of Eugene V. Debs's American Railway
Union, a shop-wide union of locals organized by departments was
formed in the spring of 1894. Debs, the long-time editor of the
Fireman's Magazine, had been an ardent spokesman for a federation of railroad brotherhoods. Disappointed in this effort by 1893
he advocated a single industrial organization for all railroad workers. The American Railway Union was born at a convention held in
Chicago in June 1893. Its membership requirements were so
broadly stated that the Pullman locals could be accepted on the
grounds that the company operated twenty-odd miles of rails in the
model town, and therefore all its workers, no matter what their
occupation, worked for a railroad.[8]

The blacksmith strike of December prompted the *Chicago Times*
to run a series of five articles (December 10-14) on conditions in
the town. The first carried the headline: "Great Destitution Among
Residents of Pullman." According to the *Time*'s correspondent, the
town's plight was the result of a drastic drop in incomes with no
reduction in living expenses. He was particularly critical of the
company for maintaining "exorbitant" rents while reducing the
men's ability to pay them. Furthermore, he charged the company
was selling water purchased from the city at rates which in effect
made the inhabitants pay for that used by the company for industrial purposes. The writer also claimed that the gas which the company manufactured and sold to residents was so over-priced—
compared to neighboring communities—that this could only be
viewed as "tribute" exacted by a monopoly.

According to the *Times*, the employees were rapidly falling behind in their rent payments, despite the company's efforts to collect. And as debtors, the men lost their freedom to change employment, or seek cheaper quarters elsewhere. Instances were cited where the company's bank clerks pressured employees to sign and turn over the rent check, even though the amount left was less than a dollar to meet a family's needs for two weeks. To heighten their troubles, the paper's reporter found the workers were "afraid to complain for fear of dismissal."

The water rates of Pullman quickly became a football of Chicago politics. John Hopkins was elected mayor in early December, and he lost little time in becoming the model town's gadfly. The city had honored Pullman's water contract with Hyde Park until it expired in 1892. For over a year the company negotiated with Chicago officials who wanted higher rates. Now Hopkins announced that residents were being overcharged and he intended to double Pullman's payments. The company reacted by offering to turn its main over to Chicago, allowing the city to supply water to the tenants directly. The mayor, however, dismissed this move as deliberate obstructionism, while the *Chicago Inter Ocean* accused him of carrying on a vendetta against George Pullman. Finally in late April, a new contract was signed which charged the company about seven cents per 10,000 gallons. Hopkins also tried to end the town's status as an independent post office, which would mean home delivery in Pullman—then still a rarity outside of cities—and its name dropped from the mailing address. This was resisted by the company and apparently was unpopular with many residents. Whatever the reason, Hopkins was unsuccessful, and letters still continued to be sent to "Pullman, Illinois," and distributed at the post office.

The December strikes and the mayor's attacks were not all of George Pullman's troubles. A week before Christmas, his favorite brother and long-time associate, Albert Pullman, died. Hardly had he attended the funeral when it became necessary to beat off a raid by Wall Street "bears" who circulated rumors of financial weakness to drive the company's stock down, causing a 10-point decline in one day. Pullman and other officers, in an effort to bolster confidence, issued public statements elaborating on its soundness and the continuing profits from car operation. This in turn exacerbated tensions in the model town since workers wondered why they needed to suffer wage cuts while the company was reporting successes. Throughout a particularly bitter winter, Pullman complained often of fatigue, and by March 9, his wife was writing in her diary, "George is feeling very tired and disinclined to do anything but rest." He soon left for a three-week vacation in California and returned only on April 14 to preside over the board of directors who announced that the company could pay the usual 2 per cent quarterly dividend without touching its surplus. On the twenty-first, Pullman went to Long Branch but hurried back to Chicago on May 1, worried by talk of a strike. Three days later, a Friday, he inspected conditions in the model town, and within the week a committee of workers traveled to the uptown office to see him.

Throughout the winter there had been homes in Pullman without adequate heat or food. Children were reportedly going to the carpentry shop and begging for scraps that could be used for a fire. By April, one-seventh of the town's dwellings stood vacant. The men were $70,000 in arrears on their rent,[9] and many depended for food on credit extended by local merchants. There was more work than in the fall, but as the number of employees also rose, this did not necessarily bring relief to individuals. No major wage reductions occurred after December, but there had been a number of minor adjustments in various departments with fear of new cuts widespread. Resentment of local management was fed by a stream of grievances that received no redress. In particular, the men were bitter that all foremen and officers still drew salaries which remained at the same rates as before the wage slashes.[10] With the growing hostility toward their immediate superiors, many workers thought the only recourse was organizing and then appealing to the uptown offices.

Yet the men did not know what to expect from the higher officers who shared no confidences with them and appeared impervious to their needs. George Pullman had instructed Middleton to assure his workers that the company was concerned about them and doing everything to get work; but little was done.[11] Concerned with the need to appear strong in the public eye, the company refrained from telling the workers that most of the orders filled after August had been deliberately assumed at a loss to insure employment for the townspeople. Lack of communication with Pullman and Wickes, the second vice-president, eroded the confidence many of the older workers had in them. By the time an effort was made to negotiate with the uptown office, the air was heavy with suspicions and many men viewed a strike as inevitable and necessary.[12]

Throughout late March and April, American Railway locals were organized in the shops, and by early May about 35 per cent of the men were members. Most who joined were skilled workers, who lived in the more expensive homes and had suffered the greatest loss of earnings. A general committee of forty-six men was elected to negotiate for the union and, if need be, to declare a strike. In early May, this committee called on Harvey Middleton to discuss a raise. Told by him that he had no authority over wages, they arranged an appointment with Thomas Wickes, second vice-president.

In the late afternoon of May 7, the meeting took place in the uptown offices. Wickes was an urbane Englishman who had been with the company over twenty years and in charge of the works for the last two. He had a reputation for integrity and judiciousness which had endeared him to subordinates. The delegation, however, was plainly bitter and predisposed to strike. Many had been angered by the company's building a wall about the eastern end of the shops and reports of extra guards being hired in anticipation of labor trouble. They complained of not earning enough and of the constant harassment by foremen. What they wanted was either a return to the wage level of May 1893 or a substantial reduction in rent. Wickes asked them to return in two days with written charges directed against specific foreman and he would then talk further with them.

On May 9, forty-three committeemen accompanied by George Howard, the vice-president of the A.R.U., attended a conference with Wickes, Middleton, and several of the department heads.

Wickes promised a thorough investigation of all charges and the correction of any abuses. He did not, however, give them such satisfaction on the issues of wages or rents. Citing figures to show the losses on recent orders, he stated that it was unreasonable to expect a restoration of former rates under the prevailing bad conditions. As for rents, he explained that the company never had received a reasonable return on its investment in the town and could not lower them.

After two hours, George Pullman joined the group. The President read from a prepared statement which essentially elaborated on the points Wickes had made. He offered to allow an examination of the contracts so that the committee might see for itself the company's losses, of which the men had not been aware.[13] On the question of rents, he remained adamant, arguing that the company, just like any other landlord, could not consider the tenant's salary in setting rates. He cautioned them not to confuse the company's roles of landlord and employer; one had nothing to do with the other. Not having changed rents during prosperous times, he saw no reason why they should be lowered now. He added informally that the company was not making any legal effort to collect the arrears out of consideration for the men's difficulties. After Pullman had concluded his statement, he remarked that he thought of the workers as his "children," and that the town's well-being was very important to him.

At the meeting's end, Howard, who had been silent, asked Pullman to affirm an earlier promise by Wickes that there would be no retaliation against any committeeman, which he did. After the men left, Pullman and Wickes were under the impression that the immediate threat of a strike had been averted. Indeed, Howard and Thomas Heathcoate, chairman of the committee, though not altogether satisfied with the meeting, thought it a beginning. Both men —eager to avoid hasty action at a moment when circumstances were not best for labor—counselled patience to the others. The Chicago papers on Thursday, May 10, reported a sense of relief throughout the model town.

At 6:30 on the morning of the tenth, when three of the committeemen who were employed in the iron department reported for work, two were told that there was none and they should "come around again" on the following Monday. The third worked until 8:00 A.M. when he, too, was laid off. News soon spread through the shops that the committeemen had been given a "Pullman dismissal" —meaning that being told to return was merely a ruse to conceal their discharge.[14] A meeting of the general committee was called for that evening to discuss what appeared to be a violation of the company's word.

The meeting began at 10:00 P.M. and lasted until early morning. A report that a company spy had been seen peering through a window prompted a move across Kensington's 115th Street to Turner Hall. Wickes had spent the day in the town holding a hearing on the complaints, but those who had been present reported that Middleton had been allowed to insult and intimidate witnesses. They felt that nothing would come of Wickes's investigations but a whitewash.[15] Two of the men laid off in the morning spoke and presented their reasons for believing themselves fired, but the third man refused to appear, later stating that he did not believe that he had been discriminated against as a committeeman.[16]

The mood of the meeting was one of disillusionment and determination. The company seemed to be untrustworthy and intent on destroying the union. Dismissal of the committeemen was the beginning of the end unless strong action was taken. To submit quietly would only encourage further repression. A resolution to strike submitted to the floor was voted on three times. On the first ballot, three cast negatives, but none did by the third ballot. Realizing the seriousness of the action, Heathcoate persuaded the committee to refer the issue back to the locals. For this reason, no strike date was set.

As the sun rose, the men went home to wash and eat before going to the shops. Shortly after work started, a union member was reportedly told by a Western Union operator that a telegram had been sent from the uptown office to Middleton, informing him of the strike vote and ordering him to close the plant at noon.[17] Word of this reached union officials who immediately decided on walking out at once, thereby achieving the status of a strike rather than a lockout. Through prearranged signals, the workers were informed of the news by 10:30. Machines and power were turned off, and tools returned to their chests. Quickly, quietly, and with discipline the various departments trooped from the works. As the men reached Florence Boulevard, they broke ranks and waited before the gates; a crowd which formed cheered as others came out. When the girls from the embroidery department walked through, a particularly loud yell was raised. Obviously proud of the solidarity they had just demonstrated, the men were in a good mood and joked considerably.

Reporters who rushed to Michigan and Adams found an atmosphere of shock and gloom. Pullman refused to see them, but others told them that he expressed pained surprise on learning the news. He had assumed his talk had helped the men appreciate the company's position, and that there had been a tacit agreement to avoid irrevocable action until the investigation of their grievances.[18] A strike at any time tended to be viewed by employers as an expression of disloyalty, but the circumstances here suggested ingratitude as well, especially since the committee had not taken advantage of the offer to examine the books. His conviction that the workers' action was an attempt to extort concessions made Pullman resolve to resist. But the first victory went to the union. When headquarters learned that only a few hundred men—primarily foremen, clerks, and unskilled laborers—remained at work, they decided to close the shops.

Within days of the strike, company and union were to charge that the immediate cause had been the other's violation of trust, and both oversimplified. The company carefully documented a denial of having fired the committeemen or planned a lockout.[19] The union never produced more than weak hearsay to back its contention.[20] A strike which would eventually shake the nation appears to have been precipitated by unfounded rumors. Yet, the union, on the basis of the company's past hostility to labor, had little reason to be trusting in the face of what seemed new aggression. The lack of formal lines of communication between employer and employee meant that the workers did not approach upper management until cumulated grievance etched deep suspicions which predisposed the men to a hasty and emotional reaction at the semblance of provocation. Each side was convinced that the other had forced the strike, and their feelings of betrayal and injustice complicated matters further.

Whether the Pullman Strike would have occurred without a triggering incident is conjectural, but labor trouble of some sort seems to have been inevitable. The meetings held suggest the strong possibility of an impasse as both sides asserted conflicting views on what had to be done. The company believed it acted in the employees' interests by reducing pay rates since this meant lower bids and more contracts. The men wanted a restoration of the old wage scale.

To Pullman and Wickes, loss of time rather than the pay cuts had been chiefly responsible for declining earnings. If work was available, a man could approach his former pay by speeding up his performance. But the union argued that the present rates were too low for all but the ablest to earn a living wage. Most men had been forced to work harder but still could not make enough to meet expenses. The company felt the only solution was lower production costs, while to the union it was higher scales.

In April 1893, the average monthly salary was a little under $51.00.[21] A year later—just before the strike—it had dropped to slightly below $36.50: a 28 per cent reduction. This loss was well above the national average for nonagricultural work and well above even the higher 12 per cent decline for those employed in manufacturing.[22] Among the last to be affected by the depression, the Pullman employees were also among the hardest hit.

Wage reductions in Pullman varied widely, depending on craft and department, as well as on the individual. The most striking example of a general loss in earnings occurred among one hundred journeyman mechanics of the freight-car construction department. Normally a well-paid group, their average salary fell from $53.06 per month in April 1893 to $13.93 by April 1894. One, R. W. Coombs, employed in the shops for a decade, had earned only $9.00, while occupying a single-family house renting at $15.71. To make matters worse, the assistant superintendent of the department was intensely disliked by the men, who had exchanged physical threats with him.[23] It is not surprising to find that the freight-car workers were leaders in the strike. While these employees suffered, however, eleven shop carpenters actually increased their earnings from $36.72 to $46.32, and strangely enough almost 10 per cent of the total shop force was making more the month preceding the strike than the year before.

The vast majority, of course, experienced severe cuts averaging 33 per cent for journeyman mechanics, 20 per cent for apprentices, and less for most laborers. Considerable changes occurred in the distribution of wages among various occupational groups. Some suffered a much greater percentage decline than others. The mechanics of the carving department, for example, had the highest average wage of all crafts in April 1893, but were only fourteenth in 1894. Skilled workers complained that laborers were sometimes earning more than they.[24]

Along with the decline in earnings, the employees resented the apparent erratic nature of the reductions. In addition, a worker's income could change markedly from one payday to the next, and on the piece-work system two men could do the same job and yet make considerably different wages. All these variants magnified tensions and spawned resentments. Much of the criticism of lower management centered on favoritism which benefited some workers at the expense of others.

In actual earnings for April 1894, nearly one-fourth of the shop employees made $31.00 or less; about half, $31.00 to $40.00; and the remainder more. Average rental remained $14.00, which included a flat water fee. Rents went down elsewhere but not in the model town, and this was considered unfair. Aside from the "barrack" tenements, charges in Pullman had always been high for workingmen. Now during a depression, they became excessive and in instances unbearable. George Pullman had erected his community in the belief that Americans of ordinary incomes could afford superior homes built with the economies of mass production. Except for "barrack" tenements, however, good housing may have been a luxury that urban industrial workers of his time could not afford. This was probably especially true in a planned setting, such as the model town. Here, a price on parks and paved streets seemed exorbitant when families lacked necessities. The inhabitants, with no option in Pullman's plan, paid for it unassisted. According to the U. S. Strike Commission:

> If we exclude the aesthetic and sanitary features at Pullman, the rents there are from 20 to 25 per cent higher than rents in Chicago or surrounding towns for similar accommodations. The aesthetic features are admired by visitors, but have little money value to employees, especially when they lack bread.[25]

The Strike Commission after considerable investigation concluded that the strike had been caused by the company's policy of reducing wages and holding rents constant.[26] The company denied this, pointing out that only one-third of the workers rented its homes. Another third boarded in the town, but rented from individuals, and the remainder lived elsewhere. Furthermore, it argued those who were company tenants had an advantage over the others in that they could fall months behind in payment without being foreclosed or evicted.[27] This argument missed the point. To the workers it was common sense that, since the company dispensed wages with its right hand and collected with its left, the two must be co-ordinated to leave the residents something to live on.[28] Yet, Pullman had denied that his being a landlord imposed new considerations on him as an employer, or that his men had the need and right to a voice in management.

A long-time premise of American society was that respectable workingmen must earn enough to live with dignity and hope. The development of large industrial corporations with impersonal treatment of a huge labor force challenged this ideal. Pullman had tried to show that human needs could be satisfied rather than violated by the strictly business context of a model town, but in this effort he failed. His men, rubbed raw by the arbitrariness of lower management and denied easy access to upper management, struck to gain relief from what they viewed as injustices arising from policies on wages and rents. Furthermore, they fought for a union and the ability to influence the company's decisions. In doing this, they contradicted the two basic premises of the town's founding: that the self-interests of employer and employee were identical, and that these interests were served best by the "Pullman System."

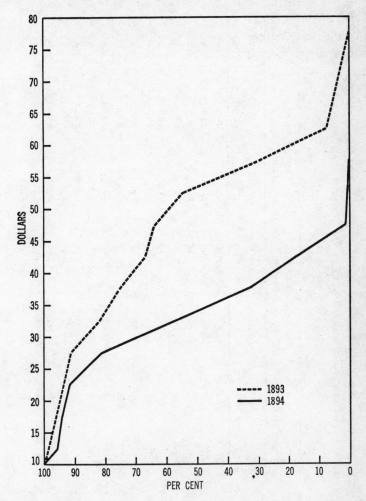

Figure 3. Graph of Income Distributions: Cumulative Earnings by Per Cent of Workers (April 1893 and April 1894).

Table 4

AVERAGE MONTHLY INCOME AND AVERAGE NUMBER OF HOURS WORKED PER MAN PER MONTH FOR JOURNEYMAN MECHANICS AT THE PULLMAN, ILLINOIS, CAR WORKS IN APRIL 1893 AND APRIL 1894

Department	Number of Men		Average Monthly Income Per Man		Average No. of Hours Per Man		Comparative Rankings*	
	April 1893	April 1894	April 1893	April 1894	April 1893	April 1894	April 1893	April 1894
Mill	37	24	$54.57	$37.76	210.71	179.79	19	20
Wood machine	97	52	58.22	46.24	220.20	210.17	15	7
Cabinet	292	187	55.46	31.35	220.94	165.89	18	31
Carving	99	12	75.09	43.06	227.54	184.00	1	14
Blacksmith and hammer	92	99	71.57	48.45	225.05	202.73	2	3
Bolt	29	20	59.63	35.54	220.03	181.35	12	22
Iron machine	122	97	60.25	35.88	251.06	186.88	11	24
Car builders	631	513	60.71	39.52	222.39	210.22	9	18
Electricians	21	14	58.45	46.25	262.10	243.43	14	6
Truck builders	13	9	60.19	43.66	242.70	222.78	10	13
Tinners	71	94	53.79	38.31	221.34	184.20	20	19
Steam fitters	62	66	61.78	46.18	235.82	200.77	7	8
Upholsterers	114	80	61.63	45.50	235.24	217.69	8	10
Brass finishers	76	54	66.90	42.36	271.91	191.69	4	15
Glass	11	10	66.74	46.10	246.27	214.40	5	9
Painters	343	312	59.23	44.60	231.37	211.35	13	12

Table 4 continued

Department	Number of Men		Average Monthly Income Per Man		Average No. of Hours Per Man		Comparative Rankings*	
	April 1893	April 1894	April 1893	April 1894	April 1893	April 1894	April 1893	April 1894
Millwright and pattern	48	27	64.46	59.29	237.85	245.00	6	1
Shop carpenters	33	11	36.72	46.32	178.27	220.55	34	5
Freight mill	42	28	51.84	35.46	226.36	172.14	23	23
Freight-car builders	147	101	53.06	13.93	203.28	90.46	22	45
Streetcar	245	140	55.49	46.98	214.26	228.04	17	4
Total	2,625	1,950	$59.33	$40.07	225.58	197.38	—	—

* The rankings combine Tables 4 and 5 into one.

Table 5

AVERAGE MONTHLY INCOME AND AVERAGE NUMBER OF HOURS WORKED PER MAN PER MONTH FOR EMPLOYEES (EXCLUDING JOURNEYMAN MECHANICS, SUPERINTENDENTS, FOREMEN, AND CLERICAL FORCE) AT THE PULLMAN, ILLINOIS, CAR WORKS IN APRIL 1893 AND APRIL 1894

Department	Number of Men		Average Monthly Income Per Man		Average No. of Hours Per Man		Comparative Rankings*	
	April 1893	April 1894	April 1893	April 1894	April 1893	April 1894	April 1893	April 1894
Store	87	63	$38.80	$37.45	251.93	231.17	32	21
Lumber	245	145	29.95	34.18	187.20	238.99	43	26
Corliss	81	58	44.78	45.24	253.00	240.64	27	11
Mill	62	31	30.73	21.19	232.77	182.68	41	42
Wood machine	57	22	32.83	25.58	245.00	206.32	38	39
Cabinet	62	28	51.52	32.29	283.08	224.25	24	30
Blacksmith and hammer	219	136	41.23	30.49	210.34	197.99	30	33
Bolt	29	11	35.86	24.19	212.17	168.00	35	40
Iron machine	87	43	38.13	26.24	224.31	186.07	33	37
Car builders	116	109	45.87	33.47	274.67	226.17	26	29
Electricians	20	11	27.83	34.34	198.80	203.18	46	25
Truck	1	2	43.20	39.28	270.00	245.50	28	17
Tinners	27	35	49.07	24.22	269.59	151.40	25	41
Steam fitters	59	93	42.12	26.34	237.97	168.87	29	38
Upholsterers	152	144	32.80	28.35	239.42	213.19	39	36
Brass finishers	24	20	53.13	34.04	269.71	231.55	21	27

Table 5 continued

Department	Number of Men		Average Monthly Income Per Man		Average No. of Hours Per Man		Comparative Rankings*	
	April 1893	April 1894	April 1893	April 1894	April 1893	April 1894	April 1893	April 1894
Glass	26	13	28.06	19.15	228.15	172.54	45	43
Painters	102	90	56.93	33.55	262.34	199.71	16	28
Millwright and pattern	14	14	67.99	48.53	402.29	266.64	3	2
Yard	83	66	39.56	41.51	238.30	276.71	36	16
Shop carpenters	7	34	29.81	16.65	196.14	151.38	31	44
Freight mill	82	40	29.64	13.04	180.74	95.88	44	46
Freight car	61	37	31.32	31.04	222.13	277.14	40	32
Streetcar	55	33	34.83	28.44	236.96	184.70	37	35
Laborers	37	33	30.02	30.13	225.68	229.97	42	34
Total	1,808	1,311	$38.68	$31.08	231.63	209.98	—	—

* The rankings combine Tables 4 and 5 into one.

13

The Conduct of the Strike

The sordid side of life that strikes generally reveal is not to be seen at Pullman. There are no close stuffy tenements . . . no overcrowding, no bad air, no poorly clad half-famished men. All is modern and perfect as science can make it, and even the strike has this character. . . . The Pullman strike is an innovation.

Chicago Daily News, May 12, 1894

Saturday, May 12, the first full day of the strike, was sunny and pleasant. Young men played baseball or lawn tennis. In late afternoon, the Pullman Band performed in Arcade Park to family groups lounging and picnicking on the grass. Those who came expecting to find a troubled community were surprised to see the workingmen behaving as though on a holiday weekend. Precautions insured that nothing would be amiss. At a huge rally the night before, a Strike Committee had been elected with Thomas Heathcoate chairman. Its first action was the formation of a rotating 24-hour guard for the works. The union claimed this would prevent property damage and undue publicity, but, as the company pointed out, the guards also established a picket line preventing the use of new employees in the shops.[1]

Only a minority of the workers had been with the company during the strike of 1886.[2] For many of the younger men, this was their first experience with labor's most powerful weapon, and they felt sure of a quick return to work on the union's terms. But over the weekend their anticipations were jolted when it was announced that all the Arcade's stores, except one, would refuse future credit.[3] Heathcoate advised his people to brace for wholesale evictions,[4]

and good-humored camaraderie faded into somber resolution. The
workers carefully husbanded their resources, looking about for outside support while new locals were formed for those still not members of the A.R.U. That Monday and for many days after the closed
factory gates symbolized the locked horns of capital and labor.

The *Chicago Record* (May 12, 1894) predicted a "prolonged and
bitter" struggle. Company officers believed the strike could last
three months. Their intention was clear: keep the shops closed until
the union broke. Pullman had once confided to a visitor that the
company in 1886 had deliberately done nothing until the men's ability to resist had crumbled after ten days.[5] There was no reason to
doubt the success of such a course in 1894. In any combat of attri-
tion, the company's vast financial power easily surpassed the worker's limited means.

Aware that the strike would be personally embarrassing, Pullman
wanted to avoid attention. On the twelfth, he left Chicago for Long
Branch, but found "Fairlawn" beseiged by reporters. He then made
his way to Maine, and the seclusion of Pullman Island in the St.
Lawrence. Later in the month he joined his wife and unmarried
daughter, Florence, in New York, where, except for brief trips to
Albion and Washington, they remained until late June.

Wickes was left in charge, although with few decisions to make.
He cautioned other officers against interviews, and limited his
statements to holding the union responsible for the strike, and expressing indifference to its length. The company, sensitive to the adverse publicity being given the model town, hoped to minimize it.
The pamphlet "The Story of Pullman" only a year before had hailed
the community as a solution to the "industrial problem" through the
"mutual recognition of capital and labor." Irony alone made the
company vulnerable.

Reporters going to Pullman generally wrote sympathetically of
its residents. The David and Goliath nature of the struggle was
evident, and people found the cause of the underdog appealing,
particularly when the workers behaved with dignity. As the strike
continued, days passing into weeks, the union strove to maintain
discipline. Assemblages heard Heathcoate and others urge patience

and propriety. They were told to keep away from the works and strongly advised to avoid drunkenness and unruliness which could only hurt their fight.

Both sides quickly recognized the importance of public opinion. The company refrained from any action that would call attention to the strike, but the union endeavored to spread its word and draw support from the outside. As the *Chicago Dispatch* (May 14, 1894) phrased it: "Pullman is called a 'model town.' It now has on its hands a model strike. The 3,000 men who threw down their tools . . . have conducted themselves in such a way as to win public sympathy and command commendation."

Though drawing some coverage from the national press, the Pullman Strike for its first month was of major interest only to Chicago papers. When the strike started, most of these, with the exception of the *Times*, believed that present business conditions made the men's action foolish and bound to fail. The *Chicago Record*'s (May 12, 1894) position was typical: "no matter what the merits of their contention . . . there is no doubt the men . . . made a grave mistake." The *Tribune* of the same day, however, went further, calling the strike "wanton, causeless, and suicidal," an ungrateful gesture toward a generous and fair employer. As the strike continued, the newspapers became concerned less with the causes of the strike than with its speedy and amicable solution. The silent and unyielding attitude of the company was soon contrasted with the conciliatory position adopted by the union. Chicago papers carried extensive coverage of the desperate situation faced by Pullman's law-abiding and resolute strikers. From all evidence, the people of Chicago and their newspapers promptly extended sympathy and support to the workers. This included the *Tribune* and others that tried unsuccessfully to distinguish between aid to strikers as human beings in need and approval of the union's demands.[6]

An attack on George Pullman was led by the *Chicago Times* who viewed the workers as starving victims of oppression. Some said the *Times* had entered into an alliance with Mayor Hopkins, for considerations in patronage.[7] Even friends of the strikers suspected the motivations behind the paper's crusading spirit. Professor I. J.

Hourwich of the University of Chicago wrote to Henry Demarest Lloyd that "the coquetry of 'The Times' with the strikers has increased its circulation very considerably." [8]

Other Chicago papers were not far behind the *Times*. Several years earlier George Pullman had received an honorary title of nobility from King Humbert I of Italy. Now, it became customary to refer to him in print as the "Baron" or "Duke" and draw an analogy between his town and a feudal manor. The famous model community was generally dismissed as a dressed-up company town, whose parks and gardens concealed exploitative rents and widespread oppression. Once an enthusiastic supporter of the town, the *Chicago Inter Ocean* (May 30, 1894) now reviled its "plan":

> Apparently to reach the high administrative ideal aimed at the management of this "model industrial tenement" by the Marquis de Pullman . . . there is nothing needed but the knout, a liberal supply of shackles, and cheap transit to Siberia.

The strikers formed a Relief Committee on May 17, announcing that Mayor Hopkins's general goods store, Secord-Hopkins, had donated flour, potatoes, and meat worth $1,500 and also $1,000 in cash. Another Kensington merchant provided a storeroom, and Hopkins allowed free use of a seven-room apartment. "Girls' local No. 269" sent its laundresses and seamstresses through the town to determine those in need. An observer noted: "Everyone seemed to know everyone and charity was administered with a friendliness unknown to Chicago soup kitchens." [9] Help came from individuals, unions, charitable organizations, and even a few business organizations. Southside policemen solicited for the Relief Committee among shopkeepers, and when some complained to Hopkins, he replied that there "was no legal objection to the police doing charitable work."

The Chicago *Daily News* donated the use of a store as the city headquarters for the Committee. A group of prominent Chicago women headed by Mrs. Fanny Kavanagh and "Mrs. Dr." Charles D. Bradley, wives of a lawyer and minister, scoured the Loop's financial institutions seeking assistance. When the two went to see Lyman Gage of the First National Bank, an altercation ensued. A founder of the Chicago Civic Federation, Gage was considered sympathetic to labor, but the women reported that on telling their mission, he lectured them severely and then, not offering them an opportunity to reply, ushered them out near tears. According to Gage, he politely told them his admiration for George Pullman and his town and that he would not hurt him in any way.[10]

Gage and other businessmen thought the strikers' plight the necessary price paid for industrial war. Others, however, disagreed. The threat of a malaria epidemic in Pullman caused a score of doctors and nurses to volunteer their services, and several local druggists filled prescriptions free of cost. An entire community of strikers was more conspicuous than the same number of strikers dispersed throughout several urban neighborhoods. In Pullman, virtually a whole town needed help, and many responded much in the way they would have if a community suffered a natural catastrophe.

In mid-May, the Chicago press gave wide circulation to a rumor in Pullman that a resident had gone insane from hunger, but the man had only suffered an epileptic seizure and was not even a company employee. Without question, conditions within the town were bad and became worse after May 22 when the workers drew their last paycheck. Those who could lived off savings already depleted by months of depression. Strikers' Relief was the only recourse for the others. By the beginning of June, over eight hundred families of workers were reported receiving assistance. Innumerable cases of individual hardship appeared in the press, which often broadcast the town's plight in banner headlines.

A sizable group of men still employed in the town were the brickyard workers. Mainly unskilled immigrants from Italy and Bohemia, these two hundred workers were not invited to join the A.R.U. and had not walked out with the others. Organized immediately after the strike, they demanded wage increases and when this was rejected left work on May 29. Chicago reporters, eager for news, rushed to the seldom visited woodframe homes adjacent to the brickyards. They found unpaved and unsewered streets lined with three-room "hovels" lacking indoor plumbing. An eight-dollar rent was considered highly exorbitant. Dubbed a "shantyville," this hithertofore ignored section of the town was now carefully scrutinized and used to embarrass the company. One paper condemned the brickworkers' homes as the "fag end of [a] modern white slave quarter." [11]

Even the rowhouses and tenements of the town proper were found wanting in certain ways. Most were well over ten years old and showing age. Visitors found the tenements' rooms small and crowded, the halls narrow and dark. The fact that row houses had only one water tap per structure was contrasted to newly built homes with taps on each floor. Pullman's residences superior by the standards of earlier days were becoming ordinary. As a journalist expressed it: "how could Pullman be a model town when its homes lacked bath tubs?" In a decade and a half multiple dwelling units had become common and public expectations higher.

The town's exterior fared better at the hands of reporters, who found its parks and public buildings attractive. But the block tenements were often derided as "barrack-like" and the row houses frequently dismissed as monotonous. Even those who were prepared to concede the town's attractive features tended to think they came at too high a cost. They criticized not only Pullman's heavy rents, but also its oppressive bureaucracy. Most assumed that all flaws should be directly attributed to George Pullman's self-seeking. Few, if any, speculated on whether the novelty of the plan or defects in its conception might be partly responsible for the present situation. On the other hand, the minority who defended the "plan" tended to be equally rigid. The tenor of the times and the excitement of the moment required black and white answers.

Within the town the community was divided between supporters of the strike and a relative handful of company men. The latter assembled daily at the Hotel Florence, while the workers congregated about union headquarters at Kensington's Howard and 115th Street. At first, there was considerable good-natured ribbing between the two groups as they passed on the street or met in stores.

One incident amused both sides considerably. The closing of the laundry presented problems to Baron von Fritsch, manager of the Florence, which he resolved by hiring a washwoman. But "when Town Agent Hornbeck heard . . . that the baron had so presumed on his position as to set up an independent laundry he was in a rage and 'dressed down' the baron during the luncheon hour." The public quarreling between two prominent officers over a washwoman provided comic relief for the whole community. But as the strike continued with no sign of a break, tension and bitterness enveloped the town. Strikers took to pinning white ribbons to their lapels and company men sported miniature American flags. By early June, a few minor incidents between the two groups had occurred.

The *Pullman Journal,* of course, was highly condemnatory of the strike, and the *Kensington Advertiser,* published by Secord-Hopkins, became the workers' organ. The division in the community was also reflected among its ministers. In mid-April, the Reverend E. C. Oggel of the Greenstone Memorial Church had preached a eulogy of George M. Pullman which narrated his rise from humble beginnings to well deserved fame and fortune. Oggel had described the model town as an experiment in "contemplated beauty and harmony, health, comfort, and contentment." Rather than being embarrassed into silence by the strike, the Reverend Oggel lost no time in using his pulpit to deliver a broadside against union leaders as "agitators" and to admonish his audience that "half a loaf was better than none." [12] Attendance at the Greenstone Church noticeably declined and within weeks Oggel left town for a vacation from which he never returned.

An interesting contrast to the conservative ideas of the elderly Oggel were those of thirty-one-year-old Reverend William Carwardine of the Pullman Methodist Church. Only in the town two years, he preached the gospel of "applied Christianity." By this Carwardine meant the recognition that "the relation existing between a man's body and soul are such that you can make very little headway appealing to the soul of a thoroughly live and healthy man if he be starving for food." [13] Carwardine had not encouraged the calling of a strike, but thought it justified by conditions in the town. In a sermon delivered ten days after the shop's closing, he refuted Oggel's praise of Pullman, by charging that the picture postcard appearance of the community was deceptive: "To the casual visitor [it] is a veritable paradise; but it is a hollow mockery, a sham, an institution girdled with red tape." [14] George Pullman was denounced for his infrequent appearances in the town and his indifference to its welfare.

Eugene Debs claimed that most of Pullman's ministers supported the workers.[15] Aside from Carwardine, however, only the pastor of the Swedish Methodist Church openly sided with the strikers. The Reverend Van Ess, powerful minister of Roseland's First Reformed Holland Church, was thought to have encouraged his congregation to return to work. Fifty of his parishioners held a meeting to consider this possibility, but union supporters flooded the room, preventing any action. Van Ess, coming under heavy criticism from the strikers, announced publicly that he was neutral in the struggle and not opposed to unions.

Carwardine's criticism of Pullman and his town attracted considerable attention in the Chicago press and drew hundreds of approving letters from across the country.[16] Becoming something of a celebrity, he began to appear before numerous meetings of church and civic organizations, where he pleaded the strikers' cause to middle-class audiences. Carwardine was concerned with demonstrating that the Pullman workers were not illiterate troublemakers, but responsible and skilled Americans subjected to intolerable conditions. In June, he began expanding his sermon into a pamphlet and contacted people who might help the strikers.[17] The fact that Carwardine and one of the town's physicians supported the workers did much to make their cause creditable and respectable.

On June 9, 1894, the *Chicago Times* claimed that an overwhelming majority of Chicagoans supported the strikers. The actions of the politicians verify this. On June 5, the sixty-two members of the City Council unanimously approved a resolution asking the Mayor to request support from all citizens for the Relief Committee. Hopkins enthusiastically complied, and a day was set aside by Chicago unions for their members to contribute money, clothes, and food. A wife of a non-striking company employee wrote the *Chicago Herald* (June 9, 1894) that so many exaggerated stories of destitution in Pullman had appeared in that paper and others that on giving her address in a Chicago store all eyes turned sympathetically towards her "as much as to say 'is it possible a resident of Pullman has the strength to come uptown.'"

The strikers of Pullman maintained discipline and avoided disorder. A reporter for the *Chicago Record,* going there on the last Sunday in May, could only write: "Drowsy Sunday peace and the entire absence of any excitement ran contrary to any preconceived notion of a strike." [18] The saloonkeepers of Kensington reported business well below normal, despite the idleness of the men. To keep morale high and also raise revenue, the union scheduled several picnics and a dance open to the public. The latter was held on May 27, and Mayor Hopkins danced with young Jennie Curtie, "chairlady" of the "girls' local" for the first promenade in the decorated second floor of the Market Building, which company officials apparently permitted to be used for the occasion.

The company, however, was less obliging on matters of more importance. As the strike continued, the Chicago Civic Federation, an association of middle-class reformers organized the year before to study municipal problems, attempted to bring about a settlement. A six-man "conciliatory committee" was appointed to get company and union together. Debs responded positively, but several letters to Wickes brought no reply. Finally, one of the committee went uninvited to his office. Wickes told the woman, Jane Addams, social worker and director of Hull House, that the company could not permit third parties to impose themselves in an issue which was "not their business." Anyway, the company would not deal with a union but only with individual "ex-employees" and under no circumstances would it arbitrate because there was "nothing to arbitrate." [19] This was to be the company's fixed response to numerous entreaties from disinterested parties for a speedy and amicable settlement through negotiation or arbitration.

A strike featuring picnics and cotillions rather than violence was a novelty in labor relations which could only be reassuring. The union, moreover, made every effort to co-operate with all efforts to end the trouble. This conciliatory posture was contrasted to the stiff-necked attitude of the company. Wickes had on several occasions remarked that the strike saved management the necessity of operating the shops at a loss, and now Chicago newspapers questioned whether the company wanted a settlement. It did, but only on its own terms.

The union knew that the men could not be out indefinitely. By mid-June the streets of Pullman were filled with moving vans as hundreds of families moved elsewhere in search of new employment. Some workers were said to have taken temporary jobs from which they contributed to the Relief Committee,[20] but this, even with liberal gifts from the public, could not support an entire community. The Pullman strikers had done all they could. Their behavior earned them broad support, including important elements of the middle class. Still few expected them to win. The Pullman Company, hoping for imminent victory, continued indifferent to public opinion. In lasting over a month, the strike was already of unusual duration, yet the workers had nothing to show for their sacrifices.

14

The Boycott, Federal Intervention, and Public Opinion

Experiencing hard times in the spring of 1894, the nation seemed poised on the edge of a catastrophe. "Coxey's Army" had disbanded in the capital, but "industrials"—groups of unemployed seeking assistance—roamed the troubled countryside. Strikes increased in frequency, and dissatisfaction became apparent in the social tinder that composed the American city. Class conflict, long a general concern, appeared inevitable to some who predicted an imminent Armageddon. In this setting the national convention of the militant American Railway Union was bound to attract attention, especially when it was known to be considering a general boycott. Reporters from the eastern press and national wire services converged on Chicago in anticipation of trouble.

Over four hundred delegates assembled at Uhlich's Hall on June 12. Nearly all worked for western and midwestern railroads, many of which had recently cut wages. Their dissatisfaction made them sympathetic to the plight of the Pullman strikers and ready for a show-down with capital. Appearing before the convention on the morning of June 16, the sleeping-car workers persuasively pleaded their cause.[1] With emotion they spoke of their "beautiful town" whose men labored hard with "brain and muscle" for women un-

tarnished by "word of scandal." Over this was superimposed the
menacing specter of a "merciless, soulless, grasping corporation."
Then came a long list of grievances and a final appeal:

> It is victory or death . . . to you we confide our cause . . . do
> not desert us as you hope not to be deserted.

Debs was eager to avoid a boycott, which he viewed as too risky,
or if that was impossible to have at least adequate justification.
Meetings were opened to press and public to escape any connota-
tion of conspiracy. Under his direction the convention demonstrated that labor preferred negotiation to force. A committee of six
delegates and six Pullman strikers was sent to Wickes who would
not meet with it. On the following day the strikers returned alone
only to be told the company would never arbitrate.

The convention now had to concede its impotence or proceed
with a boycott. Debs advised the delegates to wire their locals for
instructions, and on the twentieth a notice of intention was served
on Wickes:

> Unless the Pullman Palace Car Company does adjust the griev-
> ances before . . . June 26, 1894, the members of the American
> Railway Union shall refuse to handle Pullman cars and equip-
> ment.

This could not have surprised the company which knew that its
actions had left no alternative but capitulation. George Pullman,
returning to Chicago on the twentieth, found a radically altered
situation. The A.R.U.'s announcement had changed a local issue
into a matter of national concern. Nothing could avoid publicity
now, and he was determined to tell his side of the story.[2]

The company had a powerful ally in the General Managers' Association. A "voluntary and unincorporated association" formed in
1886 by twenty-four railroads "centering or terminating in Chicago." [3] Members tried to establish common policies on issues of
mutual interest, but the Association was little more than an ineffectual "consultative body" until 1893 when its constitution and by-laws

were strengthened.[4] Committees were now created to aid railroads in the event of a strike, and efforts were undertaken to encourage uniform wage scales.

Directly challenged by the boycott, the Association held an emergency meeting on June 25, Wickes being invited as an interested party. The railroads decided to "act unitedly" in opposing the A.R.U., and a temporary headquarters was established in the Rookery on LaSalle Street, Chicago's financial area. According to the President's Strike Commission: "until the practical end of the [boycott] the General Managers' Association directed and controlled the contest on the part of the railroads, using the combined resources of all the roads to support contentions and insure the protection of each."[5] Members were advised to fire anyone refusing orders, and the Association promised replacements. At one point, it claimed to be able to import fifty thousand eastern railroad men within forty-eight hours if necessary, and the Association actually did assign 2,500 strikebreakers.[6]

After the first meeting that Wickes attended, there was apparently no formal connection between the Palace Car Company and the General Managers. There can be no doubt, however, that each knew the desires and intentions of the other. Officers of the company and the railroads discussed developments together in their mutual clubs, and Horace Porter, for one, was on the board of several member roads.[7] The Association's official position was that it had no concern with the Pullman Strike per se, but only as it affected the railroads and their agreements with the company. It argued that members could not accede to the boycott or they would be liable to court suits by the P.P.C.C. for breech of contract.

Debs tried to co-ordinate the sympathy strike as best he could. The delegates were explicitly instructed on how to proceed on the twenty-sixth of June. Switchmen would refuse to couple Pullman cars, inspectors to examine them, and engineers and brakemen to haul any train carrying the cars. If a worker was discharged, all men on the system would walk off with further strategy to be directed from Uhlich's Hall. Service would be tied up unless and until George Pullman negotiated, or the railroads dropped his cars.

The American Railway Union and the General Managers' Association were unprecedented efforts at combination to enhance the respective power of labor and capital. An open antipathy had existed between them even before the Pullman Strike. Now they girded for battle amidst general anxiety. Debs and the railroads preempted the nation's front pages, and relegated the Pullman strike to a subsidiary position.

On the twenty-sixth, the boycott started slowly, and then spread like wildfire. The Illinois Central kept to schedule during the daylight hours. Its pleased president invited George Pullman to watch the 9:00 P.M. "Diamond Special" leave Chicago for St. Louis with the usual component of Pullman sleepers. No incident occurred then, but predictions of the boycott's failure were premature. On reporting for duty, night switchmen refused to work Pullman cars, and their example was followed by the day crew. Within two days, four thousand men were out, and I.C. trains ran sporadically. On the twenty-eighth, the "Diamond Special" was nearly derailed by sabotaged tracks a few miles south of Chicago.

By the end of June nearly fifty thousand men were away from work on all lines. Many A.R.U. locals on their own initiative transformed the boycott into strikes against the roads. These involved long-standing grievances, and confused the nature of the boycott by introducing a wide variety of local issues. Railroads throughout the West and Midwest found it necessary to curtail and sometimes suspend schedules[8] with over two-thirds of the nation affected from Ohio to California. The Illinois Populist party had scheduled a convention in Springfield over the July 4 weekend. Even though Debs approved their desire to get there any way they could, postponement was forced by the inability to find rail transportation.[9]

The A.R.U., its expectations surpassed, claimed labor's display of power and solidarity would soon bring the railroads to their knees.[10] By July 2, the Association's manager conceded a "stalemate." [11] To stem the tide, all strikers were warned that they would be permanently disqualified from further employment on all member roads. Disruption of transportation transformed Chicago into a besieged city. Prices on food, especially perishables, began to soar. Newspapers that had freely extended sympathy to the Pullman strikers competed in denouncing "Dictator Debs" and his "stranglehold" on the city.[12] The *Times*, however, continued to support him, while the *Record*, and its sister paper, the *Daily News*, attempted to be restrained. What was being called the "Chicago Strike" had superseded the Pullman Strike and was creating a crisis that could not be ignored.

From the boycott's beginning, it was closely watched by President Cleveland and his cabinet.[13] They were deeply concerned over disruption of rail service, but also feared the possibility of widespread violence. Times were tense and American cities were considered powder kegs of social disorder. Chicago seemed particularly unstable. How the nation's second city appeared to those in authority can be seen in the following description given by the strike commissioners:

> A vast metropolis, the center of an activity and growth unprecedented in history, and combining all that this implies. Its lawless elements are at present augmented by shiftless adventurers and criminals attracted to it by the Exposition. . . . [There are also] many of a certain class of objectionable foreigners, who are being precipitated upon us by unrestricted immigration. No more dangerous place for . . . a strike could be chosen.[14]

Mayor Hopkins had ordered his three thousand man police force to total readiness, but no one was certain this would be adequate. Only a few incidents were noted the first day, but soon reports suggested disorder was becoming uncontrollable both within and outside of the city. Obstructions were placed on tracks, trains halted by mobs, cars uncoupled, and switches spiked. Some of the worst violence occurred in the industrial suburb of Blue Island, just a few miles south of the city and west of the model town.

Whether the Chicago police could have handled the situation remains unclear. The commissioner of police made several contradictory statements at the time. Before the Strike Commission, however, he asserted that his men had retained control, though hard pressed. The problem was, in his words, that Chicago "is practically a network of railways, and . . . filled with railway tracks, yards, towers, switch houses and freight houses," all of which were becoming targets for mobs.[15] Rumor raced through the city, whipped by an excited and not overly responsible press.

On June 30, the Attorney General of the United States, Richard Olney, authorized the deputization of U.S. marshals at need. Ray Stannard Baker, then with the *Chicago Record*, thought the wholesale and unselective recruitment of untrained men only added to the confusion.[16] Often the railroads appointed their own people as marshals and used them as a private army, which antagonized the crowds.[17] John Hopkins and the police were accused by the *Tribune* and *Herald*, among others, of openly sympathizing with the A.R.U.

The movement of the mail was necessarily disrupted by the boycott. The Union, recognizing that this might invite federal action, offered crews for mail trains provided no Pullman cars were included, but with few exceptions, the railroads declined this arrangement. They insisted on running trains with their regular cars, and these the A.R.U. boycotted, even when they carried mail.

U.S. attorneys acting under Olney's direction obtained an injunction from the circuit court of Chicago on July 2. This court placed a blanket restraint on all actions that could impede the movement of trains and mail. One clause specifically prohibited A.R.U. officers from communicating with each other or anyone else in directing the boycott. Whatever the injunction's purpose—restoring mail delivery or breaking the boycott—it's acceptance meant the Union's defeat. A bitter Debs decided to ignore this "drag-net" and accept the consequences.[18]

For several days large mobs assembled at the Rock Island yard in Blue Island. The railroad ceased operation and demanded protection. On the afternoon of July 2, two thousand people were asked to disperse by the federal marshal of Chicago. When they refused, he returned to the city and telegraphed Olney a request for U.S. troops. Their possible employment had already been considered, and all was in readiness. A detachment from nearby Fort Sheridan pressed into Chicago on July 4. As they paraded by the nicer homes on the northern fringe of the city, attractive children ran to the marching ranks and offered flowers. When the units reached the working-class neighborhoods, however, sullen crowds taunted them. The artist Frederick Remington was with the Seventh Cavalry as it deployed about the Union Stockyards. He wrote that one soldier moving through "a seething mass of smells, stale beer, and bad language," and hearing abuse in "Hungarian or Pollack, or whatever the stuff is," pointed to the bearded immigrant workers and remarked, "Say, do you know them things ain't human."[19] Remington thought it, perhaps, unfortunate that no order was issued to fire into the crowd.

Cleveland, in ordering the intervention of the troops, had ignored the Democratic governor of the state and the city's mayor. Governor John Altgeld bitterly resented this unprecedented action, which he denounced in a telegram to the President as an unconstitutional impingement on state's rights. Cleveland defended the move as necessary and proper.[20] To some, however, it was a definite slap at a man who in granting clemency to the survivors of the Haymarket trial had enhanced a reputation as a radical. Debs charged that Cleveland's unilateralness was further evidence of the federal government's partiality toward capital. Others, however, asserted that the President's action was saving a city from a "political mayor" and a "demagogic governor," who were either incapable of or unwilling to restore order.

The presence of the soldiers did not immediately end the violence. For whatever reasons destruction actually increased. The usual Fourth of July firecracker explosions were interspersed with the ominous clanging of bells as overworked "hook and ladders" responded to scores of incendiarisms. On the fifth, a mob of ten thousand played havoc with railroad property at the Union Stockyards, while the outnumbered soldiers and police retreated before them. That night a huge fire of unexplained origin leveled many of the deserted Columbian Exposition buildings. The following morning saw the height of the destruction with the loss to railroads alone valued at $340,000.

Troops were rushed to Chicago from posts as far apart as New York and Nebraska,[21] more marshals were deputized, and the police force enlarged. Altgeld called in the state militia. Firearms and bayonets were now freely leveled at rioters, and casualties mounted. On July 7, the army systematically cleared the tracks and "rode shotgun" on trains bringing mail and food to the city. The following day Cleveland appealed to the people of Illinois for lawful behavior and threatened severe punishment for wrongdoers. A declaration of martial law was considered, but never found necessary. The mob's forays petered out in the face of gunfire and force, and by July 19 most of the troops were removed.

To Debs it was intentional that federal power in restoring "law and order" had also smashed the boycott. The hope of forcing the Pullman Company to arbitrate through pressure on the railroads could not succeed when the government's intervention made the Association unbeatable. The tide of battle had very definitely swung against labor. Union officers were openly violating the injunction and living with the prospect of imminent arrest. Press and public opinion generally held the A.R.U. responsible for the wanton rampages of the mobs, though its members were instructed to avoid trouble. Debs searched for a means of extricating his union from a situation threatening to destroy it.

On July 5, he asked for arbitration between Pullman and his strikers, promising in return to end the boycott. Nothing came of this and there was no other recourse but an appeal to organized labor. Representatives of more than one hundred Chicago trade unions attended a meeting at Uhlich's Hall on the evening of the eighth. They decided to call a general strike unless George Pullman agreed to arbitrate. Mayor Hopkins arranged for a committee of Chicago aldermen to approach the company, and it, too, met the usual frigid reception. Expected to paralyze the city, the general strike went into effect on the eleventh. But only 25,000 men participated and most returned to work the following day.[22] Fearful of involvement in a lost cause, many unions had reneged at the last moment. Debs had only labor's national leaders to turn to.

Samuel Gompers of the A.F.L., James R. Sovereign of the Knights of Labor, and several presidents of railroad brotherhoods and other large national unions attended a meeting on July 12 at Chicago's Briggs House. By now the boycott was rapidly crumbling, and the A.R.U. had given up hope for forcing the Pullman company to negotiate. It would settle for having the strikers escape penalties imposed by the Association. Eugene Debs asked Gompers to deliver personally a message to the General Managers. The A.R.U. would call off the boycott provided the men were rehired by their lines. Gompers as the most prominent labor leader was the key to the situation. Debs hoped that the A.F.L. president's appearance before the railroad association would suggest the A.R.U.'s backing by national labor.

Gompers's position was in some ways comparable to that occupied by Debs toward the Pullman strikers in mid-June. He could intervene and continue the struggle or allow its collapse. Gompers, however, had no intention of placing his Federation in the bind Debs's was in; nor for that matter was there as practical a connection between the A.F.L. and A.R.U. as existed between the latter and the Pullman locals. His presence in Chicago was only in reluctant compliance with the wishes of the city's A.F.L. trade unions. Gompers declined to convey the message to the Managers' Association, and following his lead the Brigg's House Conference offered the A.R.U. no real support. This was a crushing blow to Debs, who apparently had wanted the promise of a national general strike.[23]

The A.R.U. was beaten, and Debs knew it, but for personal and practical reasons he needed to save face. To come before the General Managers' Association with his terms would seem an abject surrender. If the A.R.U. was to survive it must appear to be suggesting a "truce," not because of expiring power, but for reasons of national interest. The message that Gompers had refused to deliver was carefully worded to avoid any suggestion of weakness. Now Mayor Hopkins agreed to carry the document to the Rookery offices of the Association, thus lending his official auspices to the effort and strengthening the desired impression of an action taken for the public good. Only reluctantly was the note accepted, and by morning it had been returned to Hopkins. The A.R.U. was clearly whipped; the railroads had no need to negotiate with the fallen foe.

By mid-July regular scheduling was restored on all but two lines where local strikes continued for another month. In early August, a special convention of the A.R.U. instructed all locals to act as they pleased. The boycott never officially ended, but simply dissolved. Most workers quit the union and were re-employed, while leaders and others who had incurred the displeasure of superiors were blacklisted. On July 17, Debs, Howard, and several associates were indicted for contempt. Unable or unwilling to post bond, they spent a week in jail,[24] and in January 1895 they received six-month sentences. On his release, Debs turned to government ownership of capital rather than organization of labor as the solution to industrial problems. The broken American Railway Union lingered on into the next century, but only as a shadow of the organization whose moment of prominence and promise had passed in 1894.

John Hopkins remained mayor until February 1895; his administration besmirched by scandal. The Civic Federation claimed that he permitted open gambling in return for graft, while the issuance of a municipal franchise to a utility company with which he was associated made him a rich man. After retirement from office, Hopkins remained active in politics, but never again sought office. A close friendship with Roger Sullivan, "boss" of the state organization, made him a power in the party until his death in 1918. What the relationship between Debs and Hopkins had been during the strike is an enigma. From one source close to the union leader, it seems Debs distrusted the apparent support of the Democratic politicians whom he suspected of ulterior motives.[25]

On July 26, 1894, Grover Cleveland appointed a three-man commission to investigate the circumstances surrounding the strike. From August 15 to August 28, the commission held sessions at the U.S. Post Office building in Chicago hearing the testimony of 107 witnesses. These included the leaders from each side, participants, reporters, city officials, and interested individuals. Its report released in late November was over seven hundred pages in length and presented the most thorough examination of a labor disturbance in American history.[26]

The commissioners in their "conclusions and recommendations" considered the significance of the Chicago strike to be the large combinations on both sides. They attributed this to the growing tendency toward concentration of capital which required labor belatedly to recognize the importance of organization. Neither of these developments were considered necessarily bad except insofar as it encouraged wasteful industrial warfare. The commissioners urged capital to recognize the need for unions and to negotiate with them on matters of common interest. Furthermore, at least in the "quasi-public" railroad industry, Congress was advised to legislate a system of compulsory arbitration.

One of the commissioners was Carroll Wright. In September 1884 Wright, then Massachusetts Commissioner of Labor Statistics, had visited the town of Pullman and had enthusiastically endorsed its plan.[27] The following year he was named U. S. Commissioner of Labor. According to his biographer, Wright was given a pass by the Pullman Palace Car Company allowing him free use of its facilities. As chairman of the Strike Commission, he believed the Chicago strike "the most expensive and far-reaching labor controversy of this generation." [28] At the strike's beginning, he had published an article critical of compulsory arbitration, but as a member of the commission his views changed. Lecturing extensively on arbitration and labor conflict, Wright, with his friends Professor Frank W. Taussig and Charles Francis Adams, Jr., played important roles in convincing both political parties to endorse arbitration in their platforms of 1896.[29] A bill introduced in Congress in late 1894 for railroad mediation was finally passed in 1898.

Other steps were taken to avoid a repetition of the Chicago strike. In November 1894, the Chicago Civic Federation convened a "Congress on Industrial Conciliation," which recommended that Illinois join other states who had established permanent arbitration boards. Altgeld called a special legislative session to consider such action. He cited the expense of the Pullman Strike, which he blamed on George Pullman's stubborn refusal to talk with his men. A bill creating a conciliation commission became law on August 2, 1895.

The social reformer Florence Kelley wrote to Henry Demarest

Lloyd in summer 1894 that the strike was a "touchstone" forcing people to reconsider their views of labor relations.[30] Some came to the conclusion that only legislation on either state or national level could prevent further conflicts. Others, however, saw the only moral of the Chicago strike to be the need for strengthening government's repressive power. In August 1894 a bill was proposed in the House "to promote the efficiency of the militia." [31] Many more bloody battles would be fought by union and management before society would reach a near consensus on labor's rights to a hearing.

15

Community Tension and
the Strike's Collapse

Years after he left office, Cleveland referred to the Pullman Strike
as a "comparatively insignificant quarrel" [1] which circumstances
mushroomed into a national crisis. From mid-June until the second
week of July, the model town, though not quite forgotten, was
overshadowed by the spectacular events of the convention, boycott,
mob action, and federal intervention. During this time the pattern
that had been already established was continued. The strikers held
their meetings, the Relief Committee dispensed aid, and reporters
came to visit. But those who wrote of the town did so in the somewhat academic manner of giving the background for the more important developments taking place in Chicago and the western two-
thirds of the nation.

On Saturday, June 30, George Pullman, accompanied by his family, left Chicago once again for Long Branch. Disorders had been
occurring with increasing frequency and it was decided not to take
his private car which might be recognized by mobs roaming the
tracks. Instead a special car was attached to a regular Pennsylvania
train which the family boarded secretly at five in the evening. Not
until the next day did the reporters on vigil before the Prairie Avenue mansion discover their departure.

The situation was considered grave enough to warrant leaving in charge Robert Todd Lincoln, son of the martyred president, who had recently become actively associated with the company. A prominent Chicago lawyer and businessman Robert Lincoln had been a member of the company's board of directors from 1880. It was only after he returned to this country from being ambassador to Great Britain in 1892 that he became, next to George Pullman, the most important figure in the company. Twice in two weeks the competent, cool Lincoln traveled east to consult with George Pullman. The strain on the latter was beginning to show. His usually controlled temper was manifested in "severe lecturing" [2] of his wife and daughter. On July 20, he went alone to Pullman Island for a rest before returning to Chicago. His family in early August sailed for Europe to remain abroad until events at home quieted.

When at the end of June violence swirled through Chicago's industrial southside, the company became concerned for the safety of plant and property in Pullman. Two focal points of disorder were Grand Crossing, a mile and a half north of Pullman, and Blue Island, a mile to its southwest. Within the model town, tension mounted and company supporters walked in pairs, armed with revolvers. The strikers for the first time were frequenting Kensington's saloons, where they mingled with idlers from the nearby volatile communities. High company officers—Wickes, Middleton, and Brown—took their turn at inspecting the shop three times daily, and the 40-man watch force was ordered to 24-hour duty, the men sleeping on the premises. On July 3, Wickes asked the mayor to enlarge the town's police detachment. Hopkins, citing the absence of incidents, declined.

Two days after federal troops entered Chicago, July 6, a Kensington mob destroyed seventy-five railroad cars, but none belonged to the company. At three in the afternoon of the same day, two hundred men forced their way into the shop grounds. Confronted by watchmen armed with riot guns they departed, though promising to return and burn the long rows of stored palace cars in the yard northeast of the factory buildings. Panicked clerks locked the company's books in a vault and phoned Wickes an exaggerated account of the "invasion." He, in turn, wired a demand for troops and deputies to Altgeld and the U.S. marshal in Chicago. By 7:30 P.M. the first of 240 men of the Illinois First Regiment arrived and took posts around the works. According to the next day's *Tribune,* (July 7, 1894) only "the presence of a strong force of military with Gatling guns . . . prevented a grave outbreak . . . at the town of Pullman last night." A reporter from the *Record* visited Kensington's bars after the arrival of the troops and reported angry and wild talk, claiming to have heard several men discuss bombing the shops.

Thomas Heathcoate criticized the troops' arrival as unnecessary and inflammatory. He asserted that the Kensington mobs consisted of troublemakers from Grand Crossing, Blue Island, and South Chicago, with only a handful of unruly Pullman workers. Pledging the strikers to remain lawful, Heathcoate requested prompt removal of the national guard. The soldiers, however, remained, bivouacking on the lawn of the Florence Hotel, which they used as headquarters. For over a week—until near mid-July—wild rumors persisted that the town would be invaded by tens of thousands reportedly organized for a march from the slums of Chicago and the shacks about the steel works of the Calumet.[3] The military commander dismissed the rumors as improbable and thought any foray could be easily handled as the broad, straight streets of Pullman permitted an advantageous use of defensive fire. He was more concerned about the possibility of dynamiters placing explosives in or around the shops. One supposed plot intended to topple the clock tower. Sentries questioned all trying to enter the grounds, admitting only those with a military pass or one signed by Wickes or Middleton.

The company's July 9 rejection of the overture from the unions darkened the mood of Pullman, which braced itself for Chicago's general strike. The following day, the factory's watch force was sworn in at Wickes's request as special Chicago police. Hopkins required, however, that each of the men had to be vouched for by local residents. By this time, relations between the residents and the Illinois Guard had become ugly. Merchants in Kensington and

Pullman were threatened with violence or boycott unless they refused to serve the troopers.⁴ The day of the general strike, July 11,
small groups congregated on corners to discuss the latest news; a
constant coming and going occurred in the small store in Kensington used by the Strike Committee. When it became known that the
Chicago unions had broken their promise most of the men went
home quietly, but an unusually large number tarried in the Kensington bars that night. Four intoxicated strikers passing a sentry
before the brickyards "taunted" and "threatened" him until he fired
in the air, dispersing the agitators. Later, a flurry of bullets was
aimed at the Florence Hotel by a sniper who fled into the night.

The defeat of the general strike was a crushing blow to the Pullman strikers and made them aware that the A.R.U. was in grave
trouble. On Saturday, July 14, the *Tribune* headline read: "Debs'
Strike Dead." The story beneath carried a report on the model
town which noted that a majority of people questioned expressed
an eagerness to return to work on any terms. Sunday was a parade
day for the National Guard. Drills were performed before an atten-
tive audience of five thousand, and at the conclusion small children
presented baskets of fruits and bouquets of flowers. Most of the
crowd had come from Chicago for the occasion, but several hundred were residents of Pullman. Many of the workers, giving up the
strike as lost, were said to have dropped their animosity to the sol-
diers.⁵

At eight o'clock Monday evening, July 16, the Pullman strikers
attended a meeting called in the hall of the Market Building by the
chaplain and officers of the First Regiment. The workers were told
that Wickes had been contacted to determine whether strikers
would be rehired if the Union pledged to return to work. Wickes
had assured the officers that the company would be favorably impressed by such action, and would consider the proposal. Now the
chaplain asked the men to authorize him to approach George Pullman on their behalf. The audience had known in advance of the
request, and according to the *Record* (July 17, 1894), roared "no"
so defiantly the windows rattled. Later that night a special session
of the Strike Committee pledged to continue the strike. Relations

with the Guard improved considerably, and no further incidents occurred until their departure, but the strike leaders were as far apart from the company as on May 11.

On the sixteenth Robert Lincoln visited George Pullman in Long Branch, and the two must have reached a decision to reopen the works.[6] On July 18, a notice was posted on the main gate that the shops were taking on workers. Eight hundred were hired by August 7. Most of these were new employees from Chicago, but they also included a few hundred "Hollanders" from Roseland who had broken with the Union. The company announced that it was getting numerous applications from Chicago's unemployed for the three thousand positions in the factory and soon expected all to be filled.[7] The strikers became restless as they realized their jobs were being taken by others.

Only gradually did the various facilities in Pullman resume operations. By the twentieth the laundry opened and two weeks later the repair shop. The opening of the laundry was the scene of a mob attack on its employees. As other shops resumed work during the next two weeks, tension increased, but no serious incident materialized. Considered sympathetic to the strikers, the community's policemen were transferred elsewhere and replaced by others who would protect the returning workers. Now the harassed Hopkins received complaints about police abuse from his neighbors. At July's end, however, the town appeared calm enough to permit a reduction in forces. Eight of the twelve militia companies stationed in the Pullman area were returned to inactive status; the remainder left within the week. In the meanwhile, the strikers' situation became critical.

By July 13, the Relief Committee was desperately low on supplies.[8] Several public appeals for help went virtually unheeded. The boycott and disorders cost the strikers the support of many former sympathizers while diverting attention from the town and multiplying the number of people elsewhere in need of aid. After the failure of the July 11 general strike, the Chicago Knights of Labor and a few unions who had defaulted on their promised support made amends by contributions, but this was a trickle compared to

COMMUNITY TENSION AND THE STRIKE'S COLLAPSE

the $300 a day needed. A Pullman doctor sought to renew interest in the residents' plight by listing malnutrition as cause on several death certificates. The strike, however, had lost its immediacy and the boycott's defeat made it anticlimactic. Indeed, the reopening of the shops had led many Chicagoans to believe the battle over. The Pullman workers were now fighting on alone and with little more than their rapidly dwindling resources for sustenance.

The second half of July saw a change in strike leadership and over-all morale. Heathcoate told reporters that there was no way for his men to continue the struggle and that he wished for a peaceful end. The General Strike Committee immediately repudiated its chairman and promised to continue the walk-out until the company admitted defeat.[9] Heathcoate's firm and responsible control of the strike now slackened.[1] The once daily meetings were being held irregularly. Strikers no longer busy with union chores found time heavy on their hands. Petty incidents between strikers and police increased. A general decline in discipline and hope were noted by reporters who also observed that more men were spending their days in Kensington's saloons. Loss of confidence made idleness a wearying burden. New and younger men began to come forth as spokesmen, but their efforts to brace the men's determination acquired an increasingly truculent and unrealistic tone. The remarkable unity of the strikers was giving way to demoralization.

On August 7, several hundred men from Chicago were hired for positions in the still closed construction department. The company announced that all remaining vacancies would be filled on the fourteenth and work commenced on the sixteenth.[11] With this the entire shop would be reopened. The strikers responded by holding several open-air night rallies; many a man emphasized his determination to remain out by going to the works and removing his personal tool chest, which was the worker's property. Others, however, gave thought to the company's promise to show preference in hiring former employees provided they resigned from the A.R.U.

When the six o'clock whistle blew on Monday morning, August 14, more than a thousand strikers were "packed forty deep" around the main gate. The men were silent and orderly, waiting their turn before a long table staffed by clerks and supervisors. "Each one, as he signed his name, drew out and deposited a soiled green card—the evidence of his membership in the American Railway Union." [12] The company, true to its word, sent back several hundred Chicago applicants without listing them. By the end of August, the shops had hired about 2,700 workers, of which all but 800 were former employees. They were paid at the old rates and the company again competed for contracts at a loss. [13]

Probably a thousand men remained without work and technically continued the strike. Some of these were union leaders, such as Thomas Heathcoate, who correctly assumed that they were blacklisted and to apply would be a futile exercise in self-degradation. [14] Others had been replaced by Chicagoans or their old jobs dropped. A hard core refused to accept their defeat. The desperation of these men was underscored on August 14 with the Relief Committee's announcement that it must close its doors for want of supplies. A ton of flour was immediately contributed by the Chicago Trade Council, which was quickly distributed. According to reporters, men were subsisting on black bread and coffee while lack of carfare required them to walk sixteen miles to and from Chicago in search of work.

After an appeal from the Relief Committee, Governor Altgeld visited Pullman on August 20. He inspected several tenement flats, talked with the occupants, and then went to the brickyard homes. In an interview with Superintendent Middleton, Altgeld inquired about the company's intentions. Middleton explained that the company planned to hire the unemployed as quickly as places occurred. The governor suggested the company rotate its men to provide work, but this was rejected as impractical. Besides, in the superintendent's opinion, efforts in this direction led to the strike in the first place. According to Middleton, the Pullman Palace Car Company would help the town's unemployed by preference for available positions; beyond that, it assumed no responsibility. [15]

George Pullman returned to Chicago on August 10. Following his arrival he avoided public appearances and stayed away from the town. To requests for interviews, he advised that his time was preoccupied with business affairs. Altgeld wrote him, describing a pathetic situation of want and suffering in Pullman and suggesting a meeting between the two to consider what the company might do in the way of relief, such as cancelling rent debts. Pullman in reply denied that extensive distress existed and ignored Altgeld's suggested meeting. In a second letter, the governor reiterated his assertions. He pointed out that since the state had already shouldered the heavy expense of protecting the company's property, it would be unfair for the public to assume the responsibility for the town's welfare.[16] Before Pullman could respond, however, Altgeld urged all citizens of Illinois and the Cook County Commissioners to aid generously the unemployed of Pullman.

The Relief Committee which had barely sustained itself was now the recipient of new interest. Several Chicago newspapers even started their own fund drives for the town. By August 23, headquarters were packed with clothing and provisions. It was announced that a family of four would receive an ample weekly allotment of four pounds of sugar, half a pound of coffee, two pounds of rice, one sack of flour, and eight pounds of meat. Contention developed, however, between strikers and Chicagoans. Strike leaders were angered that their committee had been pushed into the background by the Chicago relief group which had been virtually dormant during July, when help had been needed most. Now, its middle-class women wanted to run the fund as an outright charity with no reference to what the Pullman leaders insisted was an ongoing strike.[17] Defeated in their effort to direct the Relief Committee, the General Strike Committee tacitly admitted what all knew—they were beaten. It ceased effective functioning, though meetings were held as late as December 1894.

The town's diehards at one point decided to lead an exodus of strikers to Hiawatha, Kansas, where they hoped to erect a "cooperative" factory for the manufacture of railroad cars. Efforts to solicit capital from unions, businessmen, and banks were fruitless, and the idea died at birth. Mayor Hopkins provided jobs for a few of the unemployed on the city's parks and streets, but the number was less than a hundred and the work makeshift and temporary. Throughout late August and September hundreds of families left for Chicago and elsewhere in search of employment. In mid-October, George Pullman announced that there were only 279 former employees living in the town without work.[18] By early 1895, these had either moved or were rehired.[19]

Most families who left the town owed considerable rent. Arrears rose from $70,000 at the strike's inception to well over $100,000 by mid-August. The company made little effort to collect or evict, and consequently few residents had paid anything. In effect, it was the strikers' major financial support. Fifty thousand had been contributed to Strikers' Relief, which, while considered generous by the press, does not compare with George Pullman's handsome donation of housing.

Owning its workers' homes provided the company with a novel means of turning the screw, but a lenient policy was forced by circumstances. On three occasions, officers had told reporters that wholesale evictions were being considered.[20] Reaction to these "feelers" was critical and nothing was done. If indifferent to public opinion on the issue of arbitration, the Pullman Palace Car Company did not want the stigma of throwing penniless people on the streets. For similar reasons, it made no effort to impede movement from the town though this meant writing debts off as losses. Whatever his reasons, George Pullman did not trumpet his "generosity" and received little credit for what, properly exploited, might have placed him in a more favorable light.

On August 15, the United States Strike Commission began holding hearings twice daily in a small federal courtroom. The sessions were always crowded, but the largest audience appeared for George Pullman's testimony on the twenty-seventh. It was not every day that a giant of industry appeared before a bench of justice to defend himself, even though its censure was moral not legal. Carroll Wright began the questioning of his old acquaintance. Then the other two commissioners subjected him to a cross examination lasting more than an hour.

Pullman denied having opposed any union other than the A.R.U., but was unable to cite one recognized by the company.[21]

While agreeing that arbitration was useful in issues involving honest differences—"for instance, a question of title"—he felt that his recent dispute with the workers concerned policies that must be based on facts rather than consensus. An unhappy employee was always free to leave. Pullman defended his actions as in the best interests of his men. When the commissioners suggested that profits from other operations could have allowed a restoration of old salary rates, he insisted that wages must be determined by supply and demand. It would have been unethical for him to give charity at the stockholders' expense, as his principal responsibility as president was to enhance their investment. A stubborn and self-righteous man left the stand. His most important point had been that management must have freedom to make decisions based on business reality and which safeguarded capital. But he could not understand that labor also wanted the right to protect its own interests.

The model town was built in the anticipation that it would be an important step toward the solution of conflict between capital and labor. For Pullman believed that scientific management could increase production and thus create a larger share for all. But then, as now, there was the additional problem of division. Here he went along with the general orthodoxy of the time: wages must be decided by the market. Yet, the primary reason workers organized was to gain voice in policy decisions concerning salaries. Fearful of losing exclusive business control, Pullman and most other employers refused to permit peaceful development of means for settling industrial disputes. Consequently, these tended to magnify into widespread conflict.

The strike had cost the workers $360,000 in wages they could ill afford to lose.[22] The company's losses were probably greater and more permanent. The fame of the model town, which had served as a show place for the company's leadership in technology, business organization, and social responsibility, was replaced by world-wide notoriety. Henceforth, it was synonymous with the most serious American labor conflict of the century.

During the strike, Mark Hanna, the Cleveland industrialist and political power, commented that any employer who refused to talk with his men was a damn fool.[23] Most businessmen, however, apparently supported Pullman, and he received hundreds of encouraging letters from associates all over the country. Henry Villard wrote that, having himself experienced the calumny of the press, he could appreciate Pullman's chagrin at the way his benevolent intentions toward his workers were viciously misinterpreted.[24] Others came to similar conclusions; an editorial in *Harper's Weekly* saw the strike's moral as demonstrating that any employer who showed gratuitious interest in his men's welfare exposed himself to ingratitude.[25] For conservative businessmen, such as Charles Elliot Perkins, who had long before predicted that Pullman would one day regret building a town, the sleeping-car magnate was hoisted on his own petard. His actions had been self-entangling and founded on false hopes of harmony. The model town was an experiment never again repeated by American industry, for pragmatic businessmen would consciously avoid Pullman's mistakes.

To labor, of course, George Pullman became anathema. Samuel Gompers referred to him as "the most consummate type of avaricious wealth absorber, tyrant, and hypocrite this age . . . has furnished." [26] While some in the middle class shared this view, others tried to temper it with understanding. Jane Addams believed his intentions honorable but misdirected. In an address to a women's group, she characterized Pullman as a "modern Lear" whose ungovernable pride destroyed those he loved through insistence on directing their lives.[27] This is an overdramatization, but contains some insight. Pullman firmly believed in a stewardship of merit and assumed business success a clear proof of leadership and ability. By 1895, few could doubt that his model town was "run along strict paternalistic lines" which denied residents and workers any expression in community or factory.

Even before the Strike Commission, George Pullman insisted that the model town was a success. Asked about a statement made in 1893 that the community's environmental conditions had made his "men . . . about 40 per cent better" than ordinary workers, he replied, "that was my careful consideration at the time," and despite the strike he saw no need to modify this. As far as Pullman was concerned, agitation by an outsider, the A.R.U., had caused the trouble. To others, however, the conflict was adequate proof that his planned community did not work.

Andrew Carnegie thought Pullman a born optimist who believed everything could be made right by determination. It is not known whether he ever considered abandoning the idea of a planned town, as some of his closest friends counseled,[28] but publicly he never faltered. Till his death he fought to preserve the model community. In August 1894 the Illinois Attorney General started suit to force the company to divest itself of its large residential holdings on the grounds that these were not authorized by its charter. Without hesitation, Pullman ordered his lawyers to fight this new threat to his model town.

Memorialized for years as a public benefactor, Pullman could not help but be embittered by the odium frequently attached to his name. Called a "son of a bitch" by a public speaker at a huge rally,[29] he was commonly charged with being a cruel and tyrannical employer, a man without friends, incapable of either loving or being loved. His vaunted "Pullman System" had been dismissed as a callous exercise in exploitation, and no aspect of his life or personality was spared. For his fall from public grace, George Pullman, or at least his family, held the press responsible, and above all certain Chicago newspapers. Still he hoped that time would prove him right.

V

FROM MODEL TOWN TO URBAN
COMMUNITY, 1894-1930

16

The Separation of Factory and Town

> No longer do writers . . . resort thither to expatiate upon
> its wonders in fervid language and indulge in predictions of a
> new golden age.
>
> J. Seymour Curry, *Chicago: Its History and Its Builders*

Carwardine and Heathcoate quietly left Pullman in September 1894. The union leader became a foreman in a Chicago machine shop, and the minister acquired a Wisconsin parish. By January only a few unemployed remained as unpleasant reminders of the past summer. Bitterness lingered, however, and as late as 1900 a reporter found men who had not spoken to each other since the strike.[1] But the company's official policy was to "forgive and forget." George Pullman told his stockholders: our workers "have learnt by experience that this company was earnest in befriending them . . . and that the genuineness of the interest of this company in their welfare is far more to be trusted than the promises of the agitators who misled them."[2]

Fastidious concern with the town's appearance continued, and efforts were undertaken to heal wounds. A Men's Society of Pullman, organized in October 1894, provided for the "physical, mental, and spiritual well being of the community." Three years later, over two hundred members paid $6.00 yearly dues, and George Pullman as principal benefactor headed the list of associate members. The Pullman Athletic Club still sponsored regattas and road races which drew large crowds, while the community's athletic teams maintained their prowess. The Pullman Band, having performed with the First Regiment Illinois Guard during its stay in the town, became officially attached to the Regiment in the fall of 1894.

Quickly fading from national attention, the community found itself merely of local interest. Gone were the visitors, reporters, and social reformers of early days. Now the model town was only a curiosity associated with a brief and tragic history. As one resident later recalled, "Pullman was never the same after the strike."[3] On the surface all remained as before, but the town experienced an irreparable loss of pride and self-respect.

For several months after the strike active harassment of George Pullman continued. Chicago's two Democratic morning papers, the *Times* and *Herald,* in early October 1894 featured stories of Republican election activity in Pullman. They claimed that several hundred "starving employees "were drawn up in a line and addressed by [Republican] candidates"—a "humiliating exhibition of the slave driving methods of the Pullman corporation."[4] After the meeting, politicians and company officers dined at the Florence on "trussed fowl," toasting "Baron Pullman" with Mumm's brut. The Republican *Inter Ocean* (October 10, 1894), checking these facts, came up with another version. The candidates' visit had been neither solicited nor heeded by the company. What they ordered at the Florence was not reported, but the Republicans dined alone and paid their own bill.

More serious attacks on the company came from another direction. Governor Altgeld tried to raise its taxes and, when this failed, sought state regulation of sleeping-car rates.[5] In the Populist stronghold of Nebraska, thirteen different bills aimed at the sleeping-car industry were introduced before the legislature. Six other states and Congress also considered action. Nothing, however, came of this activity and another decade would elapse before the P.P.C.C. was subjected to public control.

In June 1895 an Illinois Circuit Court upheld the company's right to own the land and residences of Pullman. Altgeld and prominent Chicago Democrats denounced the action as a travesty of justice, and some hinted that the company's power had influenced the judge's decision. Attorney General Maloney expressed surprise and confidently stated that the decision would soon be reversed. Until 1898 the town would exist under a legal cloud and with its future uncertain.

The national economy and car construction continued slack, but by summer 1895 a semblance of well-being returned to Pullman. The workers were averaging $2.23 a day, or 10 per cent higher than April, 1894. This increase was due to more regular work since wage rates remained the same. Pullman's announced policy was to minimize time loss through restrictions on the size of his force.[6] Only 2,572 men were on the rolls, a hundred less than in August 1894. The piece-rate system was retained and rents were as before, but a new procedure to measure morale was introduced. Workers who resigned were asked their reasons, which were then forwarded to General Manager Brown of the uptown office.[7]

As late as February 5, 1897, *Railway Age* reported that the P.P.C.C. was still taking car construction contracts at a loss, but an upturn soon occurred. The financial report of October 1897 noted that employment had recently increased to four thousand with an average annual wage of $500. The nation was entering a new period of business growth and general prosperity. George Pullman, however, did not live to see it; and his death marked the beginning of the end for his town.

Business affairs kept Pullman in the east much of the time, with visits to the town infrequent. The strike hearings revealed two important facts about his job as president of the company. One was the astonishing smallness of his cash salary, which in 1890 had been only $10,000 complemented by a stock bonus and option.[8] The other was how far he had removed himself from day-to-day operations. His vagueness about its affairs prompted Carroll Wright to ask whether he was the "active business manager"—"that is do you take charge of the details of the company's affairs?"—to which Pullman replied: "No sir . . . the officers of the company report to me."

Pullman personally supervised all difficult contract renewals, and retained final say on important decisions. Otherwise his principal work was investing the company's large surplus in the stocks of other businesses. At the same time he risked his own money and thus multiplied his personal fortune while increasing that of the P.P.C.C. From 1895 to 1897, Pullman backed a Chicago consortium which founded the National Biscuit Company and sought to control the Diamond Match Company. Starting as businessman-promoter, he finished his career as a financier, an apparently common pattern.

During 1896, the sleeping-car king suffered from frequent headaches and general irritability. Two events, however, cheered him considerably. The jury at an international contest held in Prague found the town of Pullman superior to similar efforts by European industrialists, such as Krupp, and "without peer" in the entire world. This was the closest his ideas would come to vindication, and it was with strong pleasure that he received a medal from the Austro-Hungarian Empire for the world's "most perfectly planned town." Even critical Chicago papers jingoistically rejoiced at the triumph of a native son.

On April 29, 1896, Pullman proudly gave his daughter Florence in marriage to a rising young Chicago lawyer, Frank O. Lowden. A tendency toward alliances between American heiresses and impoverished European aristocrats had stirred deep general distaste, and the fact that Pullman's daughter was marrying a "manly American" —native born and self-made—rather than a "bowing and scraping Von who's it" was viewed with favor by press and public. A wedding reception in the Prairie Avenue home was attended by a thousand guests from Chicago society, the railroad industry, and American business and government. The city's newspapers acclaimed the occasion "one of the most brilliant in many years." Among those present were the Andrew Carnegies, the John D. Rockefellers, and the Henry Flaglers, as well as the widows of U. S. Grant, James G. Blaine, and Phil Sheridan. Three justices of the Supreme Court— Brown, Field, and Harlan—also attended. Though aglow with dignitaries, the reception was simply conducted, costing less than $4,000, and generally considered in good taste by a nation still sensitive to social extravagances.

The public was unaware that the couple's courtship had weathered parental difficulties which offer interesting insight into George Pullman's personality. Florence Pullman first met Frank Lowden aboard the liner *Normandy* in August 1894 when with her mother she fled the strike. On their return home, the two continued seeing each other. Like many girls of her background, Florence had promised to ask her father's permission before an engagement. Instead he was told only afterward and irately demanded she break with Lowden to restore his faith in her integrity. When writing the young lawyer, Florence offered a ray of hope:

> I have a strong feeling that the moment I have submitted to Papa's stronger will . . . he will feel that his position has been maintained with dignity, and there will be nothing that he will not do to promote my happiness.[9]

She obviously knew her father. Within three months the stubborn though not unkind Pullman consented. A proud man, he always demanded from family, friends, and business associates that his "position . . . [be] maintained with dignity." According to the long-time porter of his private car, none but the family ever addressed him by his given name. Punctiliously observing propriety, he insisted on others doing the same.

Despite his initial difficulty, Lowden found he liked his father-in-law, whom he admired as "frank [and] candid"; a man who did "not deal in mystery." [10] After his death, Lowden and other friends tried to undo the injustice they believed he had suffered. The son-in-law thought Pullman's sincere concern for social welfare had been obscured by his placing it in the context of a business philosophy. Yet, more important in blemishing his reputation had been an unyielding behavior during the strike of 1894. Acting honorably by his own standards, Pullman had eschewed compassion as inconsistent with principle. Others, however, who did not share his convictions, viewed this unbending posture as indifference to his men.

The Pullmans spent the summer of 1897 at Long Branch. They usually returned west in mid-September, but a spell of warm weather prolonged their stay. Beman and Barrett visited often to work on plans for redesigning the "cottage." Finally, on October 8, Pullman boarded his private car for Philadelphia and then Chicago. On October 16, although he had been unwell for several days, he insisted on guiding a party of railroad men through a walking tour of Pullman.[11] It was his last visit, for three days later he died, in his sixty-sixth year, of a heart attack.

Flags were lowered in Pullman, and a thousand workers packed the Arcade theater to resolve:

> We have . . . recognized his high and broad aims to make his employees to a greater degree than before sharers in the results of good work. . . . We should always cherish his memory.

Saddened, Duane Doty confided to a reporter for the *Chicago Record* (October 21): "probably no man in recent years has been more misrepresented, more frequently subjected to the ingratitude of those whose best interests he strove to subserve."

Obituaries tried to give Pullman his due. They praised his business genius and the importance of his innovations to modern travel. Most acknowledged high motives in regard to the model town, but none thought it an unqualified success or meriting imitation. Instead they usually pointed out that the town's experience showed the need for planning to be set in a democratic context and compatible with "the spirit of American institutions." [12]

The unpleasantness of Pullman's last few years was carried to the grave. Buried on October 24 in Chicago's Graceland Cemetery, his memorial was a simple Corinthian column designed by Beman. To forestall efforts at posthumous revenge by labor radicals, tons of steel and concrete were laid over the casket.[13] The Reverend Mr. Hollis of the Central Church described Pullman in his eulogy as "reserved, loving silence, and simplicity, he did not wear his heart upon a sleeve."

Pullman's estate, initially estimated at $8,000,000, was more than double this before final division in 1903 and included 58,000 shares of P.P.C.C. stock.[14] Most of this fortune went to the family, with friends and retainers handsomely remembered, but $130,000 was donated to Chicago charitable and educational institutions. His final act for Pullman was a bequest of $1,200,000 to build and sustain "a free school of manual training for the benefit of persons living or employed" there. Lowden and the will's executors, Robert T. Lincoln and Norman B. Ream, along with four others named by George Pullman, were to comprise a board of directors. The Burlington's Charles E. Perkins, who had been cynical about the model town, gladly served on the school board until his death in 1908.

A canvas of the town's families in 1899 found over a thousand children wanting to attend the school. Advice was obtained from prominent educators, such as the University of Chicago's president, William Rainey Harper, and also from Duane Doty. Pullman had hoped that the school would serve as a model for others, thus ending American dependence on immigrants for higher industrial skills. Intending to build the school while alive, he had discussed his plans with Doty. The car magnate's plan, according to Doty, was a first-rate technical institution superior to the best in Germany, which would offer thorough training in practical skills and a general education.

Moving slowly to allow the bequest to grow, the school's directors acquired a site only in 1908, and not until 1914 was the cornerstone laid. Finally, the following year, the first class of 106 students started their training. Frank Lowden rendered yeoman service in the protracted negotiations which led to the Pullman Free School of Manual Training, and thereafter the family continued a keen interest until its closing in 1950.

Named director of the Pullman Palace Car Company in 1897, Robert Todd Lincoln was its president four years later. He acquired a corporation with assets of over $60,000,000 and competent officers. After Pullman's death, the company's stock declined sharply, but by summer 1898 it stood thirty-five points higher than the previous fall. In July, Lincoln declared a special dividend of $20.00 a share. Both passenger and construction departments were busy, and new workers were hired. Vainly sought by George Pullman for years, the absorption of the Wagner Company occurred in 1899. Two hundred thousand shares of the P.P.C.C. stock, valued at $220 each at market price, were given to the Wagner Company for distribution among their shareholders as a purchase price, and William Vanderbilt and J. P. Morgan joined the company's board of directors. More than ever the P.P.C.C. was synonymous with the sleeping-car industry and vulnerable to charges of monopoly.

Changes in policy occurred quickly. For a brief period in 1899 the company experimented with an "ordinary," a sleeper that charged half the usual fare but lacked the beauty and luxury associated with a Pullman. The P.P.C.C. found to its chagrin that rather than creating new business, the "ordinary" was drawing customers from the more expensive sleeper, and quickly discontinued the experiment. At this time, however, the company declared its first nationwide fare reduction, explaining that Jim Hill of the Northern Pacific had cut that line's sleeping-car rates, and the P.P.C.C. needed to follow suit. Some reporters thought this reasoning intended to suggest a competitive situation where one did not exist, and a suspicious press viewed the reduction as an effort to curry public favor and thus reduce growing pressure for federal regulation.[15]

By 1900 rival firms were manufacturing steel freight cars and the Pullman company began using this metal for car frames. Though less attractive, metal cars were cheaper and safer than wooden ones and soon revolutionized the industry. Eight years later the company converted to all steel construction of both passenger and freight cars. In the process, the nature of production and the work force were altered with important consequences for the community of Pullman.

Under Lincoln's direction, the company's huge surplus was rapidly distributed among stockholders, increasing capitalization. Frequent stock bonuses, known as "cutting a melon," kept the company in the news and before the public. Capitalization soared from $36,-000,000 in 1897 to $120,000,000 by 1910. Critics argued that this could only have been accomplished through watering or exorbitant profits and demanded an investigation by federal agencies.[16]

As prosperity returned to company and shops, the town of Pullman began a decline. In October 1898 the Illinois Supreme Court, reversing the lower court's decision, ordered the P.P.C.C. to sell all land not used by industry. George Pullman, anticipating this action, had reportedly planned to incorporate a new company which would buy the town and sell its stock to P.P.C.C. shareholders.[17] Now the company did not even request a rehearing. Reporters were told that Marshall Field and other important stockholders were privately delighted to rid themselves of the town.[18]

Dismantling of Pullman's plan began immediately. Sewage farm and brickyard were sold in 1898. As the shops required additional facilities, the lake front was filled in and used for a round house and a yard. The picturesque, ornamental wall along Florence Avenue was replaced by a high iron fence. On April 29, 1899, the *Chicago Inter Ocean* headlined "Pullman is Doomed." Though not generally known, the land used for Lake Vista, the factory front lawn, and part of Arcade Park was owned by the I.C., which now reclaimed its right of way. Lake Vista was filled in and a street parallel to the I.C. tracks was cut from 111th Street to 107th Street. A reporter found "very little interest . . . manifested by merchants or residents . . . at the contemplated changes" [19]

By September 1899 only one park, the truncated Arcade, remained, protected by a guardrail to minimize maintenance costs. The *Chicago Sunday Chronicle* (September 24, 1899) complained that "a blighted and devastated Pullman greets the eye from the passing . . . train." A reporter who visited the town heard from an officer that the company was no longer interested in the town and that it "had no more concern for the employees than they have for the company." Its only preoccupation was with those matters that bore exclusively on business interests.

When a minister and local newspaper charged a pharmacist in the Market Hall with operating a "blind pig"—selling liquor without a license—the company took no action. Only after considerable publicity did the city police arrest the man six months after the original charge was raised. The *sub rosa* support Pullman had given many of the town's social organizations was ended, with the exception of the band and shop sports teams. No longer able to sponsor road races and regattas, and without playing fields and boat house, the Pullman Athletic Club disbanded. Membership in the Pullman Men's Society dwindled, and the library would have been in serious trouble except for aid from Mrs. Pullman.[20] In 1902 the Arcade theater closed for want of patronage.

After much prodding from the company, Chicago assumed municipal functions in July 1899. The P.P.C.C., however, continued to maintain Florence Boulevard and Arcade Park because of their proximity to the works. The town's population rose slowly and by 1897 numbered eight thousand, but many apartments remained empty. Rents in and around Chicago had fallen steadily since 1893; and in 1899 the company lowered their rents an average of 15 per cent in an effort to fill vacancies.

A court agreement required the company to sell the town by February, 1904. At that time, however, the company requested a five-year deferment because of a tight real estate market. Finally, in early 1907, buildings were appraised and circulars describing purchase terms distributed. The Pullman Loan and Trust handled all sales with residents given first option. By November 1907, over $1,000,000 worth of property had changed hands, or about half of what was available.

Low prices, usually set at one hundred times rent, combined with small down payments and long term mortgages were intended to encourage workers to buy. Many of the row houses, at an average cost of $2,000, were purchased by residents.[21] The larger tenements and public buildings were, of course, beyond the means of most Pullman employees. Florence Pullman Lowden, "proud to identify herself with her father's town," paid $352,000 for the tenements on Fulton and Stephenson.[22] Pullman's widow "for sentimental reasons" bought the Arcade building, already in serious disrepair, and the Greenstone Memorial Church was purchased by a Methodist Congregation for $16,000.

To comply with the court order, buildings which had not been sold were transferred in title to a bank clerk in April 1909. Within the next ten years this remaining property was sold, except for the school. As early as 1905, the company had offered to sell the school building to the Chicago Board of Education which had rented it since 1899. The Board declined, citing as reasons the building's antiquated plant and, also, its dangerous proximity to ungraded tracks. The school's location was an obvious flaw in the town's physical layout which apparently escaped notice until then. Not wanted by anyone, the school building was demolished in 1913. After 1909 many of the buyers were realtors and speculators. Nearly $40,000 worth of property, including vacant lots, was purchased by J. P. Morgan's Chicago realty agent.[23] According to E. F. Bryant, president of the Pullman bank, the company had expected to realize $4,000,000 from the town's sale, but obtained only half that amount.[24] Pullman as a company town and model community had come to an end.

Arcade Park was donated to the city in 1910. The gift's terms prohibited the construction of any structure except for a memorial to George Pullman. Until World War I the company gratuitously maintained the park, but then allowed it to become little more than an unattended lot. No memorial to George Pullman was ever raised in the town, sparing him a final travesty, for his standards of beauty and order had perished with his plan.

In 1908 the Illinois Circuit Court reported: "the company has now no relation to the people of Pullman except as to those engaged in its manufacturing plants, and that relation is merely employer to employee." By 1910, except for the plan's architectural residue, Pullman was an ordinary industrial community. No longer a "show place," the town was neither controversial or newsworthy. Little attention was given the plan's dismantling. The company, like other American concerns, allowed expediency to determine relations with the community. Nothing more was expected by a society that assumed the responsibility of business to be solely business.

By the twentieth century the national mood had undergone a transformation. The public no longer stood in awe of industry's titans nor thought their behavior necessarily in the general interest. Government was strengthened and empowered to regulate business. The Progressive Era marked the beginning of the modern ascendancy of community over private enterprise. Corporations were expected to obey restrictions and refrain from throwing their power about, while legislators, not the businessmen, were held responsible for solving social problems. George Pullman's "plan" was readily discounted as "utopian paternalism," an "unsatisfactory . . . domination of community interests by . . . industrial authority." [25] Hailed in the Gilded Age as a "model in the present, and a pattern for the future," it was already an anachronism by 1900. The strike of 1894 and the town's own experience played an important role in this new emphasis upon legislative rather than entrepreneurial reform.

17

The Loss of Community Identity

> The story of Pullman so far as its significance for today is con-
> cerned, centers largely in the developments whereby the feudal-
> istic power was dislodged and shifted to the shoulders of the
> community.
>
> Graham R. Taylor, *Satellite Cities*

Though no longer landlord, the company continued to be important to the town. By 1905, the P.P.C.C., having changed its name
to the Pullman Company, was the only sleeping-car firm in the nation and one of three leading manufacturers of railroad cars. The
Hepburn Act, passed the following year, empowered the Interstate
Commerce Commission to regulate the sleeping-car industry, but
not until 1910 were rates ordered lowered. The company now
needed to challenge federal control for the first time. It ingeniously
argued that a sleeper provided accommodations rather than transportation and, therefore, was a hotel, not an interstate carrier.[1]

Public opinion and the newspapers strongly supported the I.C.C.
Peter Finley Dunne's famed "Mr. Dooley" told "Hennessy": "th'
next toime I feel like riding in th' upper berth av a Pullman Car I'll
go into th' pantry, climb onto th' upper shelf, put a cinder in one
eye, and throw tin dollars out av th' window." An everyday fact of
modern life, George Pullman's innovations were no longer above
reproach but were critically scrutinized by a society always insist-
ing, in the words of one newspaper, "on more for less." The courts
upheld the jurisdiction of the I.C.C. amidst general relief that one of

the nation's more powerful corporations was finally responsible to a public agency.

Though prosperity returned in 1897, not until 1900 did annual wages of Pullman workers equal that of 1893. In the next decade, however, they rose "astronomically." By 1908, nearly ten thousand men and women worked for an average wage of $828.73. As the cost of living did not rise accordingly, the increase in salaries resulted in a higher standard of living and greater security. This unprecedented local and national prosperity was only briefly interrupted in 1904, 1907, and again in 1913.

The company's opposition to unions continued, but efforts at organizing the shops began again in 1902 and met with considerable success. After several small strikes, the company closed the works in September 1904 for two weeks "on account of a shortage of contracts." When they reopened, only men who pledged to "act towards the company as individuals" [2] were rehired. With the union broken, the company reduced the work week to fifty-four hours, allowing the men to vote on whether to divide this into a five- or five-and-one-half-day work week. Wages were always liberal for a non-union shop, and in 1914 a pension program was initiated. No further serious labor trouble occurred until after World War I, but relations between management and men were still strained. Rumors of arbitrary and inequitable practices freely circulated in the shops, and for a politician to be viewed with favor by company officers usually meant sure death at the polls.[3]

From 1905 to 1910, over $5,000,000 was invested in remodeling and enlarging the shops. New buildings were added to old with no concern for consistency in architecture or site. The once self-contained industrial sections spilled over into the residential area and enveloped the lake front. A state legislative commission even investigated charges that the company had filled the equivalent of twenty city blocks in Lake Calumet and used this land without paying taxes or acquiring title.[4] Other firms, such as the Sherman William Paint Company and the Chicago Drop Forge and Foundry Company, moved to the area south of 115th Street. By 1910, the homes of Pullman were surrounded by industry on all sides but the west.

The use of steel brought increasing reliance on coal. Late into the night smelters issued an eery light while tons of soot gushed forth to darken homes and streets. Along with this dirt came the clamor of industrial noise from powerful new machines. Observing those unpleasant developments, an ex-resident stated:

> It is now [1917] obvious . . . that all the land east of the Illinois Central Railroad tracks from 103rd to 115th Street should have been reserved for industrial plants only, and that the entire residential portion of this district should have been located west of the Illinois Central tracks.[5]

After 1907, cabinetmakers, gilders, and polishers were replaced by riveters and crane operators. These new skills were more easily acquired than the older ones. Rather than the long apprenticeship needed to master carpentry tools, a metal worker learned to tend a machine expertly in a matter of months. Already in 1900, the company reported that skilled workers had declined to only 40 per cent of the total force. Soon the proud title "journeyman mechanic" was discarded, and by 1908 "an army of steel workers . . . fanned the flames in the furnaces and leased the lash of sand blast, air hose and gas flame."

An effort to retrain older workers was largely unsuccessful, many preferring to leave. One asserted that car construction was no longer a "white man's" industry. Several complained that Italians and Poles who "don't seem to have any nerves" were the only ones capable of "standing the racket." In 1893, only seventy-five Italians worked for the company, primarily in the brickyard, but twenty years later, more than eleven hundred were employed in the shops. By 1911, there were over five hundred Greeks engaged in car construction, and when the Balkan War erupted, two hundred were thought to have left Pullman to fight for their motherland.

The town's middle class began an exodus shortly after Pullman's death. Bryant and Hopkins, banker and politician, left in 1898 when the first changes became noticeable. By 1910, few professional and company officers remained, most having moved north to the communities of Hyde Park and Woodlawn. These areas offered newer residences and more central locations, while "convenient to businesses [and] employment in Pullman. Beginning about 1905, many of the older skilled workers also left the town, usually settling in the immediate vicinity. More and more apartments in Pullman either stood vacant or were occupied by families from southern and eastern Europe, which speeded the departure of older residents. Lured by advantages elsewhere, they were clearly dissatisfied by the "diminishing attraction of Pullman as a place of residence." [6] By 1920, Poles and Italians were the two largest ethnic groups. [7]

The final blow to George Pullman's "order and beauty" came from the residents who were no longer restricted by a plan. The homes had been originally sold with a stipulation limiting their use to residences only. But this soon expired and "different houses formerly occupied as dwellings [were] remodelled into stores, so that the business of dry goods, meats, groceries, drugs, etc. is no longer centralized in the Arcade and Market Hall. [8] By 1915, Pullman contained fifteen saloons, including one located in the Market Hall. Already suffering from the loss of middle-class customers, the older merchants were now hard pressed by competition from improvised establishments and an increasing tendency to shop in Roseland. By 1918, a third of the Arcade stores were vacant and the remainder received substantial rent reductions.

Dr. John McLean's autobiography vividly describes the changes in his former home. The residence, as it faced the main gate on 111th Street, had been used as a clinic. For this reason, McLean did not leave the town with his friends but bought the building in 1907, remaining until his retirement in 1914. Then he sold the home and moved to Hyde Park. Returning for a visit a few years later he found what had formerly been his front lawn, "bright and cheerful with growing flowers," [9] now occupied by a wooden store. A "thrifty Italian" sold sandwiches "to the men as they entered and left through the big gate." For want of customers the Arcade—"built to last"— was used by the company for office space after 1922 and demol-

ished in 1926. The "thrifty Italian['s]" store, at present writing a
brick extension run into the face of the original structure, still is
open for business.

A prominent Chicago minister active in the social gospel and settlement house movements, Graham Taylor, visited Pullman in 1915
in search of material for his book *Satellite Cities*. "A Saturday afternoon stroll show[ed] many a householder working to improve his
own dwelling." Residents fixed their homes to suit themselves.
Porches, shutters, and garages were added to Beman's work, and
the original brick was sometimes covered with paint. Taylor found
the buildings previously maintained by the company at a uniformly
high rate, now varied in appearance and repair, while the "old
lawns which made each street beautiful in the old days are kept up
or not, as the present owners happen to elect, and often adjoining
premises show a glaring contrast." [10]

The tenements in particular had badly deteriorated. While interiors were adequately maintained, their lawns were merely "hard,
bare ground." But the worst problem was overcrowding. The tenements were now almost exclusively occupied by the newer immigrants. One couple with eight children took in several boarders, all
sharing a two-room flat. A common complaint was that eight or ten
men would occupy a single, small apartment with no consideration
for the necessities of housekeeping. Even some of the new homes
had been cut up to accommodate more families than originally intended. Community leaders decided to develop some form of self-
discipline to replace the former control from above.

In 1908, a Pullman Homeowners Association was founded to restore the town's "original quality." Its first action was a petition of
ten thousand names demanding that the Illinois Central grade its
tracks.[11] The railroad would not comply for five years until a series
of fatal accidents occurred and it was forced by the passage of a
city-wide ordinance.[12] The community was more successful on another issue. The Board of Education acquired a site for a new school
building, and announced it would be named the Henry George. Led
by the *Calumet Record*, a local paper, citizens demanded the future school be called the George M. Pullman school. The Board's

president gave in, explaining that, after all, the single taxer was only a thinker, while the businessman as a doer was clearly the greater person. [13] The public school, when built in 1913, was hailed by Graham Taylor as a splendid example of how the people through government could provide for themselves, but the Chicago architect Irving Pond dismissed the new building as a "barn" compared to Barrett's old structure.[14]

By 1920, a fourth of all residential buildings in Pullman were owner-occupied, and ten years later this had increased to half. Despite home ownership, the community continued to decline. Its population fell 20 per cent from 1910 to 1930. Losing their library, theater, shopping center, and social organizations, the residents were forced to go elsewhere for the amenities of urban life. After a few ineffectual years, the Pullman Homeowners Association ceased functioning, and no group took its place. The original residents, except in some of the private homes, were almost completely replaced by newcomers seeking the cheaper rents of Pullman. Instead of the social reformer come to study a model experiment, the social worker visited to report on tenement house conditions. Unaided by the company, the community was powerless to resist these changes, and Pullman, fading into obscurity, became just another industrial neighborhood.

One change which even George M. Pullman would have been unable to prevent was Chicago's engulfing the town. An Englishman visiting the fair in 1893 had been surprised to find the city's south side nothing more than little villages surrounded by prairie and farm. The streetcar eventually transformed these suburban towns into a city settlement. Car lines were first laid on a north-south axis from 1892 to 1898, and then for the next ten years east to west. Unlike the train, which stopped only at stations miles apart, the "trolley" handled passengers by the block. This more flexible transportation system permitted widespread settlement, and the former cluster of homes about the railroad station now began to spread and merge. The towns were drawn closer to each other and to the city's center, while population and shopping shifted.

Roseland's Michigan Avenue became the local center of streetcar transportation. At its intersections passengers transferred to lines going in another direction, and the street was now the area's major shopping thoroughfare. By 1910, Roseland's three banks included a branch of the Pullman Bank,[15] and the community had a "splendid movie palace." With newer homes and more services, and at a distance from industry, the old Dutch settlement soon surpassed Kensington and Pullman in importance. By 1910 its population had risen to 20,901, while Kensington's was only 6,328. A community whose very ordinariness had caused it to be ignored dominated "bumtown" and the former "model town."

Ironically, the same streetcars that changed the map of Chicago and accelerated Pullman's decline were made in the company's shops. In 1886, the company had added a streetcar division under the direction of Charles Pullman, younger brother of George. By 1900, it was the country's largest producer of "intra-urbans," and in 1907, the shop turned out the first of the famous "Red Rockets," the prototype of all later cars. In many ways the streetcar's role in urbanization paralleled the transcontinental's importance in western settlement, with the company's contributions in both areas equally significant.

By 1908, Roseland had expanded eastward to Indiana Avenue and in time would have covered all the remaining prairie to the I.C. tracks, but inadvertently George Pullman's "cordon sanitaire" between his town and the other was perpetuated. In 1908, Chicago and the Pullman Free School of Manual Training both acquired adjoining forty-acre tracts on Indiana, between Roseland and Pullman, one for a campus, the other for use as a park. This coming of a municipal park was a significant sign of the area's loss of rusticity.

The Pullman Land Association, excluded from the court decision of 1898, was not obligated to sell its vast holdings. To take advantage of interest in land along Michigan Avenue, however, it began placing tracts on the market in 1903. By 1915, it had disposed of six hundred acres but still retained another 2,500, being the city's biggest owner of contiguous vacant land. This was probably not by choice since after 1900 the overbuilding of the previous decade led to depressed land prices.

What construction took place before World War I was principally southwest of Roseland where International Harvester had recently built a plant. In Pullman's vicinity, only a few buildings were erected north and west of the town. These were usually two- and three-family brick "bungalows," a type of urban dwelling which gained favor after 1900. Graham Taylor, commenting on these new residential subdivisions and their "haphazard growth," complained that the builders and realtors had "focused on the profits to be derived out of given plots rather than upon the development of the whole area in accordance with modern scientific planning." [16]

Although the shop's work force rose to 15,000 in 1913 and exceeded 20,000 in the next decade, Pullman's population continued to decline from 7,931 in 1910 to 7,451 in 1920 and finally 6,404 by 1930. By then few single men boarded in the community and many of the families preferred to pay the much higher rent of nearby areas. Deprived of the company's assistance and lacking a middle class, the community no longer could afford the "superior facilities" with which it had been originally endowed. The Casino became a laundry, while the top floor of the Market Hall was used for professional wrestling matches and then stood vacant until destroyed by fire in 1931. The Greenstone Church's congregation could not properly maintain the building and broken stained glass was replaced by clear glass and eventually by cardboard. Even the Pullman Bank finally left the community in 1927 for new quarters in Roseland.

In 1926, Edith Abbott, dean of the University of Chicago's School of Social Service Administration, directed a young student, Mary Adams, to study Pullman and two other South Side industrial neighborhoods: South Chicago and Deering. Miss Adams found that the problems noted earlier by Graham Taylor had worsened. The model housing was nearly fifty years old and ancient by Midwest standards. Unlike Roseland, Pullman lacked a balanced variety of building ages necessary to encourage new home construction. Built at one time, Pullman had also aged at one time.

Private homes were usually well maintained, Miss Adams reported in 1926, with many renovated for modern facilities. "The front yards . . . are adorned with shrubs and plants more often than not. The vista presents an aspect of substantially built, but not pretentious, buildings." The tenements, however, lacking bathtubs and electricity and with hall toilets and sinks, were far below contemporary standards. Front yards and alleys were strewn with trash, while rear windows directly overlooked the car yards. A "fretwork of iron fire escapes which scars [their] face" had been added to comply with a new ordinance. After school and on weekends, children congregated on wooden steps leading to dark hallways. "The dreary aspect, then, corresponds to one's concept of an old-fashioned orphanage." [17]

Still, Pullman was superior to the other two neighborhoods. With their excellent brick construction, even the tenements offered "better shelter" than the newer but jerry-built "smoke-dyed frame houses of the South Chicago area near the mills." Miss Adams concluded: "Mistaken as Mr. Pullman was in his idea of company ownership, he yet rendered service to his employees when he built for them homes worthy of the name."

The physical contrast between the privately owned row homes and the rented tenements extended to other areas. Home owners were almost always Americans or older immigrants of north European stock while the families renting in the tenements were usually recent arrivals from southern and eastern Europe. This social stratification of the community aroused concern, as did a tendency toward the creation of ethnic enclaves which was noticeable by 1926.[18] Pullman, however, never really developed ghettoes. The outbreak of World War I and the National Origins Acts of the 1920's ended the flood of immigrants. By 1930, for the first time, a majority of residents were American-born, though usually first generation. This permitted a greater community stability and eased the differences between nationalities. More and more of the newcomers and particularly their children left the tenements to purchase row homes.

The years 1924 to 1930 were ones of general affluence. Wage increases steadily outpaced rises in the cost of living. The real estate market quickened and home construction jumped. The area west of

Pullman, between the I.C. tracks and the municipal park, saw new and relatively expensive homes go up until an unimproved lot became a rarity. In North Pullman, about forty homes were built just east of the tracks. Only north of 103rd Street did sizable vacant land remain, and this was reserved for industrial growth when in 1923, following New York's lead, Chicago adopted zoning.

Within Pullman's residential areas, zoning simply affirmed the reality of land use imposed by Barrett and Beman in 1880.[19] Pullman ceased to be an independent postal drop in 1910, and most of the streets were renamed in 1919. Fulton, now called Langley, was zoned for apartment buildings, and streets containing row homes were set aside for family residence. This barrier to further industrial encroachment may have saved the homes from near total destruction. Land values in Pullman increased by between one-third and one-half from 1915 to 1925 but were still considerably lower than industrial property, and the companies were exhausting vacant land for expansion.

By 1930, the community, at the brink of the nation's worst depression, was a run-down, lower-working-class neighborhood pocketed with blight. The once controversial rents of Pullman were now well below the surrounding area. The median was less than a third of Roseland's, while median home value was $3,910 as compared to $9,722 in Roseland.[20]

Prosperity in the twenties made the movie theater ubiquitous and introduced the radio, first as a luxury and status symbol and then as a household necessity. Yet, at the decade's end, Pullman still lacked a movie house, while only half its residents owned radios.[21] By 1930, it had demonstrably changed to a deprived neighborhood. In 1880, George Pullman built a model town to escape the city slums and to show that American workers could afford the best. A half-century later his model community was part of the city and fast showing signs of a slum, while its residents lacked necessities that progress had given their neighbors.

From 1920 to 1930, home ownership in Pullman doubled, reaching 50 per cent of all buildings. Although considerably higher than surrounding areas, this by itself could not restore the community to health.[22] As was expected, people maintained and improved their own homes. But home ownership of the row houses could not deter the deterioration of the tenements or alter the loss of public facilities. These problems, plus the unpleasant proximity of industry, threatened the community. By 1926, owners wanting to sell and move elsewhere were unable to get a fair price. Some complained that they had lost mobility and were dependent on jobs in the vicinity though more lucrative employment could be found elsewhere,[23] which makes one aware that George Pullman would have been vulnerable to grave charges if his original plan had included home ownership.

But after 1894, most Americans agreed that a major flaw in Pullman's plan was the very exclusion of home ownership. To many, widespread residential holdings was a panacea for all community ills. Graham Taylor, who first visited Pullman in 1885, sadly noted in 1915 its "forlorn air of faded glory." Nevertheless, he had a firm belief in the "instinctive righteousness and good judgment of the 'plain folks,'" assuming hopefully that the community, owned and governed by its residents, would experience a renaissance.[24] Twenty years after the town's sale by the company this had not occurred. Subjected to industrial change and social transformation, the people of Pullman did not develop effective self-help.

Conclusion

To George Pullman, stable communities could be achieved by planning. His model town was built to reinforce virtues of self-help and personal discipline such as industry, frugality, and cleanliness, which he perceived as threatened by the impact of industrialization and immigration on the cities. A harmonious community of contented workingmen living in comfortable housing amidst rural surroundings and enjoying superior facilities would be created not through philanthropy or utopian ideas but by practical recognition of interlocking self-interest rationally organized along a business philosophy of order and efficiency.

The town of Pullman offered a unique opportunity for comprehensive planning of factory and homes. Artists and engineers collaborated with a businessman to demonstrate that the utilitarian and the aesthetic could be combined to benefit all and satisfy everyone. The community was expected to encourage workers to remain in one place while fostering advancement and improvement within the company. This desired stability was not achieved. Pullman, built upon a business philosophy of success, was intended to epitomize American get-up-and-go initiative, and it is not surprising, therefore, that many who came here to earn a livelihood left when opportunities seemed better elsewhere By the end of the nineteenth century, Americans knew full well that attachment to community must be subordinated to the advantages of mobility. But the community also had problems peculiarly its own.

The model town was an experiment in transferring business experience and technology to a community. Yet these proved less successful when applied to social control than they had been when solving the technical problems of production and distribution. The difficulty of imposing an impersonal system was clearly revealed in the homes and workshops of Pullman. Rules intended to insure control from above and provide equity at the bottom wound worker, resident, and company officer in red tape. Decisions made at all levels of authority often resulted in injustices which only strengthened the impression of a ubiquitous company and made inhabitants and employees rankle at its arbitrariness. No clearly defined manner of expressing and resolving industrial or community grievances existed, so that they tended to overlap and fester. As an early experiment in what the twentieth century would call social engineering, the model town of Pullman was a disappointment. It was not only unable to resolve existing social problems but indeed engendered new ones.

Contemporaries variously interpreted the Pullman experience but all agreed that it should not be repeated. To businessmen, it illustrated the folly of assuming responsibility for a community's welfare and especially one accessible to general scrutiny. Any incident suggesting company interference in the personal lives or private politics of the inhabitants had been quickly reported by the nearby urban press. Public opinion, already uneasy over growing corporate power, became increasingly displeased with business ownership of the town after 1894. Other industrialists were well aware that Pullman's experiment had limited his freedom and proved a general liability. Few company-owned and -managed towns ever again were placed in proximity to large cities.

For over a decade the model town had been generally hailed as showing that rational ordering of a community could achieve high standards and meet social needs. When events underscored Pullman's shortcomings, they were assumed to be the consequence of paternalism rather than planning. While the impressive physical appearance and organization of Pullman were credited to "scientific planning," all of its flaws were attributed to George Pullman's imposition of his tastes and self-interest on the town. This was partly due to Pullman's own insistence that his system had succeeded and partly due to the fact that most critics wanted to believe that it was possible through rational forethought to improve upon the normal community's casual growth.

To urban reformers, the experiment seemed to indicate that planning would work only when combined with self-government. Jane Addams, Richard Ely, and Graham Taylor feared the concentration of community power in a company, but believed government could enlist the voluntary support of all groups to meet social problems effectively through democratically originated planning. George Pullman's own conviction that the interests of business and community were identical and that the businessman was competent to determine both was refuted by his town's experience. Many instead assumed that professional planners could devise standards of order and beauty acceptable to all. As Taylor noted in his foreword to *Satellite Cities:* "The main thing to be desired is the cooperation of public officials, working people, and enlightened citizens to secure better living and truer democracy," [1] and this was to be done through "applying . . . the new science of town building."

Clearly the model town of Pullman is of little practical interest to modern city planners. The arrangement of residential and industrial sections offered neither direction for growth nor flexibility for change and was little more than a blueprint for instant town building along the normative values of the time. Yet, its significance for the American planning tradition is considerable. Until George Pullman built his community, town planning was little more than the laying out of streets and platting of lots. As a consequence of growing concern with urban problems, it soon entered a more ambitious phase. Pullman's theme that municipal beauty and efficiency were complementary and should be made paramount through forethought was given brilliant setting by architects and landscape designers who collaborated under Daniel Burnham to plan the Columbian Exposition of 1893.

The order and utility of the "white city" strikingly contrasted with the sprawling chaos of the unplanned city and captured the public imagination as an urban ideal. Movements for municipal reform, already well developed, soon espoused urban planning as a necessary concomitant of the industrial city. For the next several decades a city beautiful movement scored considerable success as municipalities vied for self-improvement through enhancing parks and boulevards and constructing civic centers. By 1909, Daniel Burnham, under the auspices of the Chicago Commercial Club, had prepared the first comprehensive plan for an American city of regional scope.

Though with a different and broader context, Burnham's famous Chicago plan bears strong resemblance to George Pullman's ideas for his model town. The planner and the industrialist both asserted that "good order is essential to material advancement" [2] and sought "well ordered, convenient and unified" communities. Burnham's success in selling his proposals to the city's businessmen rested in part upon his emphasis on planning as an instrument of social control and industrial economy.

The Chicago plan assumed that cities would continue to expand indefinitely; George Pullman, however, hoped that planned industrial towns offered an alternative to urban growth. Part of his model town's charm and appeal rested on the sight of industry located in a community whose scale suggested the familiar and manageable size of the New England small town. Somehow it also seemed more reasonable and natural to contemporaries that workers were being trained in the old ethics of industry and frugality amidst a background of flowers and greenery. Without question, Pullman was eager to show that industrialization, which he and others considered a beneficial development, was not necessarily married to urbanization, viewed as disruptive to health and morals. Though his experiment failed, it was the forerunner of the later garden city movement and other efforts to resettle men and industry in planned communities away from the cities.

Historians have only recently realized that the nineteenth-century businessman was not always an enemy of reform. Instead, the formerly perceived antithesis is now being emended by more sophisticated exploration of the relations between the two. The model town of Pullman, with its use of an industrial system for purposes of social experimentation, suggests that modern America's search for control and order through city and regional planning may have been derived in part from the early activity of the business community in its quest for industrial efficiency.

Note on Sources

Pullman Incorporated—the successor company to Pullman's Palace Car Company and the later Pullman Company—has given the Newberry Library of Chicago the following scrapbooks, primarily consisting of newspaper and periodical clippings:

I. Scrapbooks, Miscellaneous
   Series A, Vols. 1-34 (1865-1925)
   Series B, Vols. 1-9 (1883-1924)
   Series C, Vols. 1-2 (1896-1908)
II. Scrapbooks, Strike, Vols. 1-11 (Jan. 1894—Aug. 1897)
III. Scrapbooks, General Superintendent's Office, Vols. 1-12 (1882-1908)
IV. Scrapbook, Company in Europe, 1873-78

Presently in the custody of the Newberry are records, correspondence, and other material of George M. Pullman, of the executors of his will, and of the Pullman Palace Car Company and several of its affiliates. Subsequent to completing this study, the author has catalogued this material. The diaries of Mrs. George M. Pullman, and the correspondence with her husband are in the possession of Dr. and Mrs. C. Phillip Miller.

Those interested in a bibliography, and a fuller documentation than deemed suitable here, are referred to my doctoral dissertation done for the Department of History, University of Chicago, and on deposit in Harper Library.

Notes

CHAPTER 1

1. "In Memoriam: James Lewis Pullman" [1893].
2. J. Seymour Currey, *Chicago: Its History and Its Builders* (Chicago: S. J. Clarke and Co., 1912), III, 7.
3. *Chicago Journal,* October 19, 1892.
4. Stewart H. Holbrook, *The Story of American Railroads* (New York: Crown Publishers, 1947), p. 317.
5. Quoted in Lucius Beebe, *Mr. Pullman's Elegant Palace Car* (Garden City, N. Y.: Doubleday and Co., 1961), p. 73.
6. Joseph Husband, *The Story of the Pullman Car* (Chicago: A. C. McClurg and Co., 1917), pp. 28-9.
7. *Chicago Railway Review,* May 21, 1868.
8. On September 19, 1865, U. S. Patent No. 49,992 was given to Pullman and Benjamin Field for the hinged chair and upper berth.
9. Frederick F. Cook, *Bygone Days in Chicago* (Chicago: A. C. McClurg and Co., 1910), p. 285.
10. A. T. Andreas, *History of Chicago from the Earliest Period to the Present Time* (Chicago: A. T. Andreas Co., 1886), II, 625.
11. Cook, p. 257.
12. *St. Louis Dispatch,* May 26, 1865; *Daily Missouri Democrat,* June 6, 1865.
13. *Western Railroad Gazette,* April 20, 1867.
14. Letter to George M. Pullman, April 27, 1866. Pullman Company Scrapbooks, Miscl., Series A, Newberry Library.
15. A statement made April 26, 1867, and quoted in a memorandum

in Pullman Company Scrapbooks, Miscl., Series A, Newberry Library.

16. *Boston Sunday Herald,* January 15, 1882.

17. *Portland Evening Star* (Oregon), June 11, 1868. In 1870, Kimball and Ramsey were bought out and the company was known as the Pullman Southern Palace Car Company until its absorption in the late 1890's by the parent company which had always controlled it.

CHAPTER 2

1. The other four members of the board were: H. E. Sargent, General Superintendent of the Michigan Central; Robert Harris, General Superintendent of the Chicago, Burlington and Quincy; John Crerar; and Norman Williams, Jr. (*Chicago Railway Review,* May 21, 1868). Mr. Pullman was thought to have a controlling interest in the company (*Springfield Republican,* June 7, 1869).

2. Andrew Carnegie, *Autobiography of Andrew Carnegie* (Boston: Houghton-Mifflin Co., 1920), pp. 159-61. Carnegie served on the board of directors of the Pullman Pacific Car Company until 1873, when he found it necessary to sell this company's stock to protect his steel interests.

3. *Railway Age* (Chicago), July 3, 1879.

4. *Louisville* (Kentucky) *Medical News,* July 19, 1879.

5. *Elmira* (New York) *Daily Gazette,* May 10, 1873. This organization was retained until after 1900.

6. Carnegie, *Autobiography,* p. 162.

7. *National Car Builder,* January 1875.

8. *Chicago Times,* October 12, 1875; *The New York Times,* October 15, 1875; *Railway Age,* October 16, 1875; *Chicago Tribune,* October 23, 1875.

9. *Chicago Tribune,* February 22, 1880.

10. *Chicago Evening Post,* August 12, 1869.

11. Twelve issues of *The Transcontinental* appeared, and these can be found in the Rare Book Room of the New York Public Library.

12. "Annual Report of the Company," *New York Commercial and Financial Chronicles,* September 27, 1879.

13. *Aurora* (Illinois) *Herald,* January 30, 1880; *Chicago Times,* February 22, 1880.

14. Frederick F. Cook, *By Gone Days in Chicago* (Chicago: A. C. McClurg and Co., 1910), p. 261.

15. John McLean, *One Hundred Years in Illinois, 1818-1918* (Chicago: Peterson Linotyping Co., 1919), p. 229.

CHAPTER 3

1. Arthur Meeker, *Chicago with Love* (New York: Alfred A. Knopf, 1955), p. 34.

2. Senator Sterling Morton to George M. Pullman, January 22, 1879. Morton, a Democrat from Nebraska and best remembered as the sponsor of Arbor Day, became a lobbyist for railroad interests after leaving the Senate.

3. Horace Porter to George M. Pullman, May 26, 1872, and August 24, 1877. Pullman Collection, Chicago Historical Society. Porter became vice-president in charge of the P.P.C.C.'s New York office at $10,000 a year.

4. For the activities of the P.P.C.C. in Europe, see George Behrend, *Pullman in Europe* (London: Ian Allen and Co., 1962).

5. John Jacob Blessner, *Should Auld Acquaintance Be Forgot* (Chicago: privately printed, 1924), p. 19.

6. Bessie L. Pierce, ed., *As Others See Chicago* (Chicago: University of Chicago Press, 1933), p. 271.

7. Ernest Poole, *Giants Gone: Men Who Made Chicago* (New York: McGraw-Hill, 1943), p. 271. Also see pp. 199-200.

8. *National Car Builder,* February 1872.

9. *Cincinnati Enquirer,* June 28, 1882.

10. The *New York Morning Journal* gave Pullman's wealth as $4,000,-000 in 1886 and placed him sixty-fifth on a list of America's two hundred wealthiest men (April 25, 1886).

11. *Chicago Department of Health Report,* 1881-82.

12. Ibid.

CHAPTER 4

1. William H. Osborn to William Ackerman, May 31, 1882. Illinois Central Archives, Newberry Library.

2. A. T. Andreas, *History of Chicago from the Earliest Period to the Present Time* (Chicago: A. T. Andreas Co., 1886), III, 230.

3. Budgett Meakin, *Model Factories and Villages* (London: T. Fisher Unwin, 1905), pp. 41-64.

4. William Ackerman to the Rev. R. Clark, November 25, 1882. Illinois Central Archives, Newberry Library.

5. *New York Sun,* December 9, 1883.

6. Alfred T. White, *Improved Dwellings for the Laboring Classes: The Need, and the Way to Meet It on Strict Commercial Principles, in New York and Other Cities* (New York: G. P. Putnam's Sons, 1879), pp. 16-17.

7. Ibid., p. 20.

8. Roy Lubove, *The Progressives and the Slums: Tenement House Reform in New York City, 1890-1917* (Pittsburgh: University of Pittsburgh Press, 1962), p. 37.

9. Pullman's model town was the subject of frequent articles. The most informative of the early reports are: Anonymous, "A Chicago Notion: Ideals Realized in the New Town of Pullman," *Boston Herald,* August 1, 1881 (copies of this article were mailed to

company stockholders in September 1881); *New York Sun,* December 9, 1883; Helen Starrett, "Pullman—A Social and Industrial Study," *Weekly Magazine,* September 16, 1882.

10. Pullman's testimony, *United States Strike Commission's Report on the Chicago Strike of June-July, 1894,* Senate Executive Document No. 7, 53d Congress, 3d Session (Washington, D. C.: Government Printing Office, 1895), p. 529. This document will hereafter be cited as *Strike Rep.*

11. *New York Sun,* December 9, 1883.

12. Lewis Mumford, *The City in History* (New York: Harcourt, Brace and World, 1961), p. 454.

13. Bessie L. Pierce, ed., *As Others See Chicago* (Chicago: University of Chicago Press, 1933), p. 266.

14. *New York World,* December 25, 1892.

15. *Hour Week Journal of New York,* August 5, 1882.

CHAPTER 5

1. Henry Demarest Lloyd, "Pullman" (Har.-H.D.L.), p. 1. In November, 1881, Lloyd wrote an article on the model town. A revised version of this article was accepted by *Harper's Magazine* in 1882, which sent him the galley proofs some time in 1884. Lloyd found the articles greatly enlarged. Indignant, he refused permission for publication and marked the article to indicate his writing. Both the article written in November 1881 and the galley sheets are in Wisconsin Historical Society, Lloyd Papers, Box 36. The former will henceforth be cited as Lloyd, "Pullman," while the latter will be referred to as Lloyd, "Pullman" (Har.-H.D.L.), or Lloyd, "Pullman" (Har.-ed.), depending on whether Lloyd or the unknown editor composed the section referred to.

2. *Private Laws of the State of Illinois by the Twenty-fifth General Assembly* (1867), II, 337.

3. Records of Pullman Land Association in the collection of P.P.C.C. material in the custody of the Newberry Library. See Note on Sources.

4. Diary of Mrs. George M. Pullman, September 16, 1897.

5. J. Farrell to George M. Pullman, June 8, 1880. Pullman Papers, Chicago Historical Society.

6. Irving K. Pond, "Pullman—America's First Planned Industrial Town," *Illinois Society of Architects Monthly Bulletin,* June-July, 1934, p. 7.

7. Ibid., p. 6.

8. *Railway Review,* December 23, 1881.

9. *Chicago Times,* October 23, 1881.

10. *Chicago Times,* July 26, 1886.

11. Lloyd "Pullman" (Har.-ed.), p. 1.

12. Letter of August 17, 1881.

13. *Industrial World,* September 22, 1881.
14. Ibid.
15. For a fuller description of the use of rails in car production, see *Ottawa Daily Press,* September 9, 1882: "In building a car as the work progresses it is passed from one shop to another until it is ready for the road." It is interesting to consider whether this early example of moving a product to the worker influenced the later development of the assembly-line technique.
16. Bessie L. Pierce, ed., *As Others See Chicago* (Chicago: University of Chicago Press, 1933), p. 264.
17. *Strike Rep.,* p. 500.

CHAPTER 6

1. *Chicago Tribune,* April 12, 1883.
2. Bessie L. Pierce, ed., *As Others See Chicago* (Chicago: University of Chicago Press, 1933), p. 270.
3. *St. Louis Spectator,* September 30, 1882. Another interesting description of the journey from Chicago to Pullman is in the *Boston Herald,* August 1, 1881.
4. *Chicago Inter Ocean,* December 27, 1881; *Strike Rep.,* p. 534.
5. T. C. Crawford, "Pullman Company and Its Striking Workmen," *Harper's Weekly,* XXXVIII (July 22, 1894), 687.
6. Charles H. Eaton, "Pullman and Paternalism," *American Journal of Politics,* V (1894), 575. A Methodist minister, Eaton was a friend of George Pullman and received his assistance in writing the article, which was a defense of the company at the time of the strike of 1894. A manuscript differing somewhat from the published article is in the possession of Mrs. C. Philip Miller. As Eaton had a rare opportunity to examine company records, it contains much valuable material. When Eaton's manuscript, rather than the article, is referred to, it will henceforth be cited: Eaton (MS.). Eaton also testified before the U. S. Strike Commission, see pp. 526-8 of *Strike Rep.*
7. *Chicago Inter Ocean,* November 25, 1882.
8. *Report to the State of Illinois on the Status of the Town of Pullman,* 1885, p. 44. Duane Doty, a former superintendent of Chicago schools, assisted Beman in designing the school building.
9. Quoted in William T. Stead, *If Christ Came to Chicago!* (Chicago: Laird and Lee, 1894), p. 89.
10. Daniel H. Burnham and E. H. Bennett, *Plan of Chicago* (Chicago: The Commercial Club, 1909), p. 44.
11. According to the Reverend Eaton, land west of the I.C. tracks was leased to the two churches "without compensation for ninety-nine years." Eaton (MS.), n. p.
12. Eaton (MS.), n. p.
13. *Boston Herald,* September 1, 1881.

14. Part of this land, though owned by the Pullman Land Company rather than the P.P.C.C., was managed by the company indistinguishably from its own holdings.

15. *Chicago Inter Ocean,* September 6, 1888.

16. Richard T. Ely, *Ground Under Our Feet: An Autobiography* (New York: Macmillan Co., 1938), p. 168.

17. *Pall Mall Budget* (London), April 6, 1883.

18. George M. Pullman to S. S. Beman, June 13, 1892. This letter is in the possession of Mrs. Spencer S. Beman of Winnetka, Illinois, the architect's daughter-in-law. Beman was to receive payment in addition to the retainer fee for "strictly architectural building work."

19. Irving K. Pond, "Pullman—America's First Planned Industrial Town," *Illinois Society of Architects Monthly Bulletin,* June-July, 1934, p. 7. A recent study has asserted that "Queen Ann" was not a true style, but merely a catch-all term used indiscriminately by nineteenth-century writers. Sadayoshi Omoto, "The Queen Ann Style and Architectural Criticism," *Journal of the Society of Architectural Historians,* XXIII (March 1964), 29-37.

CHAPTER 7

1. Richard T. Ely, "Pullman: A Social Study" *Harper's Monthly,* LXX (1885), p. 459.

2. *Chicago Herald,* February 21, 1886.

3. *Strike Rep.,* p. 463.

4. Quoted in *Report of Commissioners of the State Bureaus of Labor Statistics of the Industrial, Social and Economic Conditions of Pullman, Illinois* (1884), p. 13. This work will henceforth be cited *Report . . . State Bureaus of Labor Statistics.*

5. E. R. L. Gould, *Eighth Special Report of the Commissioner of Labor. The Housing of the Working People* (Washington, D. C.: Government Printing Office, 1895), p. 332. This work will henceforth be cited as *Eighth Special Report.*

6. Duane Doty to George M. Pullman, September 22, 1890. This letter and other company records are presently in the custody of the Newberry Library.

7. *Eighth Special Report,* p. 432.

8. *Boston Herald,* August 1, 1881.

9. Pierce, *As Others See Chicago,* p. 272.

10. *The Story of Pullman* (Chicago, 1893), pp. 29-30. Also, Mrs. Duane Doty, *The Town of Pullman* (Pullman, Ill.: T. P. Struhsacker, 1893), p. 35.

11. During the strike of 1894 it was charged by the workers that the company's policy was to lay off first those who lived outside Pullman, but available evidence contradicts this. See p. 247, n. 27.

12. *Strike Rep.* pp. 516-17.

13. *Strike Rep.*, p. 506; *Eighth Special Report*, p. 331. The tables in *Strike Rep.*, pp. 506-7, give a total of 1,799 dwelling units; 20 boarding houses and 43 homes at the brickyard have been subtracted from this total in the following computations based on these tables. See Table 3, p. 90.

14. *Eighth Special Report*, pp. 330-32.

15. The average monthly rental per room in Pullman was $3.30 as compared to $2.86 per room in the manufacturing towns of Massachusetts. *Report . . . State Bureaus of Labor Statistics*, p. 11. The company pointed out that for tenements the average was only $2.50. On the other hand, for the single-family house studied in *Eighth Special Report*, the cost per room was $3.60, and in other single-family dwellings, it was higher.

16. *Strike Rep.*, pp. 531-3, where a copy of the lease may be found. The lease held the tenant responsible for observing all rules established by the company, and these were posted in the town agent's office.

17. Eaton (MS.), n. p.

18. Almont Lindsey, *The Pullman Strike* (Chicago: University of Chicago Press, 1942), p. 69.

19. *Strike Rep.*, p. 530.

CHAPTER 8

1. *Chicago Tribune*, April 12, 1883.

2. *New York Sun*, December 9, 1883.

3. Ibid.

4. *Progressive Age* (Philadelphia), February 12, 1882. This newspaper's description of the town was filled with inaccuracies. It erroneously asserted that the company owned and operated all stores and had sold the homes to the workers so as to anchor them to the town and render them defenseless before exploitation. The editor of the *Arbeiter Zeitung* not only criticized the town in his paper but on at least one occasion denounced it at a public meeting. *Chicago Times*, February 16, 1882.

5. Henry Demarest Lloyd, "The Housing of the People." Unpublished article in the Henry Demarest Lloyd Papers, Box 38, Wisconsin Historical Society. This article is an interesting exposition of anti-urban sentiment by an important figure in the American reform movement of the times. He wrote of the "hideous protuberances into the air of our great business buildings and apartment houses." Lloyd wanted to see a decentralization of population and small cities situated in parks.

6. *Report . . . State Bureaus of Labor Statistics*, p. 22.

7. Richard T. Ely, "Pullman: A Social Study," *Harper's Monthly*, LXX (1885), 452-66.

8. Lloyd, "Pullman" (Har.-H.D.L.), p. 11.

9. Handwritten note at the top of the first page of galley sheets, dated July 28, 1884. Henry Demarest Lloyd Articles, Box 38, Wisconsin Historical Society. In her biography, Lloyd's sister claimed that Alden wanted Lloyd to make "more laudatory mention of Mr. Pullman" and when he declined, *Harper's* refused to publish it. Cara Lloyd, *Lloyd*, I, 144. Not only is this contradicted by the note on the galley sheet, but the article published by *Harper's* and written by Ely was critical of the town.

10. Stewart L. Woodford to Andrew D. White, January 16, 1883, Andrew D. White Papers, John M. Olin Library, Cornell University.

11. Andrew D. White, *Autobiography of Andrew D. White* (New York: Century Company, 1917), II, 378-9.

12. Stewart L. Woodford to Andrew D. White, March 28, 1884. Richard T. Ely to Andrew D. White, May 28, 1884. On July 3, 1884, George Pullman wrote to White, declining to visit Ithaca.

13. Walter E. Barrows to Richard T. Ely, March 8, 1885. Richard T. Ely Correspondence, Box 1, Wisconsin Historical Society.

14. Henry W. Alden to Richard T. Ely, October 14, 1884. Richard T. Ely Correspondence, Box 1, Wisconsin Historical Society.

15. Ely, *Autobiography*, p. 168.

16. Walter E. Barrows to Richard T. Ely, March 8, 1885. Barrows resigned from the Palace Car Company in December 1884, "because I would not sink myself or be melted up and run into [George Pullman's] mould."

17. Charles Dudley Warner, "Chicago," *Harper's Magazine,* LXXVII (June 1888), 127.

CHAPTER 9

1. *St. Louis Globe Democrat,* September 6, 1881.

2. Richard T. Ely, "Pullman: A Social Study," *Harper's Monthly,* LXX (1885), p. 461. The following company officials were officers of the township: William Berry (Trustee, 1881-83); Edward Henrick (village clerk, 1882-85; treasurer, 1885-86); E. T. Martin (treasurer, 1886-88); Joseph Wood (Trustee, 1888-89). Other men, in one way or another connected with the company, had important positions in Hyde Park government. James Bowen, who had handled real estate transactions for George Pullman, was a trustee until his death in 1881. William W. Stewart, a counsel for the company, was the township's prosecuting attorney, 1881-82. H. R. Hobart, the manager of the important trade publication, *Railway Age,* was president of the Board of Trustees, 1881-82. George Pullman at one time had rescued *Railway Age* from financial disaster through a large loan (letter from E. W. Talbot to G. W. Angell, June 25, 1877, Pullman Collection, Chicago Historical Society), and in 1884 he "donated material for a private car" to Hobart. *St. Louis Railway Register,* July 26, 1884.

3. *Chicago Tribune*, December 3, 1893. For his early life, see John W. Leonard, *The Book of Chicagoans* (Chicago: A. N. Marquis and Co., 1905), p. 295.
4. Hopkins and Secord filed a court suit against the Pullman Palace Car Company in 1891 for violating the rebate agreement. A court of appeals finally found in favor of the company in 1898. *Chicago Tribune*, January 11, 1898.
5. *Chicago Times*, April 21, 1889.
6. Returns in Hyde Park Township on annexation were calculated from precinct voting tabulation published in the *Chicago Tribune*, June 30, 1889. Of the precincts totaled to give the figures for Pullman, 22, 25, 35, and 36 were entirely within the town's boundaries, and 20, 21, and 23 were partly without. The location of several non-Pullman precincts could not be determined, and they were excluded from calculations.
7. George M. Pullman to Harriet Sanger Pullman, February 19, 1883.
8. Ely, *Autobiography*, pp. 169-70.
9. Thomas Burk Grant, "Pullman and Its Lessons," *American Journal of Politics*, V (August, 1894), 194.
10. *Chicago Times*, May 7, 1890.
11. Eaton, "Pullman," pp. 573-4.
12. *Arcade Journal*, June 14, 1890.

CHAPTER 10

1. *Annual Report of the Trustees of Hyde Park, 1884-1885*, p. 94.
2. Eaton, "Pullman," p. 577. Another observer commented on the model town and its neighbors: "A mile or two away [from Pullman] in the west [one] sees Roseland, a straggling village of the old regime, and in the south Kensington, a cluster so devoid of unity of plan as to violate every law of harmony, contrasting these with the order and beauty of Pullman, produces a feeling of unreality." Unidentified clipping (1886). Mrs. George M. Pullman's Scrapbooks, I, 23. Chicago Historical Society.
3. William T. Stead, *If Christ Came to Chicago!* (Chicago: Laird and Lee, 1894), p. 89.
4. "Pullman: A Social Study," *Harper's Monthly*, LXX (1855), p. 459.
5. Estimate based on examination of occupations listed for residents of Kensington and Roseland, in *Hyde Park [Township] Directory*, 1883, 1887, 1889.
6. *St. Louis Railway Register*, November 4, 1882.
7. Eaton, "Pullman," p. 575.
8. Clipping from the *Chicago Inter Ocean* (1885). Mrs. George M. Pullman's Scrapbooks, I, 15. In 1884, there had been 75 pianos and 30,000 volumes in the homes of Pullman. *Report . . . State Bureaus of Labor Statistics*, p. 10.

9. Ely, "Pullman," p. 462. The Chicago *Journal of Commerce* (April 25, 1883) was so impressed with the various means of "inculcating taste" in Pullman that it editorially urged "village improvement societies" to adopt them.

10. Ely, "Pullman," p. 463.

11. In the fiscal year 1885-86, Pullman averaged a $4.80 school tax, as compared to $2.83 for Kensington. Interestingly, second place for all township communities went to Roseland, with $4.16, as compared to $3.60 for the wealthy residential suburb of Kenwood, which was third. *Annual Report of the Trustees of Hyde Park, 1885-86,* p. 45.

12. Percentages derived through an occupational count of the residents and club officers listed in the *Hyde Park [Township] Directories* for 1883 and 1889. Information on club officers in 1889 was supplemented by lists for organizations found in the *Directory* for 1887 but omitted in the later one.

13. Ely, "Pullman," p. 463.

14. *Strike Rep.,* p. xxiii.

CHAPTER 11

1. Charles E. Perkins to T. J. Potter, May 10, 1886. Chicago, Burlington, and Quincy President's Letters, 9:558 B. A. Burlington Archives, Newberry Library.

2. Jane Addams, "A Modern Lear." This paper is printed in its entirety in Graham R. Taylor, *Satellite Cities* (New York: D. Appleton and Co., 1915), the above quote being on page 73, footnote 1.

3. Alfred Lief, *It Floats: The Story of Procter and Gamble* (New York: Rinehart and Company, 1958), p. 59.

4. Ibid., p. 64.

5. Horace Porter, "Railway Passenger Travel," *Scribner's Magazine,* IV (1888), 310.

6. When the Illinois State legislature was considering rate regulation, the company's counsel, A. O. Lochrane, wrote a pamphlet presenting the company argument against such a policy: *An Act to Regulate Fares in Sleeping Cars* (Chicago: C. N. Blakely and Co., 1883). Earlier, James F. Wilson had written, at the company's behest: *Are Sleeping-Car Fares Unreasonable? Are They Subject to State Regulation?* (Davenport, Iowa, 1881). These may be found in the Pullman Palace Car Company Records in the custody of the Newberry Library.

7. House Records 7107; 52nd Congress, 2nd Session. Also, *St. Louis Post Dispatch,* May 19, 1894.

8. *Chicago Tribune* and *Chicago Times,* February 19, 1884.

9. William Carwardine, *The Pullman Strike* (Chicago: Charles H. Kerr and Co., 1894), p. 11. In his testimony before the Strike Commission, George Pullman was asked: "Are you at the town of

Pullman much?" He replied: "Not much; not a great deal. It is impossible for me to spend a great deal of time there because of my duties elsewhere." *Strike Rep.*, p. 538.

10. *Railway Register* (St. Louis), May 16, 1885.

11. *Railway Age* (Chicago), March 25, 1886.

12. *Chicago Tribune*, March 22, 1886.

13. George M. Pullman to Andrew Carnegie, May 5, 1886. Andrew Carnegie Papers, Vol. IX, Folio 1445. Library of Congress.

14. *Chicago Tribune*, October 12, 1888.

15. *Strike Rep.*, p. 487. The company spent an average of $700 yearly on drugs and prescriptions alone. Some of the men complained that McLean always acted in the interests of the company by advising injured workingmen not to sue for compensation, and also writing reports that made it appear that the accidents had been due to personal negligence.

16. Charles E. Perkins to T. J. Potter, May 10, 1886. Chicago Burlington and Quincy President's Letters, 9:558, B. A. Burlington Archives, Newberry Library.

17. "Special Agent Report" with covering letters from Manager Brown and Superintendent E. F. Doran. Pullman Palace Car Company Records in the custody of the Newberry Library.

18. "One just cause of complaint is what in government affairs would be called a bad civil service in respect to the employment, retention and promotion of employees. Change is constant in men and officers, and each new superior appears to have his own friends, whom he appoints to desirable positions." Richard T. Ely, "Pullman: A Social Study," *Harper's Monthly*, LXX (1885), p. 463.

19. *Strike Rep.*, p. 422.

20. See Richard Graham's letter complaining of his superior to George Pullman, February 1, 1887. Pullman Palace Car Company Records in the custody of the Newberry Library. Also, *Chicago Inter Ocean*, [?] 1886. Mrs. George M. Pullman's Scrapbook, I, p. 17. Chicago Historical Society.

CHAPTER 12

1. Anonymous, *The Story of Pullman* (Chicago, 1893). The author was a "visitor" who came to Pullman in the summer of 1893 and stayed at the Hotel Florence. Several other works on the model town were prepared by individuals, such as Mrs. Duane Doty, *The Town of Pullman* (Pullman, Ill.: T. P. Struhsacker, 1893), and by commercial firms for sale to fair-goers.

2. Anonymous, *The Story of Pullman*, p. 6.

3. *The Press* (New York), June 1, 1893. Six months later, Pullman repeated these ideas to a reporter from the *Chicago Tribune*, January 22, 1894.

4. *Strike Rep.*, p. 577.

5. *Strike Rep.*, p. xxxiii.
6. Members of the A.R.U., who had been employed by various rail-roads at the time of the boycott, in their testimony before the Strike Commission frequently complained of ill-treatment by fore-men, e.g. *Strike Rep.*, pp. 110, 112.
7. A list of workers barred from future employment with the company was prepared by Harvey Middleton on December 23, 1893. A copy came into the hands of the strikers who presented it to the Strike Commission. *Strike Rep.*, p. 421.
8. Section thirty-one of the constitution of the American Railway Union, which appears in toto in *Strike Rep.*, pp. 52-7.
9. According to company records, residents owed $180,000 in rent from August 1893 to April 1894, but only paid $110,000 or about 60 per cent of the total. Pullman Palace Car Company Records in the custody of the Newberry Library.
10. Defending this policy, Pullman testified before the Strike Com-mission that the salaries of higher officers were too small a part of the entire cost of car production to warrant cutting, and that he feared losing his better men. When asked about superintendents and foremen involved directly in car manufacture, he replied: "That might [have] come; we [could] not do everything at once." *Strike Rep.*, p. 567.
11. William Carwardine, *The Pullman Strike* (Chicago: Charles H. Kerr and Co., 1894), p. 88.
12. *Strike Rep.*, pp. 417-19.
13. Before the Strike Commission, a union leader said that the men believed the company books doctored, or coded and, therefore, had no desire to see them. Ibid., p. 425. Events occurred so rapidly between the meeting on the ninth and the strike on the eleventh that probably the men made no definite decision concerning the books.
14. Ibid., p. 588.
15. Carwardine, p. 36.
16. *Strike Rep.*, p. 587.
17. Ibid., p. 589; Carwardine, p. 37.
18. *Chicago Record*, May 12, 1894.
19. It presented notarized affidavits by the acting superintendent of the iron department and its foreman to the Strike Commission. Both stated that they had in no way discriminated against the committeemen. Ibid., pp. 587-8.
20. Howard of the A.R.U. testified before the Commissioners that he did not think Wickes or Pullman knew of the committeemen's lay-off, but that the superintendent of the men's department was re-sponsible and had acted because the three men had criticized him in the meeting with Pullman. Ibid., p. 7. Also see Carwardine, p. 36. The union never mentioned the telegram in its statements after the first several days. Newspapers reported that the Western

Union operator denied everything, and it was said that the man who had told the union of his conversation with the operator left town very quickly after the strike.

21. The company presented detailed tables showing how much was earned by various departments and crafts in April 1893 and in April 1894. These tables were arranged, however, to buttress the company's argument that the difference in pay between the two periods was not too considerable, and they were presented in a somewhat oblique manner. Enough data was provided, however, that a further analysis permits the construction of Tables 4 and 5 found at the end of this chapter. The original company material is in *Strike Rep.*,pp. 592-3.

22. U. S. Bureau of the Census, *Historical Statistics of the United States* (Washington, D. C.: Government Printing Office, 1896), p. 92; Department of Commerce and Labor, *Thirteenth Census of the United States, Abstract* (Washington, D. C.: Government Printing Office, 1913), p. 439; C. Hoffman, "The Depression of the Nineties," *Journal of Economic History*, XVI (June 1960), 150-51.

24. In order to establish a basis for judging the comparative movement of crafts and departments in distribution of wages between April 1893 and April 1894, a "Rank Order Correlation"

$$\text{rho} = 1 - \frac{6 \, \Sigma \, D^2}{N \, (N^2 - 1)}$$

was utilized. If there had been no change in rankings, a correlation of 1.0 would have obtained; a total change would have resulted in 0. The actual correlation was .69, which can be interpreted as indicating an over-all stability of rankings, but significant differences which help explain the strong feeling of relative deprivation among the groups hardest hit.

25. *Strike Rep.*, p. xxxv.

26. Ibid., pp. xxxvii-xxxviii.

27. Of 3,284 shop employees on April 30, 1894, 563 (17%) owned homes and 560 (17%) rented homes that were outside the town. One thousand twenty-six were tenants of the company, and 1,135 boarded in Pullman. Ibid., p. 598. A comparison of these figures with those given on p. 83 challenges the charge heard both before and during the strike that the company tended to lay off first those who lived outside the town. During the boom period in September 1892 and the depression month of April 1894 the percentage of men living outside Pullman was about the same.

28. Between August 1893 and the end of April 1894, company employees in Pullman earned $1,080,226 in wages. It can be assumed that the men who rented company houses earned approximately one-third of this figure, or $360,000. If they had paid their entire

rent for the period, this would have been about $180,000 or half of their income. Figures taken from Pullman Palace Car Company records in the custody of the Newberry Library.

CHAPTER 13

1. *Strike Rep.*, p. 417.
2. At the time of the strike, 277 of the shop employees had been employed less than a year, and more than half less than five years. George M. Pullman quoted in *Chicago Tribune*, October 19, 1894.
3. The Arcade Mercantile Company was the largest store in Pullman. It had been formed in 1889 to occupy the premises vacated by the Secord-Hopkins firm. There was considerable speculation in the town that the store was operated for the company, but Hopkins asserted that the real owners were Edward F. Bryant and Duane Doty. Whoever owned the store, at least once, in July 1891, an appraisal of its profits and management was submitted by the town agent to the uptown company officers. Pullman Palace Car Company Records, Newberry Library. On May 12, the store closed down for the duration of the strike. A store operated by Charles Corkery and located in the Arcade remained open and continued credit. *Kensington Advertiser*, May 15, 19, 1894; *Chicago Times*, May 15, 1894.
4. On May 12, Assistant Superintendent Parent told reporters that he thought the company would soon evict strikers. Apparently "called down for talking too much," he later said that this was his view of what should be done and not company policy. *Chicago Herald*, May 14, 1894; *Chicago Tribune*, May 15, 1894.
5. Bessie L. Pierce, *As Others See Chicago* (Chicago: University of Chicago Press, 1933), p. 273.
6. As early as May 19, the *Tribune* stated: "Relief must be had for the residents of Pullman."
7. *Chicago Evening Journal*, March 7, 1894. The *Times* had been purchased by the late Mayor Carter Harrison and was being managed by his two sons, who had political ambitions.
8. I. J. Hourwich to Henry Demarest Lloyd, August 3, 1894. Henry Demarest Lloyd Correspondence, Box N (April-October, 1893), Wisconsin Historical Society.
10. For the *Chicago Times*'s story and letters to the editor by both the ladies and Mr. Gage, see the June 7 and 8 issues.
11. *Chicago Inter Ocean*, May 30, 1894.
12. *Chicago Times*, May 20, 1894.
13. William Cawardine, *The Pullman Strike* (Chicago: Charles H. Kerr and Co., 1894), p. 14.
14. *Chicago Mail*, May 22, 1894.
15. *Kensington Advertiser*, May 15, 1894.
16. Several of these letters were published in Carwardine, pp. 127-35.

17. William H. Carwardine to Henry Demarest Lloyd, July 6, 1894; August 3, 1894. Henry Demarest Lloyd Correspondence, Box N April-October, 1894), Wisconsin Historical Society. Carwardine, in his first letter to Lloyd, stated that he had carefully written his pamphlet in "the hope of reaching the class of people who are so prejudiced against the strikers."
18. *Chicago Record*, May 28, 1894.
19. *Chicago Mail*, June 1, 1894; *Chicago Herald,* June 2, 1894.
20. *Chicago Record*, May 29, 1894; June 1, 1894.

CHAPTER 14

1. *Strike Rep.*, pp. 87-91.
2. At this time, George Pullman gave interviews to the *Chicago Herald, New York Sun,* and *New York Tribune* among others. These interviews may be found in ibid., pp. 578-85.
3. "Proceedings of the General Managers' Association in Chicago, May, 1886–February, 1890," p. 3. Mimeographed. John Crerar Library. This library also has "Proceedings . . . January, 1892–September, 1893" and "Minutes of Meetings Including Amended Constitution, November, 1893–December, 1894."
4. David L. McMurray, "Labor Policy of the General Managers' Association," *Journal of Economic History*, XIII (Spring 1953), 167.
5. *Strike Rep.*, p. xliii.
6. Ibid., p. 252.
7. Ibid., p. 625. Porter played an active role in the Association. "Proceedings of the General Managers' Association, August 17, 1893," pp. 32-4.
8. A detailed daily report of their operations during the Chicago strike and incidents were submitted by member roads and are to be found in "Minutes of Meetings General Managers' Association, November, 1893–December, 1894," pp. 97-211.
9. M. H. Madden to Henry Demarest Lloyd. Henry Demarest Lloyd Correspondence, Box N (April-October 1894), Wisconsin Historical Society.
10. *Chicago Times,* July 1, 1894.
11. *Chicago Tribune,* July 3, 1894.
12. A too critical analysis of the Chicago and national press may be found in Almont Lindsey, *The Pullman Strike* (Chicago: University of Chicago Press, 1942), pp. 308-20. He is correct in thinking the press played an important role in discrediting the A.R.U. through spurious questioning of Debs's character and exaggerated reports of violence which the Union was held responsible for. The assumption that this resulted from an affinity between the capitalist press and business interests neglects the excitement and confusion of the moment which captured the press as much as it

was perpetrated by the reporters. Debs's views of the Chicago press are expressed in the *Strike Rep.*, p. 157, and those of George Howard on p. 19. They believed the Union supported by the *Mail, Dispatch,* and *Times,* while the *News* and *Record* were impartial. The *Herald, Inter Ocean, Tribune, Journal,* and *Post* had opposed them. The problem of analyzing these papers is represented by the *Herald.* On April 29, 1894, it had published a story on the town of Pullman which emphasized the harmony between labor and the company. After the strike began, the *Herald* enthusiastically championed the men. It first approved the A.R.U. boycott but about-faced when violence occurred. See Howard's comment on this paper, ibid., p. 19.

13. Lindsey, p. 149. One member of the Cabinet, Secretary of State Walter Gresham, was a close personal friend of George Pullman, and the two had met in Washington in May 1894.

14. *Strike Rep.*, p. xliii.

15. Ibid., p. 354.

16. Ibid., p. 370.

17. Under authorization of the U. S. Marshal in Chicago, the railroads deputized two thousand non-strikers who operated trains, receiving an additional compensation from the railroads. Olney did not learn of this practice until after, when he expressed disapproval. Carroll W. Wright to Nicholas E. Worthington, November 24, 1894. Correspondence of the U. S. Strike Commission, No. 350. Social and Economic Branch, Office of Civil Archives, National Archives, Washington, D. C.

18. Eugene V. Debs to Henry Demarest Lloyd, July 24, 1894. Henry Demarest Lloyd Correspondence, Box N (April-October, 1894), Wisconsin Historical Society.

19. Frederick Remington, "The Great Strike," *Harper's Weekly,* XXXVIII (July 21, 1894), 681.

20. Grover Cleveland, *The Government in the Chicago Strike of 1894* (Princeton, N. J.: Princeton University Press, 1913), pp. 40-49.

21. The federal units used in Chicago and suburbs, their permanent posts, and their deployment may be found in "Minutes of Meetings General Managers' Association, November, 1893–December, 1894," p. 222. The total was just short of 2,000 officers and men. In addition, there were 3,600 U.S. marshals and 3,600 national guardsmen, pp. 223-7.

22. *Chicago Times,* July 12, 13, 1894.

23. *Strike Rep.*, pp. 155, 189.

24. Florence Kelley to Henry Demarest Lloyd, July 18, 1894; L. W. Rogers to Henry Demarest Lloyd, July 11, 1894. Henry Demarest Lloyd Correspondence, Box N (April-October, 1894), Wisconsin Historical Society.

25. Ibid.

26. Wright wrote Cleveland's private secretary: "Will you kindly say

to the President that . . . the investigation was conducted fearlessly, impartially, and in a searching manner, and was a thorough success." Carroll W. Wright to Henry T. Thurber, September 3, 1894. Correspondence of the U. S. Strike Commission, No. 135. The release of the published report provoked considerable interest. Of the press reaction, Wright thought "about three-fourths of the newspapers of the country commended the report fairly. . . . Half of the other fourth undertook to criticize it intelligently. . . . The remainder simply abused it. . . . The difficulty with the press was that a garbled abstract was sent out surreptitiously by a correspondent here in Washington, who put in all such matters as related to criticism of roads, etc., to the exclusion of criticisms of the other side." Carroll W. Wright to Susie L. Austin, March 26, 1895. Correspondence of the U. S. Strike Commission, No. 67.

27. Wright probably wrote the "Report of Commissioners of the State Bureaus of Labor Statistics on the Industrial, Social and Economic Conditions of Pullman, Illinois." James Leiby, *Carroll Wright and Labor Reform* (Cambridge, Mass.: Harvard University Press, 1960), p. 160.

28. Leiby, p. 160.

29. Ibid., pp. 168-9. Carroll W. Wright to John D. Kernan, September 15, 1894. Correspondence of U. S. Commission, No. 180.

30. "I think this strike has proved the long needed touchstones which finally separates the active elements of the two classes the exploiting and the exploited." Florence Kelley to Henry Demarest Lloyd, August 15, 1894. Henry Demarest Lloyd Correspondence, Box N (April-October, 1894), Wisconsin Historical Society.

31. Lindsey, p. 329.

CHAPTER 15

1. Grover Cleveland, *The Government in the Chicago Strike of 1894* (Princeton: Princeton University Press, 1913), p. 6.

2. Mrs. George M. Pullman's Diary, June 30, 1894.

3. *Chicago Tribune,* July 8, 1894; July 13, 1894.

4. *Chicago Record,* July 11, 1894; *Chicago Tribune,* July 11, 1894.

5. *Chicago Tribune,* July 16, 1894.

6. Mrs. George M. Pullman's Diary, July 16, 1894.

7. *Chicago Record,* August 7, 1894.

8. Ibid., July 13, 1894.

9. *Chicago Record,* July 17, 1894.

10. *Chicago Tribune,* July 16, 1894. Heathcoate did not attend the meeting of the General Strike Committee on the sixteenth.

11. Ibid., August 8, 1894.

12. Ibid., August 14, 1894.

13. George M. Pullman in "Supplement to Company Report" in *Chicago Tribune,* October 19, 1894. He stated, "There has been

no substantial change in car building business and the contracts taken by us . . . since the strike are being executed at prices which bring no profit."

14. *Strike Rep.*, pp. 420-21.
15. *Chicago Record,* August 21, 1894.
16. Ibid., August 22, 23, 1894.
17. Ibid., August 30, 1894.
18. "Supplement to Company's General Report," in *Chicago Tribune,* October 19, 1894.
19. *Pullman Journal,* April 18, 1895.
20. On May 12, Assistant Superintendent Parent told reporters that the company would soon evict those who owed rent. This was retracted two days later. *Chicago Times,* May 15, 1894. On July 30, an unnamed official told a reporter that strike leaders would soon be evicted. *Chicago Record,* July 31, 1894. Wickes on August 12 stated that within the week, eviction proceedings would be started. Ibid., August 13, 1894. A day later he announced that no evictions would occur for the present. Ibid., August 14, 1894.
21. *Strike Rep.*, pp. 563-4.
22. Ibid., p. 566.
23. Thomas Beer, *Hanna* (New York: Alfred A. Knopf, 1929), pp. 132-3.
24. "I can well understand the disappointment and grief which you must naturally feel at the shocking ingratitude and dastardly conduct of the very people whose material well being and social elevation you made as much your life work as the progress of your company. That a man to whose true public spirit and genuine benevolence, the town bearing his name, forms the greatest monument . . . should have been attacked, tempts one to almost despair of human nature." Henry Villard to George M. Pullman, July 20, 1894. Quoted in Ruth Lawrence, *Pullman, Sanger and Allied Family Histories* (New York: National American Publications, 1957), p. 24.
25. *Harper's Weekly,* XXXVIII (July 21, 1894), 674.
26. Quoted in Almont Lindsey, *The Pullman Strike* (Chicago: University of Chicago Press, 1942), p. 229.
27. Jane Addams, "A Modern Lear," printed in Graham Taylor, *Satellite Cities* (New York: D. Appleton and Co., 1915), pp. 68-90.
28. The Reverend Charles H. Eaton, in his original manuscript of "Pullman and Paternalism," suggested that the company sell the homes to the tenants, but whatever the reason this was omitted from the published article. Eaton knew Pullman well, as his wife had been a longtime companion to Pullman's mother. He had appeared before the Strike Commission in an effort to defend the model town. *Strike Rep.*, pp. 526-8. The Eatons were remembered in Pullman's will, and by coincidence, were the last people to see him alive.

29. George Howard used this phrase in charging Pullman with callously forcing his older sister to seek charity by refusing help. *Strike Rep.*, p. 43. Pullman had only two younger sisters to whom he was always generous.

CHAPTER 16

1. *Boston Evening Transcript*, February 17, 1900.
2. George Pullman in "Supplement to Company's General Report," quoted in *Chicago Tribune*, October 19, 1894.
3. John McLean, *One Hundred Years in Illinois* (Chicago: Peterson Co., 1919), p. 227.
4. *Chicago Times*, October 5, 1894.
5. *Chicago Tribune*, September 26, 1894; March 5, 1895.
6. *Chicago Evening Journal Examiner*, July 7, 1895.
7. Harvey Middleton to George F. Brown, June 18, 1895. Pullman Palace Car Company Records in the custody of the Newberry Library.
8. *Strike Rep.*, p. 628.
9. Quoted in William T. Hutchinson, *Lowden of Illinois* (Chicago: University of Chicago Press, 1957), I, 47.
10. Ibid., I, 64.
11. Mrs. George M. Pullman's Diary, October 16, 1897. This entry was written several months later. Mrs. Pullman, grief-stricken by her husband's death, neglected her diary until some time in 1898, when she filled in the missing entries.
12. *Chicago Journal*, October 20, 1897.
13. On December 15, 1895, "infernal machines" had been mailed to George M. Pullman and Phillip D. Armour, but they had been warned in advance. On investigation it was discovered that the informer, who had claimed to have overheard a conversation between anarchists in a saloon, had actually sent the bombs in an effort to collect a reward. *Chicago Tribune*, December 16, 1895.
14. Records of Pullman's executors in the custody of the Newberry Library.
15. *New York Journal*, April 10, 1897.
16. *Chicago American*, December 20, 1909.
17. *Chicago Inter Ocean*, October 5, 1895; *Chicago Tribune*, October 26, 1898.
18. *Boston Financial News*, October 26, 1898; *Chicago Evening Post*, January 7, 1899.
19. *Chicago Times Herald*, April 29, 1899.
20. The company continued support of the library, though in greatly reduced form, until January 1908, when Mrs. Pullman personally assumed the cost of its operation, but gave control to a committee

of local businessmen. In July 1908 its membership fee was discarded. After the destruction of the Arcade Building, the library and a site on 111th Street and Indiana were given to Chicago on condition that the institution be named after George Pullman. For the closing of the Arcade theater, see *Calumet Record,* November 20, 1902.

21. Graham R. Taylor, *Satellite Cities* (New York: D. Appleton and Co., 1915), pp. 37-8.
22. *Chicago Daily News,* November 9, 1907.
23. *Chicago Tribune,* February 20, 1909.
24. McLean, p. 284.
25. Taylor, p. 34.

CHAPTER 17

1. *Chicago Record-Herald,* May 27, 1910.
2. *Chicago Tribune,* September 28, 1904.
3. Graham R. Taylor, *Satellite Cities* (New York: D. Appleton and Co., 1915), p. 61, 63-5.
4. *Chicago Tribune,* May 15, 1909.
5. John McLean, *One Hundred Years in Illinois* (Chicago: Peterson Co., 1919), p. 285.
6. Ibid., p. 268-9.
7. Ernest Burgess and Charles Newcomb, eds., *Census Data of the City of Chicago, 1920* (Chicago: University of Chicago Press, 1927), pp. 574, 583.
8. McLean, p. 284.
9. Ibid., p. 287.
10. Taylor, p. 37.
11. *Chicago Record-Herald,* May 24, 1908.
12. Taylor, p. 50. In a period of twenty-two months, forty-one fatal accidents reportedly occurred on railroad crossings in and around Pullman.
13. *Chicago Examiner,* June 5, 1909.
14. Taylor, pp. 54-6; Irving K. Pond, "Pullman—America's First Planned Industrial Town," *Illinois Society of Architects Monthly Bulletin,* June-July 1934, p. 8.
15. *Chicago Tribune,* April 13, 1909. This was the Roseland State Bank, opened with $200,000 capital on 115th Street and Michigan. John Runnels, the Pullman Company vice-president, was the bank's president and E. F. Bryant was in charge of its operations.
16. Taylor, p. 59.
17. Mary Faith Adams, "Present Housing Conditions in South Chicago, South Deering and Pullman" (unpub. Master's diss., School of Social Service Administration, University of Chicago, 1926), pp. 121-123, 144, 149-51.

18. Ibid., pp. 153-55.
19. "Chicago Zoning Ordinance, April 5, 1923," Maps 42, 43, and 47. Municipal Reference Library.
20. Computed from data in Ernest Burgess and Charles Newcomb, eds., *Census Data of the City of Chicago, 1930* (Chicago: University of Chicago Press, 1933), p. 588.
21. Ibid., pp. 605-6. In Pullman, only 52 per cent of the families had radios, while in neighboring tracts the percentages ranged from a low of 67.8 to a high of 81.4.
22. Burgess and Newcomb, *Census . . . 1920*, p. 485. Burgess and Newcomb, *Census . . . 1930*, p. 588.
23. Adams, p. 144.
24. Taylor, p. 67.

CONCLUSION

1. Graham R. Taylor, *Satellite Cities* (New York: D. Appleton and Co., 1915), pp. vii-viii.
2. Daniel H. Burnham and E. H. Bennett, *Plan of Chicago* (Chicago: The Commercial Club, 1909), p. 4.

Index

Abbott, Edith, 224

Ackerman, William, 39

Adams, Mary, 224–5

Addams, Jane, 176, 200, 230

Alden, Henry Mills, 100, 103

Allen Paper Wheel Company, 26, 51, 52, 56, 57, 70

Altgeld, John, 115, 185, 188, 192; on government intervention, 184; visits Pullman, 196; and G. M. Pullman, 197; attempts to regulate Pullman rates, 206

American Federation of Labor, 185–6

American Railway Union: established, 152; constitution, 152, 246n8; organization of Pullman shop workers, 152, 155, 169; organization of brickyard workers, 172; 1894 national convention, 178–9; boycott, 179–87; railroad opposition to, 180; boycott of mail trains, 183; leaders indicted, 187; after strike, 187; Pullman workers forced to resign, 195–6; in hearing testimony of G. M. Pullman, 198, 201. *See also* Debs, Eugene; Pullman Strike, 1894

Arbitration: Pullman Company declines to submit to, 176, 179, 185, 186; compulsory, 188

Arcade Building, 67, 68, 72, 85, 88, 112, 214; description, 61–2; rents, 68; demolished, 220–21

Arcade Mercantile Company, 248n3

Arcade Theatre, 63–4, 112, 214

Barrett, Nathan F., 209, 226; town plan, 50–51, 71–2, 74

Barrows, Walter E., 102, 104, 242n16

Beman, Solon Spenser, 54, 64, 133, 209, 226, 240n18; town architecture, 50–51, 73–4

257

258

Bowen, Colonel James H., 11, 25, 26–7

Brook Farm, 92, 93

Brown, George, 115, 191, 207

Bryant, Edward F., 81, 86, 128, 219–20, 248n3, 254n15

Burnham, Daniel, 66, 231

Calumet region, 25–6, 38, 84–5, 109, 123, 222–4. *See also* Hyde Park Township

Carnegie, Andrew, 140, 208; on G. M. Pullman, 3, 15, 16, 18; and Central Transportation Company, 14, 15, 16; and Pullman Pacific Car Company, 16, 236n2; and West Shore Line, 137

Carwardine, Rev. William, 143, 144, 174–5, 205

Central Transportation Company, 14, 15, 16

Chicago: early history, 4–5; and Pullman Company, 18; Prairie Avenue, 29, 33, 34, 50, 61, 208; population, 34, 123; social problems, 34–6; plant location, 38–9; ethnicity, 80, 90; annexation of Hyde Park Township, 109, 111–17; politics, 114–17; transportation, 123, 222–3; Haymarket Riot, 140; strike violence, 182–5; general strike, 185, 192–3; Burnham plan, 231. *See also* Chicago newspapers; Hyde Park Township; Pullman Strike, 1894

Chicago, Alton and St. Louis Railroad, 12

Chicago and Alton Railroad, 5–11 *passim*

Chicago Civic Federation, 172, 176, 187, 188

Chicago Commercial Club, 32, 33, 101, 231

Chicago Manual Training School, 33

Chicago newspapers: Pullman distribution, 119; on town, 129, 152; on Hopkins, 153; on Pullman Strike, 170–71, 248n6; on G. M. Pullman, 206; role in strike, 249n12

Chicago strike, 181. *See also* Pullman Strike, 1894

Cleveland, Grover, 114, 115, 182, 190; intervenes in Pullman Strike, 184, 185; creates U. S. Strike Commission, 187

Columbian Exposition, 115–16, 123, 147–8, 184, 231

Commission of State Bureaus of Labor Statistics, 98, 188, 251n27

Corliss engine, 54

Crerar, John, 31

Darrow, Clarence, 68

Debs, Eugene V., 175, 176, 193, 250n12; founds American Railway Union, 152; and national rail strike, 179–87 *passim;* indicted, 187. *See also* American Railway Union

Detroit, Michigan, 12. *See also* Pullman car shops

De Wolf, Dr. Oscar, 34, 35, 79

Diamond Match Company, 208

Doty, Duane: editor of *Pullman Journal,* 84–5, 128; as town official, 84, 88, 89, 107–9; on Pullman residents, 95; on municipal problems, 117; on G. M.